D0893317

SKY DETERMINES

Also by Ross Calvin

RIVER OF THE SUN
Stories of the Storied Gila

LIEUTENANT EMORY REPORTS:
*A Reprint of Lieutenant W. H. Emory's
"Notes of A Military Reconnoissance"*
Introduction and Notes by Ross Calvin

SKY
DETERMINES

AN INTERPRETATION OF THE SOUTHWEST

by Ross Calvin

illustrated by Peter Hurd

ALBUQUERQUE
THE UNIVERSITY OF NEW MEXICO PRESS

CONTENTS

FOREWORD

"In New Mexico whatever is both old and peculiar appears upon examination to have a connection with arid climate. Peculiarities range from the striking adaptation of the flora onwards to those of the fauna, and on up to those of the human animal.

"Sky Determines. And the writer once having picked up the trail followed it with certainty and, indeed, almost inevitably, as it led from ecology to anthropology and economics. In the succeeding chapters, the thesis is buttressed with proof from some ten different directions; and if the theory had been preconceived—which it was not—the facts brought out in the study would have fitted into it with gratifying regularity.

"Dealing with climatic matters and their consequences, the present treatise attempts to present some hitherto overlooked but abiding features of the New Mexico scene. While the observations which follow are not, when properly understood, inaccurate, they are necessarily incomplete; and, being so, are designed quite as much to stimulate future research as to furnish information. The writer's aim throughout has been to indicate not only for the general reader but for students of anthropology, history, and regional geography a fresh but permanent approach to the arid Southwest, a new and creative interpretation of its life.

"But there hovers over many of the pages a shadowy ulterior purpose of pointing out to a bedevilled humanity that in the world of roots and clouds and wings and leaves there exists no Depression; that in its beauties and simplicities rather than from divers, bewildered senates and parliaments is man's peace most likely to be derived; that as life progressively adapts itself to its background of sun and soil, it gains in wholesomeness and sincerity.

"Though the writer had not in mind the dire psychological consequences of the world Depression, the present treatise on sky, desert, and mountain, which encompass life with freedom, silence, and majesty, may possibly be received as a contribution in that direction. . . . Much of this thrillingly interesting world is still unpaved and without a roof or electric lights." Thus I wrote in 1934, when the Macmillan Company brought out the first edition of Sky Determines.

Some years before that I had come to the Southwest for reasons of health, and had been advised by physicians to stay outdoors in the sunshine as much as possible. So I had rested, imbibed large doses of sunshine, and then, after months of improvement, had begun taking long walks over the foothills near Silver City, New Mexico.

It was a fascinating landscape there, dotted with junipers, dwarf pines and oaks, and rich in the other plant species that belong in their society. Oftentimes fatigue turned my walk into a contemplative rest on a ledge of limestone; and attention then would naturally busy itself with the plants nearest at hand. Of them all, one family, by its grotesque novelty, its hardiness—which often seemed to border upon immortality—its exotic beauty, and above all its supreme adaptiveness, stirred my curiosity. It was the cactus clan. On them aridity seemed to have left its most legible imprint.

I could find no one who knew anything much about them; and at that time, in the late 20's, very little literature on them was readily available to the general reader. But I secured a State College pamphlet which gave classifications, and presently began to collect some of the species and make small experiments with them.

On hundreds of field trips I amassed and checked data—for field trips had already superseded golf and other conventional pastimes. Then the facts which observation revealed, photography recorded and preserved for minute study. In ecological matters it provided the tool which has since furnished an unequalled supplement to my written notes.

And further study of desert plant life kept continually revealing newer levels of adaptation. The winter annuals, for instance, were growing by December; by March, with the aid of stored-up soil moisture, they were blossoming or else going to seed; by late April many of them had turned yellow and withered, thus completing their life cycle ahead of the sun's raging might in June. But among the foothill grasses the case was very different, for among them signs of life scarcely appeared before the advent of Rainy Season in July. Then, spurred by the seasonal concentration of moisture, they grew amazingly for ninety days or so, bore seed and so matured before the late October frosts. The adaptation, although different, was effective in both cases. And so by observing the same process at work in species after species, I gradually became a pretty fair amateur in plant ecology—as this kind of field botany is called. The conclusion was always that while soil, temperature, sunshine, and other factors matter, it is the available water supply here in the arid Southwest which matters first and most.

Then one day the thought occurred to me that if plant life in the desert had been forced to adapt itself to aridity or else perish, the same must be true in greater or less degree of animal life also. Though a lifelong observer of bird life in the Middle West and in the East, I had only the sketchiest acquaintance with Southwestern mammals. So some hard and special effort was necessary here to amass the knowledge required to buttress my thesis.

The best inspiration of all came one day with the thought that in the human species, too, who have inhabited the arid Southwest, the same kind of harsh adaptation should be discoverable. That indicated the study of archaeology. This, fortunately, was less difficult than might have been expected, since materials were everywhere at hand, and the scientific literature was both copious and interesting. By reading and by a great many personal contacts, I found it simple to discover the evidences whose presence I had suspected. The next step was to investigate that archaeology which in New Mexico and Arizona still persists as a living mode of existence. So I observed Indian pueblos along the Rio Grande, went gleaning for Stone Age vestiges which are still discoverable among the Navahos and Apaches. At length, on arriving at the native Spanish-speaking people and the Anglos—as we are here called—I found myself on the firm ground of sociology and history, where, in the earlier stages at least, it was easy to read the influence of the Sky Powers.

With the recorded facts spread out before him, I believe that the unbiased reader can hardly fail to agree that Sky Determined the general character of plant life and animal life in the arid Southwest, and influenced the history of its various populations and shaped their cultures until the resources of twentieth-century science afforded partial control of the waters. Proof of the thesis was particularly abundant in the drouth year of 1946.

In truth, that which man determines here has never at any time very completely repealed that which Sky Determines. In 1946, for instance, newspapers reported that owing to the extreme dryness of the ground cover, forest fires had been raging in many mountains of the Southwest, and that cattle were being shipped from our parched ranges to pasturage elsewhere. Dispatches said that at Albuquerque water was being rationed; that at Santa Fe users were being required to curtail their consumption of it or else face legal penalties for disobedience; that at Silver City water could be drawn from the mains only during six designated hours out of twenty-four; that many irrigation reservoirs in New Mexico and Arizona were running dangerously low or drying up.

And the state game warden was quoted as saying that both in the Sangre de Cristos and in the Mogollons, mountain streams were drying up, leaving the trout an easy prey to their natural enemies, the bears, raccoons, snakes, and hawks; that the deer were beginning to suffer, and that many game birds on account of the drouth would not nest during the year. The Sky Powers were once more testing out the survival strength of their species.

In the 1948 edition, the main thesis of Sky Determines was set forth without change.

I added a word about my Spanish-American friends, whom I have called "Mexicanos." The section on them was written during the darkest months of the Depression. I was living among them and know what they endured then. But life is easier for them now, and better.

When Rexford Tugwell, formerly one of President Roosevelt's "Brain Trust" became chancellor of the University of Puerto Rico he sent me a copy of his first address to the student body. It was delivered in the University Theater, Rio Piedras, on August 27, 1941. Starting with *Sky Determines,* he pointed out to his students the determinants that have existed and continue to exist in the American Southwest. He mentioned then "that Puerto Ricans were dominantly Spanish as New Mexicans were, both being of the Conquistador Breed." After continuing with some of the environmental factors familiar to us he says, "If Calvin had been writing of Puerto Rico he would have said, I am sure, as some of our own writers have said, that the fall of seldom-failing rains, the generosity of these soils, the ever-blowing trade winds had been no less determinant. He would have found the basic elements of culture in sky, earth and the surrounding sea."

The fact is, the scholarly chancellor distinguished clearly between what the writer aspired to do and what he did not aspire to do. Hopefully the writer was aiming, yet without presumption, to produce a book that would not be merely scanned, but one which could be twice read.

Ross Calvin

SKY DETERMINES

CHAPTER ONE

THEME STATED

IT IS A FACT THAT ONE CANNOT think very penetratingly about New Mexico without observing unity in its confused and manifold variety — a complex, large-scale unity. The state lies in the belt where aridity is the dominant climatic factor, and the sky, as source of life-giving moisture and of the desert-making heat, determines not only its plant and animal life, but has created the peculiar environment which, until the introduction of driven wells, a little more than eighty years ago, determined likewise the direction of its human activities and pursuits. Climate effects an intelligible unity.

It is no accident that in New Mexico plant life is generally grotesque in appearance; that prehistoric man here attained a level of culture elsewhere unequalled within the boundaries of our country; that today Indian life persists unchanged here long after it has disappeared in other parts; that the native Mexicans as a rule are a miserably poor folk; and that over most of the state the Americans have followed the historical dependence upon stock raising for a livelihood. Nor are these phenomena unrelated. So directly are they results of the same causes and so organic is the unity among them, that it would not be possible to alter the picture in any of its larger features without modifying them all. Indeed, it can be demonstrated that facts as diverse as the ability of certain desert animals to live without drinking, and the fortress-like architectural style of the prehistoric Indians and their burial customs, can be strung, like the beads of a necklace, upon the one same strand of aridity.

Yet, in general, the history of the arid Southwest has been treated hitherto in the same conventional manner as that of the humid East, or of England and northern Europe, notwithstanding the fact that the four centuries of recorded history and the millennia of unrecorded history are only half-intelligible when divorced from the peculiarities of their climatic setting. It is as if a treatise on the development of architecture were written without cognizance of climatic exigencies and the character of the building material available. Buildings stand out of doors; hence the amount of snowfall determines the pitch of roofs; the amount of wind stress, the strength which must be built into walls and towers; even more imponderable matters like the type of background and the amount of sunlight in a given region will also be weighed and considered.

In like manner, the only comprehensive way of studying great marches and explorations, the long-drawn Indian warfare, the homespun operations of ranching, farming, and mining will be to take into account the out-door factors of the story. In New Mexico, history has not taken place under a roof.

The wiser way would be to compile the record of man's struggle with his environment and with his neighbors, not in a library but out in the open, where the struggle took place and still takes place. After viewing in detail the natural setting of sky, of desert, of forest and

mountain, one can say definitely that "Thus and thus it would have to work out." It is because a culture and its background cannot be separated that history should be studied with regard to its proper setting.

And no one factor can be completely dismissed without some loss. With a different topography, the course of drainage and the location of the great trails would have been different. With a different topography, the forestation would have been different, and that change would have vitally affected lumbering, grazing, and agriculture, and what is probably of equal importance, the whole future of the state as a paradise for sport and recreation. Thus the peculiar relief of the country, which includes extremes of temperature and rainfall, which ranges from arctic to sub-tropic, has influenced the sequence of events and the direction of cultures from the time of the cliff dwellers, and it will not cease to be meaningful for residents and tourists in generations to come.

Yet the topography joins hands on the one side with geology, without which vast mining and agricultural developments would be unintelligible, and on the other with the biological sciences and meteorology. The types and amount of vegetation, which affect the amount of cover and the abundance of food, determine rather narrowly the limits of animal life; the amount and fertility of the arable soils, the availability of the water supply, the kind of crops which will mature — all affect the land's usefulness for human occupation. And its mineral wealth may yet go much farther in undoing the handicaps of an otherwise unfavorable enterprise.

Thus the ideal account would allow due weight to sunshine, soil, water — elemental factors of the environment from which man emerges. Whereas in more conventional scenes they aid man's purposes without his notice, they have here retarded and embarrassed them in a thousand intangible, unguessed ways; and where nature has dealt so harshly with her plants and all her other animals, it seems neither far-fetched nor visionary to conclude that she would not be over-indulgent with her human species. So an attempt to delve into such peculiarities can hardly fail to be rewarded by a new understanding of a strange, beautiful history.

To convey an accurate and comprehensive notion of New Mexico in a thumbnail sketch lies beyond the writer's power of condensation. But if, for the sake of clearness, one were to describe it as the Land of Desert, Mesa, and Mountain, the description would not fail.

Of desert in the strictest physiographic sense, there is little; and yet of arid land, which by comparison with the humid East appears desert, there is very much. Over a great deal of the country no plants thrive without special adaptation, and the grotesque appearance and general thorniness among them, as well as an unusual abundance of predacious types of birds and animals, indicate that here competition for life is fiercer and the penalty for incompetence more fatal than elsewhere.

And like the word desert, mesa is also ill-defined. A mesa in its clearest sense is, no doubt, a flat table (Lat. *mensa*) lying somewhat higher than the surrounding country, and capped with stone. Yet the level edge of the great tableland or plateau from which the middle Rio Grande Valley is carved is called a mesa, and often the word means no more than a horizontal bench bevelled at the edge by an arroyo — or to use another undefined word, canyon. But since there is no inevitable term for the high grazing country that slopes gently in vast tablelands from the Continental Divide, mesa is as good a makeshift as another. It may well suggest a gaunt land, a red land, turfless, but held together by harsh bunch grasses, curing in the sunshine to buff-colored hay, that stand through autumn, winter, and spring. The green dots on the landscape are dwarf cedars and pines. Over all spreads a turquoise sky that — outside the rainy season — will be clear on nine days out of ten.

The mountains have a sudden uniqueness of their own. Upon the hot cactus-and-yucca plains they often lie like islands of the northland. On their high skylines appear the slim Canadian shapes of spruce and fir. Fur-bearing animals roam the dark solitudes and leave marks of their treadings on the winter snowfields. Summers are cool and rainy. Ascending towards the 10,000-foot level. one finds himself in a different world.

In the arid setting of desert and mesa, culture has since time immemorial localized itself in the valleys. The Forgotten Ones gave up their wanderings for a sedentary life beside the waters, and there pooling their strength for the defense of the cornlands upon which they settled, they built communal dwellings that served also as fortresses. And as their one surviving art form, they created a pottery so conspicuously fine that it is the wonder of modern archaeology. Then in the fullness of time their culture was extinguished. By what agency — *¿quién sabe?*

Of some undetermined relation to the prehistoric men, the puebleños follow the same general mode of life. Sky rendered impossible for the Tewas and Keresans, as for their progenitors, a nomadic life like that of the plains tribes, who subsisted merely by following the buffalo, and anchored them permanently to a settled habitation in the arable valleys. Good Catholics though they have been for a dozen generations, they still rely upon the incantations of the cacique for the maturing of their corn, and to this day there remains welded upon their Faith a purely heathen liturgical drama, the Rain Dance.

Hither in 1540 came Coronado on the most golden adventure. It must never be forgotten that with the Conquistadores came the Franciscan padres, of mettle exactly as indomitable. Say what you will, they came to bestow the religion of Catholic Spain. And they bestowed it. But so violent was the recoil of the native sun-and-rain religion that the great Pueblo Rebellion of 1680 left not a Spaniard alive in northern New Mexico. And here, too, history appears predestined.

And Santa Fe, founded more than three centuries ago, is older than New York, older even than Boston. Yet it has a population of 34,000. That also is peculiar. (Though the population of Santa Fe has in the meantime increased by several thousands, the main thesis here is as true today as it was when first proposed.)

Today the progeny of the Conquistadores is a mixed race, backward, illiterate, poor — disinherited in the land of their fathers. They retain a mellow quaintness — but because they cannot help it. For them, wealth and progress were not in the cards.

Clinging to them for the space of two and a half centuries, the Apache harriers stung again and again like a cloud of angry bees. The Apache was the earliest of all American Indians to make war on the white man. Yet the white man conquered him last.

The Americanos, though a part of their energy was diverted into the search for metals, have been over most of the domain, like the Mexicans before them, primarily ranchers. But it was for them, in addition, to build the great trails and bring in machinery. With machinery, they not only robbed the mountains of their treasure, but they brought up from underground depths the water with which ranching expanded and on which agriculture and the growth of towns relied. In this most recent chapter of history, they gained command of the water, thus dominating and humanizing the whole environment.

So the pageant has for its setting the intoxicating splendor of the desert, the green magnificence of the forest, the mystery of barbaric mountains, the serene openness of a sky whose eye is the desert-making sun;

and for its incidental stage properties, terraced pueblos drowsing from an aboriginal past, Spanish missions, haciendas, and herds of longhorn cattle; American stage-coaches, silver mines, wind-driven pumps, and irrigation dams. Acting their part and speaking their lines, each in his own tongue, prehistoric cliff dwellers, rain priests, and ceramic artists pass in review, busy at their appropriate tasks; and so, likewise, El Dorado, the Gilded Man with his European explorers and conquerors, and the brown-robed Franciscans upholding the Cross; Spanish governors with their retinue of caballeros riding along the Camino Real to Santa Fe; mountain men and traders from the Missouri Valley; and in the later scenes, cattle rustlers, train robbers, Apache renegades, troops of cavalry, government engineers, miners, and ranchmen. A crowded canvas! And for the confused interlocking themes of the plot, the evolution of a primitive culture and its reaction to Latin Christianity and the arts of civilization; the development of a Mexican village into a desert-bound, isolated commonwealth, and finally its conquest by a virile new nation, the *entrada* of the steel rails and the advent of the machine! Here is abiding stuff for the weaving of tradition, incident for the composing of lays and ballads, achievements and labors for heroic tragedy. A rich theme, an imperial theme!

And it will demand, so to speak, of all who aspire to treat it, a style that is stately yet compassionate and poignantly sincere; a style endowed also with the foreign riches of learning, for the sake of the contrasts and analogies involved, since it is a tale which will be studded with gemlike names from the idiom of Spain, and both the liturgy and martyrology of Spanish Catholicism, resounding afar off with the final trumpets of European noblemen and their armies in the New World.

CHAPTER TWO

SKY

To comprehend the arid and
beautifully strange Land of Desert, Mesa, and Mountain,
one begins by studying its sky. As source of the intense
heat and frugal moisture, Sky Determines climate, and
climate determines flora, fauna, and the general aspect of
the country. The sky has, since long before the dawn of
history, exercised compelling potency in shaping the destiny of the human inhabitants, and this fact permeates
all southwestern anthropology, history, and economics.
Indeed, the favorable or unfavorable alternation of sunshine and rainfall conditions everything. Sunshine makes
the land beautiful; rain makes it habitable. It is not a
mere figure of speech to say that the sky has tilted the
balance between desert and habitable country; that it has
marked out the crooked, descending lines of drainage
and trenched the sun-flooded plateaus with arroyos, and
then in the course of ages, ground them into silent, stony
canyons. It has exerted a bearing on the routes of travel,

decided the location of towns and cities, and influenced all the multifarious activities included in the anthropologist's term "culture."

It was most natural that the aborigines should think of the sky and its deities as rulers of their world. When the rainclouds formed above them and descended low into their valleys, they were readily transformed by primitive faith and simplicity into the hovering wings of the Thunder Bird; and to this day, the primeval ritual of the sky gods is preserved in such religious ceremonials as the Green Corn Dance at the pueblo of Santo Domingo.

And as the later races came upon the scene, the same gods had power upon them also, for civilized men no less than others must depend upon water. So except in the confined valleys, they were herdsmen and miners, not tillers of the soil, and herdsmen and miners they have continued to be. Finally, as the land lost its savagery under the touch of civilization, another class came flowing in at the beckoning of the sky — the health-seekers. To them the dryness of the air gave hope that their diseases might literally dry up.

Though the rain is all-important in New Mexico, when one begins systematically to study out the source of it, he is face to face with a problem which is infinitely complicated. The state is among the largest, extending through six degrees of north latitude, and, in addition, the extremely varied topography sets up local conditions which exercise all sorts of disturbing effects upon the weather. The southwestern part of the state, for instance, receives its moisture both from the Pacific Ocean and from the Gulf of Mexico; but in the southeastern section, the Pecos Valley receives no moisture at all from the Pacific.

In a matter so complex and irregular, any generalized

scheme would be of questionable value, and it is doubtful whether anything more specific can be said than that any pressure gradient — to quote from a letter by Mr. Hallenbeck, meteorologist at Roswell —"that will bring moisture-laden air up a considerable slope will result in precipitation."

But however intricate the local causes that affect weather, the general picture is clear. The mariner winds come cruising eastward from far out on the Pacific Ocean, northward from far out over the Gulf of Mexico. Bearing their quota of moisture with them, they course across the continent until they lose themselves in the vast planetary circulation which wraps the globe in its eternal aura of mist and cloud. Unseen they transport hither annually through the air above California, Arizona, and Texas, a sheet of water 340 miles wide, 350 miles long, and one foot thick. Flying overhead in magnitudes which the imagination finds incredible when set down in tons of weight, it recalls the ancient Hebrew conception of the abyss of water above the world, which is supported by the firmament.

Relying on the fact that the average precipitation at the New Mexico observation stations is just above twelve inches, and the well-grounded belief that this figure very closely approximates that for the state at large, one must see that theoretically on every foot of ground, there would rest, if it could be conserved for a twelvemonth, a cubic foot of water. The amount is of prime significance. If, for instance, there were two cubes, New Mexico would lose its proud title of Sunshine State, for invading vapors would clog and thicken the delicate clarity of the atmosphere, blurring out half the infinite responsiveness of that medium to ever-varying illumination, and prosaic agriculture would be ruefully substituted for beauty.

But if the moisture were much less — say half a cube — the country at large would lapse into a true desert, having forfeited the graciousness which nature bestows upon a soil where grasses grow.

Yet the most striking thing about the moisture is the unevenness of its distribution, and the effects of that unevenness upon myriads of life forms.

In the prudent economy of nature, a rise in altitude produces a drop in temperature, which in turn, causes an increase in rainfall. This simple law is bound up with most of the natural phenomena of the Southwest, since it accounts for the distribution of plant and animal life, which in turn, again, determined until fairly recently the distribution of the human animal over this and other regions.

Although sections of New Mexico vary in the amount of precipitation from perhaps six or eight inches to above twenty inches, most of it may be fairly called, in Mary Austin's fine phrase, a "Land of Little Rain." But everywhere nature makes the most of the sky's frugal gifts, and by a canny graduation of her resources produces for each varying amount of moisture an appropriate set of plants and animals, or, as the biologist says, she arranges her creatures into life zones. Viewed in another way, one might say that flora and fauna are arranged in well-defined bands between the low-lying desert plains and the mountain summits.

The traveller will ordinarily observe but four of them, for the upper two lie out of reach at timberline or above it. The four common ones, however, will be recognized at sight, for they are clearly differentiated. The lowest is the desert or Lower Sonoran Zone, the next higher the grazing or Upper Sonoran Zone, the next, the lumber or Transition Zone, and the last, the water-storage or Canadian Zone. Beginning somewhere near the timberline, lies the Hudsonian Zone, and above it on the highest peaks, the Arctic-Alpine Zone; but the first four are the important ones.

The Lower Sonoran Zone, as seen in the Rio Grande Valley and on the Deming plain, has many characteristic

thorny denizens, but none more so than the mesquite — that low, armored, sprangling shrub with the odd habit of lying buried, all but its head, in a sandy, red-earth dune, until some Mexican wood-digger exhumes it for his fireplace. It probably is the greatest water-collector in the world. I once paced off the length of an exposed root — twenty-seven feet. Literally, it is invincible by drouth.

And then there is the creosote bush, so named from its odor when wet. After a steaming summer shower one never forgets it, nor the little varnished leaves which stay green all the year. Be the harsh desert gravel ever so bare, the creosote still carries on, even after the cacti have dropped out of the race.

While mesquite and creosote are the conspicuous markers of the zone, other vegetation does not, of course, except in peculiarly unfavorable spots, drop out of the race. Cacti of many kinds store up within their leathery hide abundance of moisture for any drouth, and recompense the desert with bizarre and lovely blossoms. And yuccas of two or more varieties, the ocotillos, and the dagger-leaved *lechuguillas* or — to use another term about equally obscure — agaves, appear to thrive as well on heat and drouth.

Among the stones of this zone the horned toad lurks unseen because of its protective coloration, while little lizards dart hither and thither with a swiftness that must often elude their ancient pursuer, the roadrunner. And here one walks with alert feet, ever heedful for a tawny diamond pattern on the ground—the back of a diamond rattlesnake. Here and there, as symbols of the predacious spirit of the desert, stand little burrowing owls, while overhead flap curious white-necked ravens — although without having the bird in hand, one would never guess the fact. And in the heated valleys, the lank, proletarian jack rabbits, commonest animal of the Lower Sonoran Zone, gallop through beds of prickly pear; on the rolling, grassy slopes, buff-and-white antelopes, most beautiful of its denizens, flee the traveller with unmatched celerity and gracefulness; but most characteristic are the undefeated, predatory coyotes which slink, seldom seen, through the creosote brush.

And though I have called the Lower Sonoran the desert zone, it is at the same time the agricultural zone, for within it lie most of the irrigable farm lands. Along with its jagged outcrops of dark lava, its barren, mineral-stained ridges, and its alkali flats, it has also its stripes of rich valley soil, from which the high temperature and the long growing season, with the aid always of water, are able to coax a bounteous yield of cantaloupes, beans, corn, and alfalfa hay and cotton. And as for grapes, let fancy toy with ardent, sunburst names, like Purple Damascas, Mission, Flame Tokay, and Golden Chasselas — varieties that have stood the tests at Mesilla Park. And here the Mexicans grow the *chiles colorados* which dry on the adobe wall in scarlet *ristras* when October and harvest come.

When the traveller, leaving the hot, shadeless plains, reaches the first piñons and junipers, dwarf evergreens, he may be sure that there ends the Lower Sonoran and that he is entering the Upper Sonoran Zone. Where the level country terminates in a dissected incline, whose little northern slopes afford economical melting for the snows and slow drying for the rains, there the junipers begin to dot the landscape with sharp shadows — they and the evergreen oaks and the tree yuccas. And the traveller may be still further assured by the presence of a bunch grass called by ranchmen blue grama, and readily identified when ripe by its tell-tale sickle-shaped head.

In altitude the meeting line of the two zones rises and falls as much as several hundred feet, according to ground slope. Says Mr. Vernon Bailey, government authority on life zones: "On east and west slopes the upper edge of this zone (the Lower) in the Rio Grande Valley conforms closely to the 5,000-foot contour, but on northeast slopes usually runs 500 feet lower and on southwest slopes 500 feet higher."

While the two zones often overlap considerably, at Silver City they are sharply defined. Coming into town on the train, one ascends a rising plain along the San Vicente Arroyo to a point within a mile or so of the station, and then suddenly on the northward slants of the side arroyos, little junipers appear. From that point over the foothills up to the yellow pine country, they extend in an unbroken band.

Mesquite and creosote have disappeared entirely. New varieties of cacti come in, and while a few overlap, many of the Lower ones drop out, unable to sustain the prolonged freezing in winter and the increased precipitation in summer. And the higher on the slope towards the Divide the tree yuccas ascend, the greater size and beauty they attain.

Here upon mounds of clay honeycombed with burrows, sit prairie dogs, bolt upright and as motionless as stakes, but when danger approaches, they scramble for underground safety.

The gaunt jack rabbit and the coyote are still as much at home as before, but the beautiful bannertail, misnamed kangaroo rat, has disappeared, and the smaller black-tailed rattlesnake has superseded the diamondback. Among the cedars the noisy Woodhouse jays go forever crying, and the tyrant kingbird, noisier still, carries on endless warfare with his fellows.

Here the dry-farmer is concerned only with the maturing of patches of corn, wheat, potatoes, and grain sorghum before the mid-October frost. The paying crops belong down in the valleys, where irrigation is practical. This belt belongs not to the farmer but to the rancher, and the white-faced Hereford is king. (This is, of course, not everywhere true, but for the present purpose quite true enough.)

Yet, in passing, something ought to be said for the apples—the kind they grow at Pinos Altos. Throughout the Rocky Mountains the Upper Sonoran is famous for its apples, and in this state it produced nearly a million bushels of them last autumn.

But in this zone, no trout is taken and no deer killed. For that sort of sport, one must go up among the yellow pines of the Transition Zone.

In the great Gila Forest, the yellow pines of the Transition Zone reach down well below the 7,000-foot level, but in the northern end of the state, contrary to one's expectation, they do not generally descend so far. Since the base level of the country is higher, it acts as a radiating surface, warming the mountain slopes and raising the zone boundary.

Here among the pines both plant and animal life are comparatively uniform. Because of the short, cool growing seasons, the country is not interrupted by cultivation, for beyond the raising of potatoes and garden vegetables for home use, little can be grown, and so the beautiful orange boles spread in a clean, open forest, untrammeled over a thousand hills. And, curiously, there is little fear of the sawmill, for in this arid country, they are more valuable standing than lying as logs. Watersheds must be protected!

At the 7,000-foot level there is in the atmosphere a tang, a suggestion of coolness and evaporation. Clouds are more frequent than over the lowlands, the rainfall is much heavier, and through much of the winter the shaded slopes are snow-covered. Here the cacti have disappeared, and the yucca, presiding genus of the two lower zones, yields place to the fierce century plant. The larger black-crested jay supersedes the Woodhouse species, and the showy, plume-tailed Abert squirrel attracts one's attention from the humbler rock squirrels.

Here, where black-tailed (mule) deer browse, the mountain mahogany and wild turkey lurk in the thickets, takes place most of the big game hunting. Here, if one may judge by the deep-furred pelts in ranchers' homes, brown and cinnamon bear must be rather common; bobcats are taken in traps, and great mountain lions, which prey incessantly on deer and cattle, are hunted in the fall with packs of dogs.

As one goes higher, the life zones diminish rapidly in extent. The Lower Sonoran covers some 18,000 square miles, all in southern New Mexico, and the Upper Sonoran, still larger, some 92,000 in all parts of the state; but the Transition covers only 10,000, and the Canadian, much more restricted, approximately 2,000. The Hudsonian and the Arctic-Alpine, smallest of all, constitute mere boreal islands on the map. Yet the Canadian and the Alpine summits that tower above it are to the other zones important out of all proportion to their size, for they store the water for all the thirsty lands below them.

Here from autumn until late in the spring, the snow lies many feet deep in the spruce-and-fir wilderness. A forestry official told me, on his return from the Mogollon Mountains in the second week of June, that there were then three great patches of snow on the cold side of Whitewater Baldy, and that they looked good for at least another month. At the same time he said that reports coming to him from a rancher stated that in a dark canyon on Black Mountain there was a drift thirty feet deep. Now the intelligent and providential thing about this moisture **is that until about June**, the hottest, dustiest month, much of it is held in reserve for **the valley** fields along the Gila, and then released exactly when it is needed most.

The Canadian Zone, extremely irregular in shape and broken in topography, is clothed everywhere in a somber forest of conifers. The Engelmann spruce, slenderest and most pointed of all, rising against the sky makes an unforgettable silhouette, insistently Canadian in aspect. The giant Douglas firs cover the distant slopes in practically pure stand, gloomy, interrupted only with a scattering of white firs or by a compact patch of light green, which shows where the aspen trees have taken a foothold after some ancient burn.

In the winter great snows accumulate, and in the summer, rain falls almost daily. The luxuriant forest growth springs from the soil, matures, and finally, as the prostrate crumbling trunks give evidence, is resolved again into the soil. In these high, cool, remote solitudes, the processes of life and death proceed unhurried, certain, without interference. A shy bird twitters, a spruce squirrel shows itself momentarily, but other animation is not revealed.

From the shadowed ravines trickle the fine tributaries which go cascading into chilly, willow-bordered brooks, where the trout lurk. But in the wider purposes of nature, good fishing appears somewhat as an afterthought. Up near the clouds the sky gods are paying out from their reservoirs the life-sustaining waters for their creatures below.

And thus the sky rules the whole gamut from lowland deserts to the isolated ridges and cones which pierce the void two miles above them. Yet the chief difference is only this — over the plains the sky is prevailingly cloudless, while over the peaks at an altitude of 13,000 feet or more it is, a good part of the time, cloudy.

Above the line where the last spruces stop short, the barren rocks are clad with plant life which comes down, they say, from the Arctic tundra. I don't know. I have taken a few pictures at timberline and studied the Sangre de Cristo summits with powerful binoculars, but that is all. And yet anyone must see that the immense, remote blotches of snow are valuable to the lowlands where water is given so frugally.

It is the range of temperature which begins at these arctic extremes and scales down—or perhaps up—to those of the torrid deserts, which bestows upon New Mexico its almost unparalleled richness of flora and fauna. Along the Rio Grande marshes, I have identified ibises which had strayed up clear from the tropics.

Says Florence Merriam Bailey in *Birds of New Mexico* (p. 205), "The diversity of New Mexico fauna is one of its most compelling features, a diversity found in only one other state in the Union, and rarely found by the traveller short of the Tropics, where glacier-crowned peaks look down upon groves of spreading palms. For within the boundaries of New Mexico the naturalist finds not only the birds of arid plains and coniferous forests, but Lower Sonoran stragglers from Mexico and heritages of the Arctic-Alpine summits of the northern Rocky Mountains."

The precipitation of the moisture takes place chiefly at two seasons of the year. Throughout the region which includes southeastern Arizona and southwestern New Mexico, there is a sharply defined rainy season which begins in July and extends over through August into September. In this period falls, roughly speaking, half of the annual rainfall.

In his summary of data for this section, Mr. P. O. Day, government climatologist, says: "The rains of summer are local in character and generally traceable to the influence of the mountains interposing their masses to the free passage of the rain-bearing winds. These winds in their passage over the high elevations are cooled by the consequent elevation and expansion sufficiently to cause condensation and precipitation, and while the maximum intensity of these local storms of summer is confined largely to the adjacent mountain areas, the upper currents distribute the precipitation to some extent over the adjacent valleys and plains."

In other words, the summer rains fall chiefly during mountain thunderstorms from clouds which cover only a part of the sky. For these showers no weather map is sufficiently detailed, and the customary data on barometric pressure and wind velocity have only the most limited application. But with the secondary maximum fall of precipitation during the colder months, the case is exactly reversed. Says Mr. Day again: "The precipitation of winter is the result of general storm movement over the district, induced by low areas that develop over the Gulf of California and the lower Colorado Valley, the greater part of the moisture from which, however, is deposited in regions far to the eastward. In the high elevations much of the precipitation of winter occurs as snow, and its gradual melting later in the year serves to maintain a moderate supply of water in the streams till the heavier rains of the late summer appear."

One thing is thus plain. It is on the mountain tops that the rain gods sit, pouring out frugally the life-sustaining moisture from their *ollas* (water jars).

The summer rainy season is worth more than a cursory look, for coming upon the heels of brown, dust-laden June, it is veritably a life saver. With the rains of mid-summer, spring comes back, and the whole country blossoms like the garden of the Lord. Hot weather is now ended, and among the hills that flank the Great Divide, not only the temperature, but the whole face of nature suggests the eastern May. Daily warm thunder-showers call forth the unaccustomed verdure, until at a distance the pastures wear the aspect of an immense, free-spreading green lawn; standing water for a time is common at the roadside; the lean cows grow fat, and with the first thorough soaking of the earth, the forest fires cease. The mercury rises in the middle of the day to the eighties and then stops. At night it drops to the sixties. Multitudes of waiting blossoms open, and though the rose-purple banners of the cholla and the lemon cups of the prickly pear have passed, their place is more than taken by the magnificent ivory lilies of the yucca. Among the junipers, the scarlet paint brush and the shy pent-stemons stain the fresh young grass as with spots of blood. Such is the second springtime and the second growing season, which begins when the first showers drench the Fourth of July picnickers and lasts until some time in September.

A summer cloudburst over the mountains possesses a quality all its own. Lightnings slash the pines; bellowing thunder sets the echoes surging among the peaks and reverberating down the valleys, while from the sky descends vertically a roaring opaque curtain of water — not infrequently with whips of hailstones—that blots out distances and confuses near outlines. The steep slopes shed the deluge like a roof down boulder-strewn washes, and the run-off is immense. In box canyons occur at such times what are known as "wall-floods," in which the water, on the principle of a choke-bore gun, collects, rises high upon the sides and swirls down the narrow trough in a terrifying wall. Farther down the valleys, where the torrents have lost their waterfall aspect, they go racing along the arroyos in an aqueous mixture of sand, silt, and all sorts of débris — a red-brown, unsavory emulsion. Where it has no bed, the stream spreads out; where it must maintain a course between banks, it eddies and stands on end, it foams and leaps with various antics; and where it grinds the bottom down to bedrock, it leaves the granite polished like a clean table.

Where an arroyo crosses a highway in the Southwest, the engineers build not a bridge, but an "apron," and once in so often some inexperienced or too-daring motorist risks the force of the water before it has abated sufficiently, and pays with his life for his error in judgment. The dips are equipped in many places with markers, and a driver ventures into a two-foot stage only at great risk.

But in an hour the flood has raged itself down to a trickle; the late afternoon sky is clearing, and in the twilight there is only a little heat lightning to flicker on the rosy thunderheads. And during the night, the clouds disappear, only to form again next day by noon.

After the rainy season follows an autumn of splendor. In the whole procession of months, October is most brilliant. The bright sky has banished clouds. Slumbrous noondays chill to frosty midnights. Apples hang red among thinning leaves; sere fodder cures on wayside sheds; the Mexicans spread out late peaches to dry in the sun. And then there are the scarlet peppers! At low altitudes, the valley cottonwoods flaunt their intense golden cloud against the azure. At higher levels, a little snow lies in the road under the pines. Growing season comes to an end.

November passes brightly. With the deer season comes freezing weather. Over the village roofs floats the incense of cedar firewood. This is a fragrance that once experienced is never forgotten. December brings increasing chill out of doors, higher fires indoors. For some reason or other the coldest week of the year commonly falls near Christmas, and those who go out to the forest for greens must wade more or less snow.

By January the high peaks are blotched all over with white, and over most of the country there has been a snowfall or two of respectable depth, though probably its duration on the ground has been brief. February and March have their days of cloudiness, yet even so, the ground is drier, on the average, than in summer, and the amount of sunshine in winter is but 2 per cent less than in summer. In this connection Mr. Hallenbeck makes an interesting distinction in the *New Mexico* Magazine for December, 1931. He writes: "There is no part of the country that does not have more sunshine than it wants or needs in summer. In summer sunshine, New Mexico ranks below both Arizona and California, but in winter more than makes up this difference, outranking its nearest competitor, Arizona, by 3.6 per cent. No state in the whole Union can equal New Mexico in the abundance of winter sunshine." The mountains at this time of year are buried under great snowfields, where the Sky Powers are storing moisture to start spring vegetation.

March and April see the beginnings of new growth. Fresh shoots appear at the end of tree branches; the sullen cacti respond faintly to the soaked-up soil water. This is the unloved time of winds and dust. May accelerates reluctant growth with increasing warmth, though with very little additional moisture. In June the dryness rises to a disagreeable crescendo. Roads are ribbons of dust. Forest fires send up their baleful beacons of smoke. Then after ten days of threatening, the July rains begin the cycle all over again, and *spring follows summer.*

But what happens when the customary rains fail — when the clouds form and are dissipated in vain, when the dry winter ends without a big snow? The simple answer is — Drouth. During the first half of the decade which began in 1920, there occurred memorable drouths. At Silver City, the annual records are as follow:

Year	Precipitation	Departure from Normal
1920	15.02	2.90
1921	13.91	3.89
1922	12.54	4.88
1923	16.56	.85
1924	9.67	7.70

In the first half of the decade the total deficiency was nearly one-quarter of the average amount. On the ranges great numbers of cattle came to a miserable death by thirst and starvation, and their whitened bones still lying here and there along the barbed-wire fences bear impressive witness to the power of the sky. In helpless despair, dry-farmers watched one year's crop after another shrivel away. Ranchers were forced into bankruptcy, and most of the banks over the state were compelled to close their doors. Sky Determines!

And immeasurable harm was done also to the land itself. With the resultant overgrazing the useful grasses were killed out, and noxious growths like the broom-weed — which is a reliable sign of overgrazing — sprang up to supersede them, or else the surface of the ground was trampled bare and left open to ruinous erosion. On slopes where the protective carpet of vegetation was cropped away, deep gullies ate far down into the friable subsoil. And lacking the annual replenishment of fertility by decaying roots and stems, the ground quickly lapsed into barrenness. Where the brush was destroyed, animal life disappeared on account of lack of cover. The cottontop quail, for instance, was during this time exterminated throughout a large part of its range, and even now its haunts have not become entirely restocked.

The sky is never without significance in New Mexico. Clouded or cloudless, it has an effect on the land. When it rains, the earth is being nourished; when it is clear, growth takes place at a prodigious rate, but evaporation is also immensely accelerated. Here the air, a mile above sea level, is very thin, very clear, very dry, and down through it blazes a southern sun with an ardency that sets the molecules of water dancing at a rate elsewhere unsurpassed. Such by an elementary law of physics.

And fifteen inches of precipitation along the Canadian border, where the humidity is high, the air cool, the sky often cloudy, and the altitude fairly low, is in actual effect very different from the same amount along the Mexican border where all these conditions are reversed. Some experiments at the New Mexico State University have established the fact that there the total amount of evaporation from a tank is from five to six feet per year. Similar experiments at Fort Collins, Colorado, show the mean evaporation to be only about forty inches — a little more than half as much.

One more consequence of the clear sky is the rapid rate at which radiation takes place. In the Mississippi Valley thick, muggy air and a curtain of cloud often prevent the escape of the earth's heat during the night, so that the temperature changes but a few degrees. But in New Mexico, while the rocks and the uncarpeted landscape absorb great quantities of heat during midday, the temperature drops sharply at sunset. With few or no clouds to retard radiation, so much heat is lost that even after warm days frost often nips the plants at night.

When consideration is given to rainfall, to hailstorms, to drouth, to winter snows, to high evaporation and early frost, it is small wonder that the puebl23eños, who are farmer folk dependent upon nature's bounty, are so obsessed with the importance of the religious dance. From the obscure depths of antiquity to the present, their one unchanging litany to the Sky Powers has been,

SAVE US, OR WE PERISH!

And naturally enough, the Mexican farmers retain the same idea. Over the world farmers all must depend pretty much on faith. In Merrie England through the Middle Ages, priest and people solemnly traversed the parish bounds on Rogation Days blessing the crops. Indeed — to speak with the long perspective of history — this dependence of man upon his environment endured till rapid transportation on the great trails of commerce ended it only yesterday. Along the Rio Grande and the Mimbres they feel the human dependence as of old, and annually they bless the fields with the ancient formulas on San Ysidro's Day, the fourth of April. The following sympathetic account of the ceremony is clipped from the editorial page of the *Las Cruces* (N. M.) *Citizen:*

Last Sunday San Ysidro came out of his retirement and borne on the shoulders of four residents of Old Mesilla, preceded by a hundred young women dressed in white and bearing the blue cross of the Virgin, a hundred boys with the red cross representing the children of Christ, forty choir girls singing hymns and twenty little girls with veils and crowns, paraded the streets of Old Mesilla and for the distance of a mile up and down the valley viewed the fields of the farmers. San Ysidro, who is the patron of agriculture, yearly makes this pilgrimage to insure the fertility of the fields, protect the crops from the ravages of locusts, and bring the gentle rains to the land. The figure of the saint is that of a stalwart man, well over five feet tall wearing boots and carrying a spade of American make, for the image is New York made. But George Griggs, whose Billy the Kid museum holds many a relic of historic and artistic interest, has the original San Ysidro of Old Mesilla, a small fellow only about two feet in height, carved out of a gnarled wood, and with his two oxen and ancient yoked plow quite wormeaten and decrepit.

Since the dawn of time peoples of all races and colors have in the spring of the year asked the aid of some deity, wood god, or saint, in propitiating the powers of nature, which can be so ruthless in their treatment of mankind.

Even today when we rely upon the biological survey of the United States to control the locusts, the reclamation service and irrigation district to furnish water, and the pure seed association to insure the fertility of the seed, we still feel the need of another intermediary.

The emotional and aesthetic effect of the sky is no less real than the practical one. Here one sees it all — 180 glorious, colorful degrees of it. In any direction save downwards, it fills the larger part of the view and the eye cannot lift without being aware of its magnificence. All day long it offers for the efforts of nature, celestial colorist, a stupendous dome, which for weeks on end she hangs with curtains of the sincerest, heart-comforting azure, or tiring, frescoes with idle, pearl-white angels. But when the summer rains begin, she sits and, like a squaw weaving a blanket, splashes the evening firmament with bizarre patterns of crimson and ochre edged with orange flame. And then at twilight, she paints out the whole of it and begins again with a wash of tender, uncertain greys.

Beginning when the night draws to an end, a perceptible lightening appears at the bottom of the dome where it reaches down to meet the earth. In a while the indefinite luminosity has ripened to full dawn. As the sun lifts half-way over the horizon, the furrowed margin of the mesa is tinged instantly with gold, and unguessed fractured spires and domes are thrust forth from mountain walls. The day's color transmutations have begun. Through the unwatched hours they continue until the sunset, when the whole cosmic pageant is re-enacted in reverse order.

Even the "sick man" (tuberculosis patient), prostrate upon his bed from weary dawn to wearier twilight, is cheered and sustained with gazing out upon a rectangle of blank sky, which turns, hour after hour, with delicacy beyond reach of water color, from silvery yellow to turquoise and azure, and finally to saffron and rose.

But the light is more impressive still than the color. In fact, the magic of the colors is due in no small part to the illumination under which they are viewed. To one whose conception of the sun's power is gained, say, in an eastern city, the supreme radiance of the Southwest is indescribable. It is a sort of spiritual experience, a a psychic phenomenon. It renders intelligible the rapture of the ancient Greek dramatist, when he exclaims, "Hail, holy light, the eye of golden day!" In a world of prose, this light is sheerest poetry, Promethean glory.

Coming southward on a transcontinental train, one becomes conscious before approaching the Mexican Border at El Paso of a different quality in the light. It has more than double the brightness than that to which he is accustomed — and the scientific proof is in his camera. An exposure meter shows, in fact, that a photographic plate is affected some three times as rapidly as in New York. For this the extreme clarity of the air accounts in part and the high altitude in part. Objects are not blurred and diffused by particles of floating water vapor, nor here, five thousand feet above sea level, are the ultra-violet rays screened out by the last mile of thick, dust-laden strata on their earthward journey. Here the light seems to bite into the negative as the etcher's acid bites into his copper plate. And contributing to the half preternatural brightness are the almost vertical position of the sun — especially in summer — above this southern land, the immense reflecting power of the buff, uncarpeted landscape, and the absence of shadows.

But to experience the sky, one must be alone in it — on a mountain top. Alone and still! One does not sing or shout, for the mountain silences must be respected, and echoes are commanded but by the thunder. Nor does one move about much. Small concerns are rebuked in such a place. One climbs and contemplates.

A hawk sails past, fan-tailed, and the panorama extended beneath the bird's eye epitomizes the whole domain of desert, mesa, and mountain. Over it arches a dome resembling in color the blue of the beautiful copper ore called azurite, while from near its apex beats down the transcendent splendor of noonday from the sun's unmuffled disk.

Far below, the hills withdraw from a thread of level ground pockmarked by old-time mining — Chloride Flat, the valley of silver, now as deserted as a cemetery, and marked off by monuments of red-rusted machinery. Eastward ten miles some rows of geometric dots tell the location of Fort Bayard, an outpost erected in the 'sixties against marauding redskins, and now a tranquil hospital for tuberculosis. Beyond gapes the mile-long crater of one of the world's great copper mines at Santa Rita, which more than a century ago was already worked by the Spaniards. Though other hamlets are hidden away in the foothills' red folds, a half turn of the head brings into view a lonely prospect that has been for a thousand years the same — a far-flung region of ultramarine air, empire of the sun, where from the mile-high plateau, sinister crusts of lava crop out to show the land's anatomy, and where the sleek, deceptive plain, tawny and soft-looking as fawnskin, but bitter with age-long drouth, recedes into a sky so remote as to recall the earth's curvature. Grandly the eye circles peak by peak. Along the horizon rise into the sky misty, serrated spectres — Hatchet Mountain tinted but not obscured by eighty miles of blue air; the Tres Hermanas, three accurate barren pyramids which look from the Border far down into Mexico, and a whole catalog of lesser elevations. Close in, comparatively speaking, squats one of the characteristic stone-capped formations, so common in parts of the Southwest, to which Spanish explorers gave the name *mesas*, tables. Not far behind it rises a small, skull-shaped hill ridged across the crown like an antique Roman helmet. Massacre Peak, it is called, for at its foot is a grave wherein rest sixteen bodies, victims of a raid some seventy years ago by the Apache chieftain Victorio.

Westward one faces out upon Upper Sonoran country, whose characteristic color through most of the arid year is that of its ripened grasses. Half a dozen leagues beyond the Great Divide, where the treeless hills go billowing up toward Wild Horse Mesa, these grasses give the country a sheen from October until July that looks as if some Sir Walter had flung over it a cape of golden velvet, with rich high lights where it crumpled into hasty folds; for there, as day ends, the sun's last serene magnificence alternates upon bright slopes and their amethyst valleys behind them, level full of shadow. And yet in the illumination of grey days, the dissected slopes have the appearance of a wrinkled, beardless skin, dry and of infinite age.

And in the whole immensity, smiles not one tilled

field. On that matter the Sky Powers gave their decision long ago.

"And just how transparent is this air?" asks an observer. One answer is that at night the naked eye, gazing at the bowl of the Great Dipper, can detect there stars down to the fifth magnitude and below. The reason is that at elevations ranging from five thousand to ten thousand feet, we have between our eyes and the heavens from one-tenth to one-fourth less atmosphere than we should have in the eastern states. When the moon is full, there is sufficient light for reading common seven-point type (used in national magazines), and Cook's Peak, forty miles distant, can be seen as readily — though not so distinctly — as by day.

Thought turns dreamily to astronomical diagrams, cosmic fantasies. The unmuffled sun with its white searing glory sets the ether dancing, and stirs a reverent wonder about the space above with its myriad of other suns; while in the east climbs a slow young moon, hourglass of the skies, following its path with the probity of higher mathematics.

CHAPTER THREE

DESERT

LONG AGO ONE OF THE GREEK sky gods stole the chariot of the sun. Unable to control the mighty coursers of Apollo, he permitted them to approach too near the earth, where the heat seared a broad band across its middle. To this day the scar of the burn remains. It is called the Sahara. On the other side of the earth, somewhere near the same latitude, another part of the same scar is visible, though less long and less deep. It used to be called the American Desert.

Nowhere, indeed, is the sky's determination of earth so emphatically sharp as on the desert. There the immense excess of heat and the extreme rate of evaporation combine with the insufficiency of precipitation to produce a complete though one-sided responsiveness. In New Mexico the general level of the country, which lies at an altitude of about five thousand feet, is not screened from the sun's imperial flame by the lowest, densest mile of atmosphere which so dampens its effect; consequently, the protection against its penetrating power is small, and by the very lack of density in the high air the molecules of water are enabled to pass quickly into vapor. And thus the sun becomes a desert-maker.

But the reader is warned at the outset against the vulgar error of believing that the American Southwest is everywhere and over all desert. Even by reputable geographers, it is true, the American Desert was once accepted as a reality, and only the ferocity of its perils matched the span of its area. The short-grass country, which begins in Kansas and extends to the foothills of the Rockies, was thus included, and the vast tract lying between the Texas and New Mexico line, and the strip of paradise along the Pacific was considered one unmitigated Sahara. In fact, the image which rises in many an Easterner's mind today at the mention of the Southwest includes a waste of shifting sand across which a ten-mule team draws a covered wagon with much sweat and dust, while the brave pioneer and his whole family at the end of the scene expire like the snuffing of a candle, as the sun continues to blaze.

But a truer picture is found in a government pamphlet recently issued by the Forest Service:

The impression entertained by the uninitiated that the Southwest is essentially a land of treeless wastes, cactus, and deserts is a mistaken one. It is true that there are great areas of these interesting geographic types. In addition, however, the Southwest contains millions of acres of fir and pine-clad mountains, and includes among its plants and animals species that live up to the Arctic and down by the Tropic of Cancer. Within this region lies the greatest expanse of pure pine forest in the world. The Arctic ptarmigan and the Mexican jaguar are both at home there, and from the cold heights above timber line, where only tiny Alpine flowers grow, one can see with the naked eye hot low-lying deserts, the habitat of the giant cactus.

The desert, exotic, terrible, fabulous — what is it, and where? While the reality is no myth, its fangs have been drawn. With the first highway, its terrors paled; and with the first automobile, an iron horse which neither drouth nor heat can conquer, they disappeared. Today, for the motorist speeding at fifty miles an hour or better over a resilient ribbon of asphalt, it is no menace at all. But in the back country a row of cans fastened to the running board — a red one for gasoline, a blue one for oil, and a white one for water — still exhibits a measure of respect for it. (Since these words were written, roads have been improved, cars have grown more dependable as well as faster, and even the back country is not without filling stations.)

Seen through the double window of a Pullman, the desert is a progressive experience. Yet not an impressive one, particularly. The second night out from shivering, snow-blanketed Chicago, the train speeds from Kansas across a tip of Oklahoma and the corner of Texas. At daybreak next morning, one lifts the curtain and peeps out on a world which he is likely to call desert. To his eyes there is almost a complete absence of signs of human habitation. The landscape is arid, there is a conspicuous lack of running streams, the hills are thinly spotted with dwarf cedars, and over the plain stand, scattered at random, thousands of what appear to be bushy-topped fence posts — yuccas. Such is the indefinite margin of the Land of Little Rain.

Then southward along the barren western scarp of the Sacramento Range. Out from it an immense spread of red-earth dunes heaped ten feet high by the winds, and each crowned by a scraggy, vicious mesquite bush recedes towards the boundary mountains beyond. Southward the aspect of the land grows more formidable still. Serrated, naked crags rise out of the plain in fantastic formations that resemble piles of furnace slag, and the whole face of the country suggests the action of fire. The bareness of the ground that shows between the widely spaced vegetation indicates significantly the amount of available moisture. In vain, the squinting eye searches for masses of shadow to cool and comfort.

Leaving the border city of El Paso in the early morning of a January day, the traveler experiences even from a car window the first sensation of the desert — its timelessness. To say that the desert has no seasons would be inexact, yet it creates the illusion of having none. The unfailing wonder of mornings that remain forever cloudless, the gaunt reddish mountains that never at any time lose their seared look; the absence of any motion or life that one can perceive; the grey, dusty green of a vegetation that neither freshens with the springtime nor flames with the autumn — these impressions brood over the desert, and help to infix the notion that here all the todays are like the yesterdays, and that the morrows will not be different. In the north, winter sunshine is a fleeting, precious thing that flashes with the brevity of a smile through sullen clouds; here it seems to come with the inevitability of the morning, a permanent benediction. It appears merely nature's way of beginning the day, the same for a million years. An inexpressible sense of standing still amidst the transiencies of mortality — such is the first subtle feel of the desert.

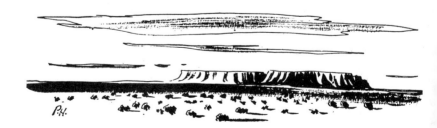

Westward strikes the route. Yesterday a disgruntled traveller remarked: "The rest of the way to the coast is all the same. Twenty-four hours more of sage brush." Yet he had seen little or no sage, and the way is not the same for any considerable distance. We skirt a lava field, a low, black, broken expanse of volcanic rock spewed out by the earth in some primeval convulsion. Jagged, burnt-out, satanic, it lies now, a favorite summer haunt of rattlesnakes. The Mexicans call it *malpais,* bad country. And though green with the shrub that one later learns to call creosote bush *(Laurrea Tridentata),* this is a spot of the real desert.

The sticky, scented plant is really worth a second glance. Shunning the depressions where a trace of moisture may contrive to elude the searches of wind and sun, it prefers to bury its feet in sun-scorched gravel slopes and defy the elements. More than the ocotillo, more than the mesquite, more even than any of the cacti, it is the spirit of the waste lands.

But the lava yields presently to red earth and a different vegetation. In the southwest corner of New Mexico, the plain rises almost imperceptibly to an altitude of 4,500 feet at the Continental Divide, yet one would start down the other side unconscious of the fact, were it not for an announcement on a large signboard. The region everywhere exhibits varying degrees of desolation and aridity, yet everywhere it is alike in the sense of being uninhabited. Miles of yucca and whitened bunch grass alternate with others of mesquite, where the red earth lies bare between high-piled hummocks, and with others, where on the pale gravel, creosote occurs in pure sand. Generally the three growths avoid invasions of one another's territory. Where the yuccas grow, one sees white-faced Herefords grazing, but elsewhere he will see no more of animal life than a hawk sailing low on tilted pinions or the retreating black tail of a jack rabbit. Yet, except for snow-dusted mountains always rising in the background, the land is not wrapped in mid-winter bleakness. The Lower Sonoran Zone — so named from a province in Old Mexico — is drenched with a sunshine that even in January warms one's shoulders, though at night the chill may reach several degrees below freezing. And the yuccas, the creosote, the ragged wire-leafed shrub called popotillo, and the prickly pears, preserve all winter long their illusory greenness and thus keep up the appearance of growth.

Near the Arizona line, one glimpses the first barrel cacti — a distinct step in the approach to the culmination of desert. Traversing a few counties more, one finds the cacti, whose lesser members he has many times noted already, culminating in the splendid sahuaro, a fluted green column that reaches a height of more than thirty feet. Its grotesque form seems to introduce a new world, yet the sight he pictures is not yet. Not until he has left Yuma, and is across the Colorado River upon the soil of California, do the heat, aridity, and sand combine to produce his ideal desert. Then at last appear the rising, wind-waved hills of brown sand. It is the Sahara which he has always pictured.

Yet these naked dunes are not really the type of the desert. In fact, so noteworthy are they that their location is marked on the maps, and their slopes are used as background for motion pictures. Moreover, their extent is a disappointment, being only some twenty-five miles in length and hardly a fourth as much in width.

Nor does the famous Painted Desert in northern Arizona better fulfill one's expectation, for it is a desolation not of sands but of parti-colored clays and marls.

Towards the horizon, its coloration is second only to that of the Grand Canyon, but it is a phenomenon by itself rather than typical desert. And the remarkable White Sands of Alamogordo, New Mexico, though now enjoying the dignity that attaches to a national monument, are still farther from the scene pictured by imagination, for they are not sand at all, but gypsum.

Two hundred and seventy square miles of it lie in unsullied whiteness spread out beneath the sky, a little less brilliant than snow, though only a little less. Unlike true sands, they reveal under a magnifier no ebony grains of mica, but are of uniform composition, size, and color. Barring the presence of scattered yuccas and a few other shrubs that appear incredibly able to sustain life without water or soil, their drifting slopes are bare, and, there being nothing to defile them, pure.

The whiteness of this desert has produced an effect known nowhere else, for, during the ages, it has actually modified the color of the animal life upon it. Only recently a scientific expedition was sent out to make a study of the white mice and other small creatures of the locality. Other deserts are tawny; this one could rival Antarctica.

Yet it is not the scientific interest of this waste, but its eerie loveliness which makes it deserve to be set aside as a reservation. In the eye-contracting incandescence of this pure desolation dwells beauty of an unknown quality. With silence not desecrated by the sound of one steam whistle, with air unpolluted by drifts of coal smoke, it is ringed round by violet mountains, and overarched by a sky whose azure approaches the darkest part of the spectrum. And over its unsoiled surface there are strewn none of the bits of driftwood and refuse with which the ocean defiles its margin. If a bit of the desert is ever preserved in the museum of paradise, it will be lifted from the virginal White Sands.

While aridity is thus seen to be a progressive experience from Chicago to Yuma and beyond, there is no general agreement as to what constitutes a desert. A plant or an animal may have half a dozen common names, but there is a Latin name which identifies it for scientists of all lands and in all languages. Not so the waste places.

Perhaps as good a definition as any would be "a place where no life form survives without special adaptation to aridity." A survey of the desert scene soon produces in an observer a vigorous recoil from the notion of Nature as mother.

The potency of desert sunshine is not easily overstated. While in terms of the thermometer the government observers keep close tab on the maxima, their instruments are always placed in the shade to prevent the mercury from absorbing the sun's direct rays, and thus since there is no shade on the desert, their accuracy is for ordinary purposes apparent rather than real. The yucca's leaf casts no more shadow than a sword blade, and the other typical growths reach to less than a man's height. In summer the wind feels like the breath of an oven. It seems incredible that without fire, air could be so hot. Only the rattlesnake, twined under the saltbush's shadow, preserves its lethal chill.

And to the heat, drouth adds its hostility. Along the Mexican Border, the rainfall amounts to about seven inches annually, and over the Lower Sonoran Zone in the Rio Grande Valley, as far north as Albuquerque, it is but little more. Most of it falls in brief summer downpours, and is quickly absorbed by the heated sands. The sky clears, the sun reappears, and all trace of rain disappears. The atmosphere drinks in moisture like a sponge, and for this reason one does not perspire — except under the hatband — for sweat dries away as it forms. Meat when exposed to the sun does not decay, but dries and cures; and for centuries the Indians and native people have been preserving meat by this method. A cartridge shell dropped on the sand lies for years untarnished. Everything gives the impression of dried-out brittleness — as in extreme coldness. A creosote branch snaps off short without bending.

The drouth alone and of itself would not have its terrific effect were it not for the desert-making sun and the desert-making wind which are in alliance with it. In a cooler region farther north, where the moisture is dissipated slowly, its deficiency would be felt vastly less. But here the wind, being intensely hot, is, in consequence, intensely dry; and, although bearing vast quantities of water from the Pacific and the Gulf of California, it becomes so highly heated over the intervening country that instead of precipitating, it is enabled to absorb more moisture. So in an area receiving but a few inches of rainfall annually, it busies itself daily in removing any unconsidered trifles of even that small amount. The twain are irresistible by any cultivated plants, unless fortified by abundance of water. The best resistance to them is leaflessness, and that the all-thorn, the blue thorn (*Zizyphus lycioides*) , and others of their kind well know. Their skeleton branches oppose the desiccating blasts with entire impunity.

On those formidable days when not a roadrunner is hunting lizards and not even a buzzard is on the wing; when the jack rabbit, panting in the shade of a yucca stalk, droops his mule-like ears for the heat, and the wind is busy at its routine of sweeping the desert floor of its powdered débris, one will observe its whirling offspring, the dust-devils. Forever on unremunerated errands, they traverse the brush back and forth, hour after hour, in purposeless haste. Turbulent and harpy-fingered — weren't the Harpies unclean snatchers who were always throwing things into a disorder? — they go coiling in a left-hand spiral, swaying among the hummocks, sucking up clouds of light dust high into the sky, only to let them aimlessly subside again. Half a dozen may be performing at the same time. Along the White Sands of Alamogordo, the whirlwinds, laden with a much heavier substance, stand erect for long moments, the slimness of their shining gypsum columns deceiving the eye by apparent motionlessness.

But the real season of dusty winds is spring. Then come upon the waste those evil, dun-colored monsters called dust storms. Less accurate is the name sand storms, for blown sand, being heavy, does not fly high but sweeps along in a thin abrading sheet near the ground. In them the irreconcilable savage in nature rises to the surface.

Drawing its substance from those portions of the desolation where the floor between the snaggy thorn bushes is of bare sand and loam, the tawny cloud, as it approaches from a distance, draws an opaque yet sunlit band across the flats and hides the base of the mountains. Then fugitive tumbleweeds begin to race like fleeing animals. In myriads they go rolling and leaping towards some faroff barbed-wire fence, where they lodge and build themselves into a four-foot wall of indefinite length, catching wind enough to loosen staples and often pull the strands from their posts. The few straying cattle stand with heads down and tails to the storm; and the desert itself, though long habituated to torments, seems trying to escape. Though the sky is without a cloud, a mountain two miles distant may, in literal fact, be invisible. The yuccas spring their stiff, gaunt forms before the blast, looking more grotesque than ever in the pale obscurity; the dried winter broomweeds are snapped off at the root, revealing bare sand where yesterday there was a little loam and dead vegetation. And the low sweep of the blast claws at the hummocks of captive sand beneath the mesquite bushes and drifts it to the leeward in tapering, rippled tails. In the interior of the turmoil, day sinks to a drab, lurid twilight which has the character of a solar eclipse. All colors are greyed, and through the obscurity of gritty, suffocating dust a copper sun burns palely.

On the desert the very air itself is different. Contorted and agitated by the heat, it quivers like water, making binoculars next to useless for objects close to the ground, since they magnify the intervening vibrations. At middays from April to November outlines of distant trees and low hills waver through the heated medium as though viewed through a running stream. In the distance mirages create for the eye tremulous, elusive lakes which vanish into clear light as one goes onward.

Isolated upon the level plain rise island-like peaks, "drowned" as geologists say, in gravel. Many of them would amount to considerable mountains in their own right, but the débris removed from the higher ridges not far-distant has been carried down by erosion and redeposited around them in a level sheet that has deeply submerged their base.

With a somewhat different result the same process has been at work on the higher ridges themselves. Exposed to the action of erosion, to alternate freezing and thawing, and to the curious fissure-widening by rock wedges, the most resistant cliff finally disintegrates, splinters into giant fragments, which lie where they fall. Disintegrating in turn, these talus deposits themselves are transported downwards and outwards by torrents to form outwash fans; and at length, the fans coalescing, form not a level sheet but a continuous sloping mantle, which adjusted snugly to every inlet and bay of the mountain's shape, enfolds it and extends from half-way up its side down to the valley level. The sheerest crags thus surround themselves with chippings of their own limestone, granite, and lava, which the floods sort out and grade into boulders and pebbles of gradually diminished size as they descend the slope. Then when a little soil has accumulated among the rocks, desert plants take up the task of reclaiming the ground, century plants and barrel cacti first, then the sotol and ocotillos. On the gravel, farther down, creosote speedily crowds out all contestants, and its dull olive green indicates the limit of outwash material as clearly as though on a colored map.

When, as in the extreme southwestern corner of the state, the mountains rise close together or stand in neighboring parallel ridges, like the Hatchet, the Animas, the Peloncillo, and the Chiricahua (the last just across the line in Arizona), there are formed by these vast outwash slopes valleys of the type called *bolsons* — "pockets." Here in these sinks, which one inevitably likens to the bottom of a bowl, the forces of desolation attain to their stark climax. The reason is in part physical, in part chemical.

The drainage of the surrounding mountain slopes, carrying in solution the salts and alkalis freed by the decomposition of rocks, descends along the small lateral arroyos to a main trunk. With no outlet it can only pour out its floods upon the lower lands to seek their own level. Having no bed, the water spreads itself over the basin in a sheet sometimes miles long and only a few inches deep; and when the valley floor is of plastic, impervious clay, it has no escape except by evaporation, and thus on these *playas* it frequently stands from the rainy season throughout the winter. Such are Animas Lake on Highway 80 south of Lordsburg, and the well-known Playas Lake farther south, which is sufficiently permanent to be marked on maps. Thick with silt, such bodies of water when roiled by the wind have an exact *café au lait* hue. Mesquite follows an arroyo to the basin and rank sacaton grass surrounds it with a margin, but neither ventures upon it.

Here in January I have chanced upon a flock of wild mallards wintering, and in the surrounding clay there were countless tracks made by the webbed feet of waterfowl. Such paradoxes one encounters upon the desert.

But when at length the desert-making sun has had its effect, and evaporation has removed the last lingering pools, the playa is desolate. Desert plants cannot endure the water, and marsh plants cannot endure the desert. So neither can capture and redeem the spot, which relapses into a mournful and perennial baldness. Stripped of the mysteriousness which water always gives, the floor of these so-called dry lakes cracks into polygons of dried, silty clay so smooth that boys could play marbles upon it.

Then over the bareness an unholy chemistry deposits a white encrustation of alkali leached from the weathering rocks. Partly it comes from the standing water and partly from evaporation of the saturated ground water. Ultimately the solution becomes so highly concentrated in such soils as to exceed the toleration of the strongest plants. But the chemical ban on vegetation is superfluous, seeing how effective is the other.

Touch this crust with the tongue and it stings like

salt, is bitter like soda. And when the tortured land lies dry and hot in summer, the wind whips the particles into the air. And along one of these lakes in northern Mexico I have seen a cloud of it drifting like a grey mist for miles, high enough and dense enough to obscure a mountain beyond. Such are the desolate leavings of what is called indifferently soda lake, dry lake, alkali flat.

There are two other chemical manifestations which seem to belong with peculiar appropriateness to the wastes. One is the white subsoil deposit of lime called *caliche,* and the other is a similar coating of calcium carbonate, which frequently is observed on black lava.

Caliche is a lime hardpan which at the surface occurs in small nodules or fragments, but often increases in density a foot or two below the surface until it forms a firmly cemented layer of almost rock-like hardness. Along the many cut-banks of the desert it is exposed as a white stratum which creates an effective barrier alike to water and to roots. It is loved only by the creosote.

The other calcium deposit is likewise hard and white. Occurring where underground waters gave up their lime long ago, it appears somehow, when coated upon black volcanic boulders of basalt, the product of some peculiarly sinister intention.

In addition to the wet-weather lakes, one chances sometimes upon a lone waterhole — for often enough while there is no water on the desert, there may be plenty under the surface. In the arroyos it flows over the sands but briefly, then, sinking out of sight, continues its course as an underground seep. Where it crosses a bed of caliche or stone, it is brought to the surface in an isolated pool.

Inevitably the place becomes a focus of animal life, and along its margin the naturalist reads signs of the creatures which are for the most part invisible. Here he may frighten up a pair of kildeers in noisy alarm, or even a wild duck, but in any case the mud tells its story. This four-toed mark as long as a cattle brand was left unmistakably by a heron. These others show where a skunk sneaked past on a nocturnal errand. And on the sand dunes which the wind has concentrated and swept together upon the bank above, myriads of other feet have left a record. This trail that looks like a dog's and moves straight ahead was left by a coyote; this other with two prints widely spaced and two others close together was made as a jack rabbit's long hind legs straddled his front ones. Mouse tracks are everywhere, especially under plants with ripened seeds. This path leading out from a red adobe mound with its several exits was worn by kangaroo rats, but significantly it does not lead to water, for kangaroo rats, like many other small mammals here, obtain sufficient moisture from cactus and hence do not drink. One of the lesser inhabitants — which one I have not been able to discover — leaves the mark of his dragging tail between his footprints. The ruinous enlargement of a ground squirrel's burrow, made by powerful forelegs and long claws, is the signature of a foraging badger. And a row of tiny depressions so faint as scarcely to have disturbed the dust is the lacy trail of a lizard.

Significantly absent among the desert folk is one animal that is elsewhere common in warm habitats — the opossum. Defenseless, fat, slow, it finds existence too savage among the swift, alert predators here. Antithesis — the pack rats which erect great strongholds in a bed of prickly pear. There they accumulate a pile of thorns, sticks, dried dung, burrs from the cholla, and other miscellany sufficient to fill a wagon. Among the signs of animal life these are the most conspicuous — unless it be the number of bones, frail, blanched relics of death, which continually the ever-drifting grains cover and re-cover.

Here, where unimposing creatures like rats build themselves impressive citadels, one may expect attack to be ferocious and continual. And in this domain of prey, so it is. King of the predators, the mountain lion readily kills cattle and deer, though like the bears, he prefers forested mountains to open desert ranges. Bobcats, while seldom seen in daytime, prowl everywhere by night, and are among the commonest carnivores to accept the trapper's bait. Coyotes, nature's trickiest full-size sneakers, make themselves at home everywhere, living indifferently upon mice or calves. Shot at, trapped, poisoned, they still hold their own, and their voice is heard on winter nights at the margin of every village. In addition, heavy-bodied, hog-nosed skunks, little hydrophobia skunks, badgers, foxes, big, long-bodied weasels — all help to keep life gaunt, alert, thin-flanked.

Competing with the jaw and fang mechanisms mounted upon four feet, there are the predators of the air — creatures of beak and talon propelled by wings — eagles, owls, hawks, and even shrikes (butcher birds) in wide profusion. Driving one January day to the Tres Hermanas Peaks, I counted six large hawks before noting another winged creature. Everywhere above the mice, rats, ground squirrels, and most of all, the unarmed and prolific jack rabbits, descends an avalanche of winged beings that pluck and rend, hungry for carnage. Then add to all the dreaded rattlesnakes.

In the plant world the case is not different. There the growing thing endeavors to encase itself in impenetrable armor against the gnawing thing. The succulent pads of prickly pear, though defended by three-inch barbed needles, show constantly the depredations of small teeth. Then the eater becomes meat for another's appetite, and thus the cycle of life rings changes unendingly on the verb *devour*. . . . I devour, I devoured, I am devoured.

But plants cannot attack. Theirs must be weapons of defense. *Voilà*, the thorn!

If the desert is not essentially a place of drifting sands, it is emphatically a place of thorns. There, as the running and creeping creatures have their fang, the vegetation stands ready with drawn dagger. In a warfare which is perpetual and of a ferocity elsewhere unequalled, water is the key, for water is life. And for life everyone fights.

The thorn was doubtless nature's first weapon. Eons before the first claw, ages before the first tooth, there was evolved the first thorn. When strife first began, the thorn was ready. In one form or another it runs all through life. It adds a sentimental interest to every rose, and it was once used on a tragic Friday to make a royal crown; but it reaches its final development on the cactus, nature's *picador* of the desert. While some plants, like the creosote bush, attain to safety by means of an ill-smelling varnish, and others, like the loco, have a juice that causes madness or other poisoning, and still others have various unusual but effective protections, the conventional weapon is the thorn. And the thorn, instead of the sand ripple, I nominate as symbol of the desert.

There is a cactus called in Spanish *bisnaga*, which at a distance has all the appearance of a giant watermelon protruding one end of its rounded form from the earth, and it, too, it filled with a juicy pulp. But there the resemblance ends abruptly. Imagine the fate of anything moistly edible and at the same time vulnerable, if left unprotected for a night among the four-footed population of the desert. But the *bisnaga*, or as we call it, barrel cactus, squats safely year after year in the same spot, guarding its reservoir as effectively as the Wagnerian dragon guards its hoard. "I lie here possessing," it says dragonwise to every passer-by. Back of the defiance is the thorn.

Equally menacing is the shrub beside it — the ocotillo, most bizarre and splendid thing on the waste. Until May it stands looking like nothing but a bundle of dead sticks in the ground. It branches grudgingly, and the dozen or so single wands seem to have nothing in common but the root. Then one day, as you go past again, the dead-looking stems, which oftentimes have yet not a green leaf, have suddenly become tipped with an unsurpassable flame of the most exquisite scarlet blossoms. Sometimes before, sometimes after they open, the stalks become covered with tiny soft leaves, but in them lurk the wickedest thorns, which stand so close together that even a lady's slender fingers can scarce grasp them without a wound.

Both these plants shun mountain and plain, but thrive on the great outwash slopes which connect the two. Their habitat is thus narrowly marked out into a band only a few hundred feet from top to bottom. Interspersed among them and limited to the same kind of terrain, the *sotol,* or dasylirion, bears on its tough, straplike leaves a margin of claws — bent, sharp, and strong enough to tear the skin viciously. And on the same stony and forbidding slopes, the century plant, or mescal, has likewise rows of very adequate marginal spines, but owns in addition a stiff terminal spike that will pierce a heavy boot. While Spanish dagger is a name applied indiscriminately to half a dozen sorts of yucca and agave, none merits the title more than this plant.

At a considerably higher altitude — up towards seven

thousand feet — a different species comes in. Its closely overlapping blades are shorter and stouter, grouping themselves into a ferocious rosette. Such is the *latifolia* mescal, from which the dreaded Mescalero Apaches, whose ferocity equaled that of the plant, took their name. Year by year one will lurk unnoticed beside a boulder. Finally comes the proud season when it decides to flower. From a circle of daggers a stalk shoots up with amazing swiftness, climbing half a foot in twenty-four hours. When the shaft is six inches across at the base and some fifteen feet tall, the yellow-and-red flowers appear. But the flowering is not alone the triumph of the plant's life, but its tragedy. Before the blossoms have fallen the leaves have turned from green to a livid purple, and it is assuming the look of death.

Common, too, are the cat-claw, whose popular name describes it well, but whose scientific name, *biuncifera* — double-clawed — describes it better; the bluethorn, a leafless shrub of glaucous hue, and the all-thorn associated with a sinister tradition. Its other name, Jerusalem thorn, alludes to the belief among pious Mexicans that it is the identical bramble from which the soldiers of Pontius Pilate plaited the Crown of Thorns.

Mesquite and yucca, two of the major plant forms of the region, are nowise inferior to the others in defense mechanisms. Yuccas of several varieties abound in New Mexico — the rigid-leafed, the narrow-leafed, the large-fruited, etc., and all bear glorious flowers. When one stands in a field where hundreds of the *Yucca radiosas*, towering ten feet above his head, outline their aspiring torches of ivory lilies upon the azure background, it is a pattern to gladden eyes and stir emotions. But all can inflict a wound.

The thorn all of these plants possess in common. And

what variety of devilish instruments! The blade of one yucca is a sword, while that of another is a tremulous rapier; that of the mescal is a wide dagger; and yet other growths are armed with claws, fish hooks, and needles. Thus it happens that none has experienced the desert who has not felt its stabs.

There remains one plant family which has gathered into itself, as no other has done, the ferocity, the grotesqueness, the protective adaptations, and the unsurpassable loveliness of the desert — cacti.

Though there is indeed a certain prickly quality about the very name, one soon learns that a cactus is not merely any plant that has stickers. A cactus is a perfectly definite growth that has no leaves and a green, leathery skin. Its stem is thick and fleshy, usually of cylindrical or globose shape, except when flattened as in the prickly pears; and spines are borne not at random all over the surface, but in small restricted areas known as areolae. The flowers, notable for size as well as beauty, have earned for the cactus the nickname "desert orchid" — which seems inadequate. In ornamentation nothing in the plant kingdom surpasses it; and in stubborn vitality, nothing equals it nor comes so close to immortality.

The adaptations of plant life to the arid environment are manifold. The ocotillo is coated with a water-tight inner bark that in both appearance and hardness approaches horn; the creosote bush is sticky with a disagreeable varnish that deters trespassers; the yucca's thick stem is filled with a tough, spongy fiber that retains water indefinitely and will not burn. On many other plants a coating of minute hairs is a common device. But in ingenuity and completeness the cactus surpasses them all.

Where it grows, the difference between life and death is simply water. Give the adventurer all that strength can supply or courage inspire, and he perishes abjectly without water. Having learned also that a sphere exposes less surface for its volume than any other solid, it turns its knowledge of geometry to tidy use. It retracts its members into itself, and becomes, presto, a sphere, or at least a cylinder, thus reducing evaporation from its pulpy interior to the barest minimum. And because leaves have a reckless way of wasting their moisture on the desert air, it serenely transfers their functions to the leathery epidermis and goes ahead without them. It develops a sap resembling mucilage which will not bleed, but quickly coagulates and seals any chance wound. It develops long, threadlike roots that absorb surface moisture from the earth for many feet around. And it has evolved a skin that withstands equally well parching heat and freezing cold. The final mark of adaptation is the thorn.

As a consequence, even in such basic matters as classification and nomenclature, the size and distribution and arrangement of the thorns are considered. Thus in the scientific lists there is a constant recurrence of such words as *polyacantha* (many-spined), *dasyacantha* (rough-spined), *tenuispina* (slender-spined); and these with the generic names such as *Opuntia* and *Mammillaria,* form the only reliable designations. Of the scores of varieties found over the Southwest, only a dozen or two have common names, and these are in the main untrustworthy. A few have retained their melodious Spanish appellations — cholla, sahuaro, bisnaga, nopal.

It is in the areolae that the different species proclaim their identity and express their individuality. One of the common chollas prefers to employ from eight to a dozen or so spines of nearly equal length; and on a single joint no larger than a small banana, the number may reach a thousand. It was, accordingly, into a clump of chollas that the Apaches used to toss their prisoners, for their practised skill in such matters could devise nothing more excruciating. The prickly pear, or nopal, on the other hand, by doubling or redoubling the length of its spines, manages to get along with only two or three in an areola, and is protected from everything but the lean jack rabbit and the smaller rodents. The *Mammillarias* bear a wheel of thorns at the end of teat-like tubercles; the *Echinocerei,* displaying somewhat more ferocity, send out a convenient number horizontally, and then add one or more longer, fiercer ones that stand erect. The *bisnaga,* not content with the ordinary "radials" and "centrals," puts out wicked fishhooks from two to four inches long that catch and hold you fast. Try to free yourself, and you are hooked and punctured in a dozen other places.

Like the good Toledo blades of medieval Spain, cactus thorns are often bravely ornamented. Some are flattened, others angled or twisted; some are bent, scimitar-fashion, and others are banded and brightly colored. Some varieties of prickly pear affect rich, deep brown thorns of needle sharpness and more than needle length that stand defiantly erect; others bear only pacific white or amber ones that bend close to the side of the stem. But the little grey ball cactus, so lacking in glory except on the three or four high days of the year, when it flaunts its brilliant rose-purple blossoms, has a bristling apex worth examination with a magnifier. Each individual spine runs from a white base through gradations of lavender to a carmine or purple tip. Beside their minute perfection, what are the thorns of rose or thistle?

Yet when all is said, it is not in the ornamented thorns, but in the flower that the plant's loveliness resides. Can anyone really doubt that it has one of the loveliest blossoms of earth? Looking at its glories of gold-and-crimson or of rose-hued purple, one has the feeling that here is color which might have been diluted through a multitude of less noble blooms, for it seems to gather into itself a rich condensation of the colors of the wasteland.

The cactus flies the gaudiest flag in a land where nature uses color without stint, and where every flowering thing must make its decorations count. It is common to see a little *Opuntia* with but a single joint or two putting forth a glorious golden cup nearly as large as itself; or a small *Cereus* with a superb purple one, four inches across. In spite of its sternly utilitarian make, probably nothing in the plant kingdom spends so much of itself for beauty as the cactus.

Studying cacti at home, in the desert, or on the mesa, one senses a certain strangeness about them, an exotic quality of beauty and cruelty, as in some old Arabian romance. It is no wonder that their perverse, bizarre charm had to wait for its exploitation until the days of modernism. Though the artists who today are designing crazy bowls for the nopal may tomorrow be promoting the poison ivy and burdock, none will deny that they have for once espoused a loveliness that is authentic yet different. Flowers ought to shine with coy grace, one is convinced, from amidst green leaves; but these iconoclasts flaunt themselves absurdly at the end of a stubby shoot, alone, without a setting; or lying as though dropped by accident in a menacing thorn-tangle. The eye at first refuses to believe, and is inclined to suspect that a flock of great lemon-yellow butterflies have folded their wings and paused to rest on the lowly prickly pear.

While most house plants speak so little of their original estate and habitat that they might have been devised to order under the glass roof of a hothouse, the cactus carries in itself perennially the savor of the arid places. Even in a city flat it is a spot forever desert. It speaks of a nativity on tawny wastes where the keen nocturnal chill of the waste alternates with searing, quivering light and heat; where through weary, rainless months, killing, oven-like winds, and toothed attack by gaunt and thirsty beasts must be endured and conquered before one single bud can open. The cactus is, as it were, the spirit of the lonely mesas, and deep-trenched arroyos, of burning turquoise skies and ragged mountains. But the cactus speaks also of an invincible life-essence moulded by privation and struggle, of a purposeful evolution which through timeless generations has wrought wisely. And it has more history than we know—for how else could be brought together in one grotesque form the barbs of Gehenna and the blossoms of Paradise?

It becomes obvious that neither through a glass window nor from the back of a horse can one discover the grotesque marvels and perfections of the desert. One must dismount and go on foot, with eyes alert, exposing himself to its actual contact, and only thus will he learn of its power of inflicting wounds, the heat and eye-contracting light, its animal life, its chemical processes, its physical make, and finally, its undeniable metallic beauty.

The truth is that man at grips with the desert — not in an automobile nor even on horseback — finds it a red-eyed savage. In summer it wilts him with the ferocity of its heat and tortures him with thirst; in winter, it not seldom freezes him and buries his road with snow. Only recently the press carried an account of snowdrifts on the Mohave Desert in California, and it has been but a few years since two automobiles stalled in the snow east of

Deming, New Mexico, with the result that five of the occupants froze to death. In short, the inhospitality of the desert to man and his beasts, and its unsuitability for his crops have ever been among its characteristics.

The consequence has been a rigid localization of culture in the valleys. There, alone, the environment suited human occupation; since there water was readily obtainable for drinking, for cooking, and for irrigation; there was the rich soil in which corn would grow rank and tall; there was wood for the camp fire and a cool canopy of cottonwood leaves to furnish shade from the sun, and an oasis where feet could tread safely in the universal thorniness. And at the waterside a living would be easier also in other ways, for there wild fruits would be far more available than in the bareness of the uplands, and fish could be taken, and game would regularly come within reach of the hunter's arrow. Indeed, there was an accumulation of advantages that caused the aborigines to shun altogether the immense arid expanses and concentrate their habitations in the green, narrow strips of valley land along the Rio Grande, the Pecos, the San Juan, the Gila, the Mimbres, and their tributaries. Incidentally, the same considerations influenced the location of the Spanish and Mexican villages, and, in fact, lost validity for the Americans only after the advent of bored wells and wind-driven pumps.

And this localization had a vastly important effect on prehistoric culture. Men were no longer thinly dispersed, but came together in numbers for mutual advantage and protection. When it was a question of holding a home and rich possessions or being dispossessed to wander upon the inhospitable desert, they would naturally retain their valley at any cost. Such need gave immediate impetus to the study of defense and finally bore fruit in the development of an architecture. A sedentary life encouraged their advance in the age-old science of agriculture, and their contacts with one another stimulated intellectual rivalry, which found expression in the making of artistic basketry and pottery. Finally, the association with the beneficence of water tended to shape their mythology and direct significantly the evolution of their religious ritual.

The ancient puebleños perfected one sort of technique for meeting desert conditions; and their modern descendants employ it to the present time. But the Apaches devised another, entirely different. Essentially they were predators. They and the other harriers, the Navahos and Comanches, were raiding the pueblos when the written history of the Southwest begins, and so, until the white man enforced his peace upon them, they continued to do. So great was the dread of these marauders that important towns on the eastern frontier of the pueblo country — Quarái, Abo, and Quivira, all at the time under Spanish tutelage, if not protection — were abandoned. "Cities that died of fear," they have been called, implying the existence of a scourge such as the ancient litany deprecates:

Deliver us, good Lord, from the Turk and the infidel.

Yet if the Apache was a scourge to the pueblos, he also surpassed the coyote itself in ability to forage from the land. The desert gods themselves were his especial protectors, and into him they injected a quintessence of hardness, fierceness, and stamina that enabled him through more than two and a half centuries to deal the white man blow for blow.

For one who has eyes to see and goes not in haste, the desert has always the lure of a beautiful strangeness.

Nothing about it is conventional. In a long rainy spell which elsewhere brightens grass and freshens the landscape, the waste glooms in abject greyness. Only in vibrant, delirious sunlight does it seem completely itself.

Out on the elevated plains nearly a mile in air, the cloud ceiling occasionally descends to earth. At such times giant masses of vapor drag their inert, ragged forms across the mountains and trail across the plain as a vertical curtain hanging from the sky — a weirdly chaotic spectacle. Inside the cloud there may be mist or drizzling rain, or when it drifts aside, the peak in the rear of it may have grown hoary with new snow.

Snow along the desert is fantastic, swirling among the yuccas and cacti, alighting upon sands and encrusted alkali. Purposes of nature seem to have gone crosswise.

But it is with the light that the desert spirits like best to play tricks. Caught once on a peak in a February rainstorm, I waited until the sun came out. Soon it burst brilliantly through, and then on the thin rear of the rain began to flash gleaming rainbows. One after another formed and faded, until four had gone. Meanwhile, we had been viewing the plain below through the bands of the iris. And then there are the eerie mirages.

The familiar summer's-day kind simulates a sheet of water lying in a depression, and never deceives a normal eye. But there is a mirage which occurs on cold mornings in winter and fairly rivals enchantment. It deceives only acute observers, for none others see it. The motorist speeding along may note gradual changes in the contour of a distant mountain, and attribute them quite reasonably to changes of his own position. But if for a few minutes he will remain stationary, he may chance to note rising from a familiar peak an unaccountable turret. There may be a tall, abrupt butte in a sector where buttes should not be, or in place of a flat band of hills at the horizon, a row of squat pyramids separated by spaces of clear light. Then one of the pyramids, when next he looks, may be surmounted by something resembling a blockhouse, and another may have assumed an outlandish toadstool outline unevenly balanced on a stem. The next glance may reveal before his astonished vision some absurd terra firma floating in mid-air. With such bafflements the simple lake of heat has little in common.

One morning from the top of the Great Divide I sketched as accurately as possible the triangular silhouette of Big Hatchet Mountain, rising eighty miles distant on the south horizon. At 10:35, on the eastern end, appeared a low round rise, and the rest of the slope nearly to the top was serrated. There was one deep U-shaped notch. By 10:38 the notch had been nearly filled and a projection was developing just at the right of it. By 10:40 the round-topped rise had acquired a sharp vertex, while the rest of the mountain resembled a tilted, regular mesa which ended in a precipice a trifle west of the summit. During all this time, the western slope remained as immobile as the neighboring Tres Hermanas, and a single look would have afforded absolutely nothing to make the eye suspicious. The steps in the transformation followed one another with the dreamy mysteriousness of the aurora borealis.

Such fantasms occur in the sky near the horizon, but the earth has its mirages also. On a morning when leaden clouds curtained the eastern light, I saw a potent beam burst through and search out a section of the plain which, distorted by the air as by a faulty lens, seemed fairly to stand on edge. The dead winter grass kindled into brightness, resembled an immense buff tapestry depending from the sky, and the very weirdness of the spectacle suggested doubts as to what really constitutes reality.

The chiefest loveliness remains forever distant from the beholder. Thorn and gravel near at hand are too insistently realistic, but effects of colored sunlight viewed through leagues of colored air claim the rank of sheer splendor. The finest spectacle in nature is, therefore, a remote desert mountain glorified in the sunset — not one with green forested slopes, but with bare crags of tinted stone.

Always the silhouette of a sharp-lined desert range rims the horizon, serrated and blue upon a sky of rose at the vesper hour — the thin, chipped edges of the firmament. And their angled outline, as though arrested in a stupendous billowing, lends fine appropriateness to the Spanish name, "sierra," a saw. Or there will be a scarp, wine-red and remote, which viewed through the clear medium turns delicately to the aerial hue of lilac petals; the same scarp in a crimson sunset will flush to warm red.

In the hour of the grey desert's splendor, it is good to be among the Rio Grande dunes down by the Border. Across their spherical curves, the sharp shadows grow long. The wind, still saturated with sunlight, whips the sand into a thin crystal sheet like drifting snow, and the yucca blades vibrate with blurred motion like steel springs. Aloft in the solitude of the firmament move high bronze clouds in the slow suspiration of air. Bright angles jut forth from the mountain, their eastern profiles sinking into amethyst obscurity. A cloud intervenes, the light changes. A red reflection tinges the lilac crags. On the sloping planes of sand lies a graded illumination like candlelight falling on blank walls. There come, riding by, two silent men — the border patrol following a smuggler's track — and their horses' feet lift the sand in little shining splashes. Down towards the edge of the mesquite, low red beams search out the doorways and corners of a ruined adobe, and in the waste it catches the high light a moment like a gravestone. What man dared the desert . . . and with whom?

In the mystery of twilight, poetic softness veils the desolation, and coolness comes with velvet touch. The yuccas vibrate no longer, and the sands awaiting tomorrow's wind, lie still. All shadows, all reflections have gone, only the west remains luminous green and silver. Upon the irregular desert pattern of light and dark something moves dimly across the distance — a coyote.

CHAPTER FOUR

MOUNTAINS

MOUNTAINS ARE THE AUTHENTIC abode of the Sky Powers, who in the beginning determined the function of lofty ridges and peaks in the economy of nature. There, in majestic councils, they deliberate upon such basic matters as rainfall for the valleys and grazing lands, coolness for tempering the desert heat, frost for ripening the corn, winter snows for feeding the trout streams. The irrigation ditches *(acequias)* are their peculiar care. And they shepherd the flocks of clouds—cirrus, cumulus, nimbus, and the others — that take shape over their realm and sail forth to dissolve their substance over the lowlands.

Excelling even the potent magic of the Indian rain priest, the mountains are the weather-breeders. Invisible air currents flowing across country ascend the slopes into the chilling atmosphere above and presently begin to condense their moisture into visible form. The higher they rise, the cooler they grow and the greater becomes their relative humidity. Soon in the colder temperature, the saturation point is reached, and some of the moisture is "squeezed out" or precipitated in liquid state. It is no vagary of nature that mist and rain are regular in the higher altitudes.

On a clear summer morning it is an illuminating and striking experience to watch a cloud form out of nothing above the head of some tall peak. Presently others come marching together out of nowhere and assemble themselves over the adjacent mountains. White at first and widely spaced, they collect and crowd against one another in serried ranks, until, like an obscure level island in the sky, they hide the sun. Then in the charged air the lightning snaps crisply, and the Thunder Bird flaps its wings in sonorous reverberations above the pines and spruces. And this, I submit, is a much more picturesque piece of myth-making than our own ancestors' invention of Aquarius, the Water Man of the zodiac.

It was precisely thus that on the afternoon of June 12 the rainy season of 1933 opened over southwestern New Mexico. By a uniquely fortunate accident, I happened to witness the whole process. The various steps were observed in the following order.

The morning air was brilliant, still, serene — the perfection of weather with which the region is endowed, although the excessive dryness of the two preceding months had left the hills sere. Driving towards the Mogollon Mountains, I noted about eleven o'clock a pearly cumulus cloud forming above the middle of the range, where currents in the upper atmosphere were slowly doming the vaporous mass into symmetry. Its shadowed base was already dark blue, but except for two or three insignificant outliers, the sky was everywhere empty of cloud.

Though it was only mid-June, I remarked to my companion, "That's exactly the way the summer rains come. Just watch that cloud till afternoon!" Then entering the hills a few miles above the point where the Gila debouches upon the mesas, we saw no more of the cloud until perhaps one o'clock, when lazy fragments, detached from a much larger mass overlying the high peaks beyond us, began obscuring the sunlight. Presently a sound fell from the sky as though someone were moving heavy furniture in the attic, and then came more thunder in half a dozen separate explosions. Soon there drifted along the high skyline on the north a thin, silvery curtain of rain; and although the edge of the dark nimbus lay pretty accurately over the mountains, unseen winds were spreading a grey rack widely above the lowlands; so very shortly a sprinkling of drops spattered down upon the dusty river bank, while instantly the air became charged with the fresh, unmistakable odor of moisture. I looked at my watch — it said five minutes after two o'clock. After some false starts, rain came down soon afterwards in a heavy gust mingled with some hailstones, and the air turned chilly. Thunder came in long-continued reverberations. Thus there was no mistaking the type of storm.

Leaving the foothills and crossing the mesa towards the highway later on, I noted a mass of jumbled blue thunderheads surmounting the entire region of ridges and peaks that stretches from Glenwood on the west to the Black Range on the east. At four o'clock I learned by telephone that rain was already falling at the Civilian Conservation Camp along the headwaters of the Rio Mimbres sixty miles distant.

Thus arrived the rainy season. While the visible effects were purely local, as they are wont to be, the wider explanation includes causes that go back to distant oceans. New Mexico, like Arizona and Sonora, as Professor Huntington points out in his *Climatic Factor* (Chapter I), lies in a world zone where high pressure and consequent aridity prevail; but here the trade winds are never clearly developed, their place being taken by relatively moist winds which blow from the south and may be properly called monsoons. In summer the interior of the North American continent, being highly heated, becomes naturally an area of low pressure; hence the winds, though irregular, tend to move across the Southwest in a flow "whose prevailing direction is distinctly northward. They form, as it were, an inward draft blowing from the Gulf of California and the Pacific Ocean on the one hand, and from the Gulf of Mexico on the other toward the continental center of low pressure."

On approaching land, the winds first become heated

and very dry, since the land is hotter than the sea, but coming farther inland, they rise on the mountains and thus at length precipitate their moisture. After the spring dry season, the southerly monsoon becomes established by indraft towards the interior of the continent, and the summer thundershowers begin to occur regularly over the higher elevations.

The summer rains proceed from the south and are equatorial in character, and so differ strikingly from those of the winter, which are characteristic of the Temperate Zone and originate in cyclonic westerly storms. Even the aspect of the sky and the architecture of the clouds is distinct. The high-piled cumuli and nimbi of August occupy only a part of the sky — never the whole of it. Rising from a flat base of rain-blue tint, they tower like genii from an enchanter's bottle until their rounded summits may reach several thousand feet above it.

The puebleño's symbol of a summer rain, the crop shower, consists of two semi-circles, round side up and lying end to end with a third surmounting them. From the bases descend black parallel lines — streamers of rain. A rather apt piece of impressionism, one might remark. There's no mistaking them for the general rains that come later in the year. The winter clouds are flattened!

In the mountains it rains and rains. Almost every afternoon in summer, following a forenoon spent in marshalling the masses of vapor, it falls like a grey-blue curtain of shivery coldness from the base of the cloud island. Lightning slashes the pine trunks — noticeably oftener upon isolated trees than in mid-forest. Thunder rolls almost continuously. One day in August, 1932, I timed the rumblings, and for fifteen measured minutes there was no cessation for a single moment. But towards evening the shower lets up and the sky begins clearing. At bedtime the stars have exchanged their fuzziness for the usual hard brilliancy, and daybreak arrives unclouded.

Everywhere there is a sense of dampness strikingly at variance with the feel of the lower arid zones. The ground does not dry out, and while on the plains and among the juniper foothills there is no dew, here the dew is regular and heavy; and often during the night white clouds of mist creep along the canyon walls, ghostly and silent. Evaporation during the cool, rainy summers proceeds very slowly, and in camp above eight thousand feet, clothes feel damp in the morning and feet slide into boots with much reluctance. An hour before daylight, the night chill sends the mercury down to 40 degrees. And to carry further the semblance to the northern forests, the Colorado spruces wear beards of greenish moss.

The later storms also suggest the north. When autumn is about half finished on the high ridges and the golden aspen foliage is being stripped from the boughs, a flurry dusts the summits with snow. On shaded slopes it lies without melting. Then one day, announced by a slaty-hued ceiling that rests inertly upon the peaks, and by slow, lowering vapors that drag through the gloomy conifers, a snowstorm comes driving out of the west. Next day the sunshine brings to view one of the supreme spectacles of nature — a mountain wrapped in snow immaculate from the sky. While the red earth of the foothills may be scarcely covered between the dwarf evergreens, the tall pines receding in the distance above them will be coated with flakes as though with giant hoarfrost; but higher yet, the scattered spruces, still half concealed by white, horizontal cloud fragments, will rise darkly upon the snows as in the far northern Rockies. In such guise, the Sangre de Cristos are an unearthly pageant, a memory past all forgetting.

And while rapt in the contemplation of such beauty, a beholder must also be impressed with the wise economy of nature in thus storing her reserves of moisture. Over a great watershed, a three-foot snowfall will assure in the dry months the flow of no one knows how many springs and watercourses. Observations are made and records scrupulously kept by the weather bureau and the forest service, both of whom have a very practical concern in the matter. The amount of spring forage for grazing animals varies directly as the amount of winter precipitation, and on the abundance or the scarcity of moisture stored in the mountains depends the livelihood of thousands of homesteaders in the agricultural valleys, and the condition of the waterworks system of towns and villages throughout the state. In a useful bulletin entitled "Public Water Supplies of New Mexico," Professor John D. Clark of the University says: "In the north central, and to a slight degree in the central portion, melted snow from the high mountains furnishes water almost throughout the year." He states that a large portion of the supply is thus derived at Santa Fe, and that Alamogordo and Cimarron likewise depend upon mountain springs. But in Silver City, on the other hand, during dry seasons the fire hazard used to be greatly heightened because of inadequate pressure in the mains; water used to be turned off during a part of the day, and few lawns were cultivated because sprinkling was either impossible or so expensive as to be prohibitive. For years, even with the present increased supply, there will continue to be a dearth of trees. Flower beds, grass, and shade were all affected.

Measurements show that precipitation is closely bound up with altitude. Over districts having an elevation of from 3,000 to 4,500 feet, the annual amount averages from eight to ten inches; from 4,500 to 6,000 feet, some fifteen inches or better; and from 7,000 upwards, it ranges between twenty and thirty inches. The mountain villages, it will be seen, receive the cream of the rain crop. Cloudcroft, only a little below 9,000 feet, receives about two feet of water from the sky, including more than six feet of snow. Alamogordo, on the desert about a vertical mile below it, averages less than one foot a year. Silver City, lying among the foothills at 6,000, averages seventeen inches, while Pinos Altos, perched on the Divide a quarter mile higher, although barely out of sight around a shoulder of the mountain, receives half again as much. Taos, though high, gets but little more than a foot on account of local topography; yet the Anchor Mine in the same county receives at 10,600 feet a total of thirty-five inches, which includes — according to the figures given by Mr. Ligon in his *Wild Life of New Mexico* — the startling snowfall of 317 inches.

Rugged mountains with their great snowfields thus appear as reservoirs vitally necessary to the rest of the country. And the magnitude of the reservoir, lying among the high, corrugated ridges, is for a warm, arid country half incredible. The newspapers of the entire country at Thanksgiving time, 1931, carried dispatches from Gallup, New Mexico, of a single great storm which overtook some Zuñi and Navaho Indians while gathering piñon nuts on the high mesas, and cut off their return with five feet of snow. More than a thousand Indians were thus marooned, and many of them perished while supply trains and pack horses were battling their way through the huge drifts, and the white man's airplanes were dropping blankets and food from the sky.

And in the middle of the following April, the Associated Press was carrying stories of the resultant floods which broke the dam and imperilled Zuñi homes, while threatening the loss of the reservoir on which their irrigation depended. In May, as spring thaws through the Colorado Rockies began to unchain the sources of the Rio Grande, that river rose to a stage at Española, New Mexico, which menaced the existence of the village. And in the lower end of the state, particularly over the Gila watershed, the winter precipitation accumulated as an immense reserve. Said the March statement of the Santa Fe weather bureau: "Quemado — up to 48 inches remain over the highest peaks, soft and melting. Mimbres — 18 inches remain over the peaks of the Black Range; settling and solid." The magnitude of such precipitation suggests fascinating studies in erosion and drainage, for the waiting stores of water cannot descend from the level of the clouds to the sea without immense attrition.

The consideration of the drainage of mountains begins obviously with the divides. The Continental Divide is the backbone of North America. On its eastern flank, the waters descend towards the Atlantic; on its western, towards the Pacific. The scale involved stirs the imagination and fills the fancy with epic pictures of great rivers, of gulfs and oceans, of gigantic land masses.

Yet the Great Divide is by no means everywhere impressive. Decreasing in elevation from some twelve thousand feet in Colorado, it sinks finally to a plain near the Mexican Border. At Pinos Altos, New Mexico, it holds a village comfortably in its saddle, but a few miles farther down, it narrows to a ridge only a few feet in width. The gentle decline faces the east; the more precipitous, the west, where it drops ultimately to the Gila River. Walking along the narrow crest, one looks down at a slope opposed directly to the sun, too warm to retain snow even in January and moist enough only for beargrass and sotol; while on the other lie crusted snowfields, whereon conifers cast stripes of shadow, blue and parallel. Here one may have the experience of climbing a warm, bare slope, and at its crest, coming upon deep snow where a party is at noisy play with skis.

For a study such as the present, the Gila is one of the most interesting of American streams, traversing as it does within comparatively few leagues the entire gamut from the snows of the Canadian Zone to mid-desert in the Lower Sonoran. From the highest peaks of the Sierra del Gila — to call it by its ancient and most descriptive name—descend its icy seeps. One of them has the liquid-sounding appellation Gilita, Little Gila (pronounced as in Spanish, "He-lee-ta") ; another is Willow Creek, which bestows its name upon a majestic mountain whereon snows linger through June. Farther down in the range on a dour, fire-scarred old peak, Whitewater Baldy, rises the West Fork of the stream. Heading up among the spruces, their tributaries are typical icy-cold trout streams whose water through the warmest part of the summer stands about 50 degrees in the morning, and, though rising a few degrees during the day, always affords the camp an excellent substitute for refrigeration.

Even while occupied with the serious business of catching a mess of trout, one is repaid for observing the age-long process of attrition here going on, for nowhere else does sky so evidently and so effectively chisel earth. Following a dim trail made by the feet of fishermen, one notes the antics of moving water. Here in effortless, jointless grace, moving in and out with serpentine line, shining, flashing, plumed with tassels of spray — here and nowhere else is the Plumed Serpent, water spirit of Indian myth.

In white cascades the stream hastens downhill over

ledges, and then retards its rush to murmur to sandbars along its way; it broadens into willow-darkened pools where one strains vision for the arrowy trout; it backs up behind a boulder, where it digs a channel round the corner and escapes with laughter on the other side. Coming from the obscurity of a shaded bend, it meets the sunlight in luminous surprise and shoots dancing reflections up at the alder leaves. It flows now over pebbles, multicolored, and now over a clean floor of stone, and anon slips through a deep notch as though poured from a trough. And there are occasional little cataracts ten feet high, where the water shoots into a churning pothole and breaks brilliantly into spray.

In places, the canyon "boxes up" — that is, the walls approach so close together that there is no longer room for a trail — and there one must wade. Through these narrows the torrent rushes like an escaping flood. Now and then one must scramble up over giant fragments of rock that have tumbled down from the overhanging walls, and with the aid of freshet-borne tree trunks and other driftwood, created a dam across the brook. Elsewhere the wild gorge widens out, and only some tall pinnacles of lava remain to indicate the line of the original cliff. Dropping rapidly — in places some hundreds of feet to the mile — the canyon floor spreads occasionally into a tiny flood plain, and there nourishes a homely tangle of grapevines, willows, and alders, while the banks are carpeted with dead white-oak leaves exactly as among creeks a thousand miles to the east.

Here and there upon slopes along the way, plunging waters working in a somewhat different way have aided in producing what are called rock slides. Ancient cloudbursts, employing the tactics of hydraulic mining, have dissolved away the meager soil and set free the boulders to go tumbling down the canyon side. Result — a field of more or less rounded fragments ranging in size from a watermelon upwards, given over in the midst of the green forest permanently to desolation. Erosion wields a tool of power.

Finally the chill, tumultuous tributaries, issuing from between their mountain walls, spread at once into slow, tepid currents, canopied by cottonwoods and — on the sunny slope of the divide — become typical arid-country streams. As these westward-facing watercourses emerge from their shaded canyons, their accompanying plant life changes almost as abruptly as though one had passed through a wall. While inside there is scarce a reminder of the desert, outside, the hot slopes sustain little else than mesquite and cactus. And on the bottomlands are fields of corn and alfalfa, the third type of vegetation within a stone's throw. And the range of the hooded oriole and the large Arizona cardinal reaches almost to the cold, somber haunts of the ouzel.

But it is for the corn that the moisture matters most, and in these valleys it has flourished for ages. The ancient Mimbreños used a cross section of its ear as a decorative motif on their food bowls, and among their burials the excavator still unearths the charred cobs. The Apaches, though by instinct tameless wanderers, had here their *rancherias* and were cultivating their cornfields when the Spanish armies marched against them in the eighteenth century. And corn is still the best crop — and the most beautiful. Contemplating its slender grace, its silken shoot and golden tassel, one can understand why the puebleños personify the plant as a maiden, and represent the Corn Maidens as the chief food-givers. When the welcome, welcome flood plashes from the *acequia* under the willows to bathe the corn roots with freshness, only then does one thrill to the poignant beauty of water in the desert. And the intelligent thing about this mountain water is that until about June, the hottest, dustiest month, it is held in reserve, and then released exactly when the corn needs it most. Finally the waters, wistfully mindful of snows and spruces, murmur down the desert towards Steeple Rock and the sere pyramids of the Peloncillo Mountains. Traversing the stark wastes to Yuma, the Gila there meets the thick, ruddy Colorado. Such is the progress of the moisture down from its storage near the cloud ceiling to the sea level.

But among the rivers which drain New Mexico — the Gila, Pecos, San Juan, Canadian, and the others — there is one which stands alone — the Rio Grande. The great Rio, as distinguished from all the others, is a stream old in story, and in its own right a stream of consequence; so one writes of it with due respect.

Rising among the clouds in Colorado, it bisects, roughly speaking, the state of New Mexico from north to south, marks out the international boundary for some hundreds of miles between Mexico and the United States, and at length discharges its tribute into the Gulf near the border of the Tropics, some twelve hundred miles from its head. Economically, it is the most important thing in New Mexico, for along its irrigated bottomlands is grown food enough to supply the entire population. Before the dawn of history it provided food for the aborigines, and later on for the puebleños who followed them. It nourished for the Spaniards plots of grain and *frijoles,* and after the Americans began to apply science to the methods of cultivation, its valley developed into an agricultural area of vast importance. The Elephant Butte Dam today supplies water for thousands of acres of vegetables, cotton, alfalfa, cereals, and today impounds the largest artificial lake in the world. (Within a very few years after this statement was made, Lake Mead at Boulder Dam became the title-holder.)

While the purpose of the present study is primarily to examine the influence of sky in conditioning human environment, it may not be amiss to glance at a larger aspect of the same influence upon the land itself. We have been considering relatively transient matters. There remains the utterly permanent, never-resting process of erosion; and the cutting, grinding action of gravel-laden water so readily observed in a trout stream, when multiplied thousands upon thousands of times and continued through the infinity of geologic ages, is obviously capable of achieving large-scale results. Of course, where the rate of flow is too languid, the pebbles, although losing about one-third of their weight from buoyancy, cannot be transported; but in mountain streams where the gradient is high, they are ceaselessly carried downward by the current, abrading whatever they touch. This eternal attrition along the sides and bottom of a thousand-mile river is incalculable, and only the shortness of our observation prevents our seeing the results.

But it is easy to picture the cycles of nature being accelerated, as in the Planetarium in Chicago. There the stars and planets are shown upon a large dome exactly as they appear in the heavens, and there Ursa Major pursued by Cassiopeia swings counter-clockwise round the Pole Star, and the whole series of constellations goes trailing across the meridian with perfect precision. But the point of difference is that while in the skies the complete revolution requires twenty-four hours, upon the dome it is completed in three minutes. Such foreshortening applied to erosional processes suggests interesting speculative possibilities. Nature progressing about five hundred times as fast as man's life, would rush through, while a human being in slow motion was filling out his threescore and ten, a term of thirty-five thousand years, which even in geology is more than a moment. What will happen in the next interval of that length? What has happened in the past one? While only the imagination can supply an answer, science nonetheless affords some valuable data. But in this unscientific foreshortening, one wishes also for another unscientific aid — a motion-picture projector through which the film could be run backwards. The trick is used sometimes in showing, for instance, how a great blast throws down the whole side of a quarry, and then the scene is reversed, so that the astonished spectator beholds the wall rising out of the pit to assume its former status. Imagination aided by such a device could picture some striking effects of sky upon earth. Tall mountains, for example, would shoot up where now are seen only worn hills, and the rounded contour of the land in many places would be superseded by bare shoulders and pinnacles of stone. Great outwash fans which spread from the bottom of dry torrent beds to join mountain and plain would disappear. Huge boulders and rock masses would spring back upwards to rejoin the parent cliff; dissected plateaus would again assume the flatness of tablelands, and pointed buttes would regain the breadth of mesas. Sluggish streams would once more be cascades, and valleys narrow down to ravines. Effects of sky! Toying with such fancies helps in comprehending mesas, canyons, and jagged desert mountains.

Very different from the tall peaks on which clouds become impaled are the low, barren desert ranges. Stark of outline and unforested, commonly of volcanic origin, rising abruptly and disconnected out of the arid plain, their serrated silhouettes confer a fantastic, burnt-out character upon the southwestern corner of the state. Not high enough to be successful weather-breeders, they are only the object of the weather's furious extremes. Bare from top to bottom, they lie in the path of all the winds, and their stony anatomy has protection neither from the sun's intensity in summer, nor the freezing of winter nights. Exposure to alternate expansion and contraction fractures their lavas into crags and pinnacles, while the lesser fragments are tumbled down the torrent beds by the force of cloudbursts.

And here is one more of the numberless ways in which aridity works. In the desert, where plant life is scanty, erosion goes on at a mad pace, because foliage is lacking to intercept the beating of the rain sheets, and rootage is insufficient to hold the friable soil in place. In consequence, the bare summits tend to emerge, clean as a row of hound's teeth in the gum, from out the enveloping talus slopes. In a storm the run-off shoots down unobstructed from their polished sides as from a vast roof, and with a head of half a mile or so, there is plenty of violence.

After one clear demonstration that sky as source of moisture has supreme power upon the lands, it is easy to understand how by the process of differential erosion, canyons and mesas are formed in the dissection of a level plateau; and, furthermore, how by the aridity which prevents the encroachment of vegetation and the consequent formation of soil, the rocky profiles are maintained always starkly chiseled and bare. Streams with a steep gradient and carrying large amounts of abrasive material wear down their beds very rapidly, especially during times of flood. One set of strata after another is revealed in succession as the deepening continues, and the structure of the earth's crust is revealed, it may be for thousands of feet. Where hard strata occur, perpendicular cliffs result; where strata are less resistant, the slopes are more gentle.

The main stream has always tributaries, which in turn carve also for themselves steep canyons, and the erosion continues to the point where at length a series of them lies close together, separated only by narrow divides. Ultimately, the original surface is all removed except where more resistant portions remain standing like islands above the new level. Such islands, called mesas, are usually capped with some hard stone, very often a lava. As the denudation proceeds further, an island becomes smaller and smaller until it is scarcely more than a spur which towers above the plain, and in that state is called a butte.

Of all the forms into which water sculptures the land, a mesa is perhaps the most interesting. Rising solitary from the interminable desert plain, it possesses a solemn weirdness which imagination cannot resist. And its summit is the loneliest place on the lonely wastes. To reach it one must scale the face of a sharp slope to the stone capping with which it is crowned; and when one has arrived at the top of the precipice and turns to look behind him, nothing is there but the wind. And a far-off horizon opens still wider upon infinity.

At the risk of seeming to invent a far-fetched instance, one may point out in passing the effect, also, of rain waters in enriching certain ore bodies, as for example those at Santa Rita. Penetrating at length to deep subterranean levels, they became charged with various chemicals. Now, the Grant County mining district lies in a hot-springs region drained by the Mimbres River, and in the remote time when igneous intrusions were forced from beneath into the country rock, mineralization took place along the contact zones. But the changes, so I am informed by a government geologist who has carefully investigated the problem, must have taken place by means of highly heated underground waters, for the magma alone, he is convinced, would have been quite incapable of producing such metamorphism. Thus in the most literal sense, sky water affects not merely human environment, but the surface of the land itself, and, indeed, the strata far beneath the surface.

More marvelous, in fact, than all the sculpture of mountain and plateau by the agency of the sky is the subterranean wonderland sculptured from strata deep within the Guadalupe Range — the Carlsbad Cavern.

In attempting to describe the Cavern, any pen, even the most gifted, achieves little more than a jumble of poetic language. The subject is too remote from everyday things, and the difficulty of finding suitable imagery is too great; and, furthermore, the sizes, shapes, and positions of its objects are not calculable from the data which ordinary experience supplies. Yet the matter is clarified by saying that a section of the Cavern, when reduced to something like a mathematical scale, is seen to be a rather flat, irregular cavity whose floor lies in an almost horizontal plane, and whose ceiling, with the exception of various domes, is roughly parallel to its floor. Or, pictured in another way, if the empty space were used as a mold, its casting would be a fairly thin, sheet-like mass, covered with a multitude of surface irregularities, both depressions and protuberances, yet few of sufficient size to mar the general pattern.

The actual erosion is the work of water charged with carbonic acid, but the resulting fairyland which the visitor sees is due not alone to excavation, but also to the redeposition of chemicals carried in solution as the water descended to successively lower levels. The explanation is as simple as it is futile. Like the building of the ice creations at Niagara, the process is pure simplicity; the product, pure wizardry.

Dimensions are everywhere stupendous. The Big Room is three-quarters of a mile in length; the ceiling of one of the domes is 350 feet above the floor; a single stalagmite is sixty-two feet high, sixteen feet in diameter; the entrance keeps descending for half a mile before one's feet find level going, and at the lowest point the trail is more than seven hundred feet underground. Finally, when one emerges from the giant portal, he has taken a subterranean jaunt of seven miles.

While men have occasionally created exaggerated structures and excavated pits whose magnitude suggests camparisons with the Cavern, its magnificence is unapproachable. No oriental potentate in all his glory ever beheld such a palace of art as this one, for, literally, walls, floor, and ceiling for miles have encrustations of crystal. Moorish columns support fairy arches of translucent onyx; vaulted alcoves are hung with shining daggers of dripstone; and from gem-like facets on the floor, light leaps and flashes as though from winter frost.

Beneath the span of the hundred-foot arch in the natural limestone, the traveller makes his descent into Avernus. Plant life, so far as is known, does not exist in the Cavern, but exploring parties have found, in addition to the bat population, some horned owls and some crickets. Beyond the safety of the gigantic blue beam of daylight which streams down from the entrance, life does not venture far. And there are yet deeps and deeps unknown. The most recent scientific expedition to gather data attained a new low level of 1,350 feet, and a new upper level of 250 feet above the one previously known, and explored ten miles of passages in addition to the twenty-one already known. Besides making a photographic record of various new chambers, and conducting interesting experiments in radio reception, they discovered the dry bed of an ancient river.

Yet the wonders which the everyday tourist beholds suffice for a lifetime. Nothing more is needed — not even the action of the President of the United States in setting it aside recently as a national park. As was said by the late Dr. Willis T. Lee, the first scientific investigator to visit the scene: "Carlsbad Cavern, New Mexico, is the most spectacular of underground wonders in America. For spacious chambers, for variety and beauty of multitudinous natural decorations, and for general scenic quality, it is king of its kind."

Inside the portal, down beyond the final, pallid reflection of day, waits unearthly, quiet, stygian darkness in a realm of unimagined weirdness and inexpressible beauty. The temperature drops swiftly some fifty degrees, for although across the desert limestone slopes above, the sun sheds a quivering heat that raises the mercury well above the one-hundred mark, here winter and summer the air remains constant at 56 degrees, and fresh by the circulation of mysterious currents. Before the dancing lanterns descending the half-mile corridor, shadows frisk and climb, while momentary high lights rest upon eerie white beasts that lurk along the fringe of darkness — hippogriffs, dragons, monsters born of primeval myth. Grotesqueness mingles familiarly with grandeur, and plutonian blackness snatches at the rear of lights and laughter marching down the descent. (Naturally, electric lights were installed later in the Cavern. The illumination is tasteful, not garish. But something of the fantastic emotional effect disappeared with the dancing lanterns. Today the imagination misses something.)

Unreality is the major impression. Things possess no definite shape of their own except such as a gleam of light bestows upon a chance profile, which is instantly modified by a swing of one's torch. And the formlessness is still further complicated by complete uncertainty about the perspective, for when dimensions are unknown, far and near are meaningless terms; and the apex of a dome may be a hundred feet above one's head, or it may be thrice as far. And everywhere the shadows, envoys of the all-surrounding and timeless night, baffle both eye and sense of proportion. It is the kingdom of Chaos guarded by Darkness; and the mind peopling each appropriate setting with actors from the gnome and kobold world, muses vaguely upon what daylight might reveal.

Then after a long distance the corridor opens into a great-domed chamber, and the plan of the labyrinth, so far as it possesses one, becomes somewhat more comprehensible, for here is a series of vast chambers, each with its alcoves and all connected by tenuous passageways. Here in the Titan King's Palace, unreality and grotesqueness yield to the sheerest unearthly beauty; and, viewing its transcendent glories by the illumination of artfully placed electric lamps, the contemplative beholder falls reverently silent. From this point onwards, description should be confined to scientific measurements or to psychological emotions, since it is adequate for nothing else. The eye being accustomed to measure receding distance by the gradual diminution in the size of known objects, here has no clue, as their actual size is unknown. So for the lack of any intelligible perspective, photography itself gives only an imperfect notion of the scene, and a picture of the Cavern invariably lacks depth, for objects appearing to have lost their third dimension seem to stand all in one plane.

In words borrowed from Dr. Lee, "The chambers about the Palace are separated from the master room by curtains and partitions of gleaming onyx formed by the deposition of lime carbonate from waters dripping from the roof. The great dome is so high that it is only dimly illuminated by the torches. Most of the ceiling is covered with dripstone. Thousands of stalactites hang singly, in doublets, in triplets, and in groups. They range from a few inches to lengths representing the entire height of the room, and in diameter from that of a small pencil to masses many feet thick. In some places they hang so thickly that they coalesce at the top, forming spiny masses weighing thousands of tons."

The stupendous Big Room lies beyond. It might be the abandoned haunt of colossal primitive gods that became extinct when creation was immature. In it awaits the final overwhelming chaos of cascades of frozen stone caught as it were in mid-motion; of pellucid draperies depending before gem-encrusted shrines; of gigantic icicles of dripstone which hang from glittering domes, and of funereal, fluted stalagmites that tower high into the obscurity like memorial obelisks. It is a place of death forever withdrawn from the mutation of all things human; a place lying cold with the death of inorganic chemic substance where life never reached. And there through the indefinite eternity, it waits and waits, where time comes not.

And when the last foolish syllables no longer reverberate along the walls, there steals back once more the encroaching silence. The brief, ineffectual lights have gone, leaving not a scar upon the darkness. Then somewhere a drop of sky water falls with velvet plash from its stiletto of stone — a symbol of the Cavern's patient making.

CHAPTER FIVE

FOREST

SKY WATER FALLS IN THE ARID
Southwest as the mountains oppose the passage of the
moisture-bearing winds, but it is the forest which conserves the supply, once it has reached the earth. Sky
determines the forest, its extent and character, while the
forest in its turn determines what is to become of the
ground water.

It is a curious phenomenon that in spite of the prevailing aridity, floods constantly ravage the Southwest.
Many years ago a rampage of the mighty Colorado created the Salton Sea, which still spreads its dead waters
upon the California Desert. In 1929 the Rio Grande
went berserk and deluged the villages along its middle
course. One of them, San Marcial, the river destroyed
and covered over. A photograph illustrating an article
by H. H. Bennett in the *Scientific Monthly* (November,
1932) shows a deposit of sand seven feet deep drifted
upon the surface there.

In myriads of less spectacular instances, floods have gone racing down arroyos causing immense waste of valuable soil and still more valuable water. Serving in a two-fold capacity, forest aids in flood prevention, and in the conservation of water supply. And this conservation is of the most vital importance to the grazing man, the agriculturist, and the town dweller who draws water from the public mains.

Silver City, New Mexico, in the early 'nineties had for its Main Street the sandy wash known as San Vicente Arroyo. Along it, in those decades, general stores raised their false fronts, and its saloons, as in all western towns, proffered refreshment to the cowpuncher whose ponies waited in three-legged repose before the door. High-piled freight wagons, drawn by six-horse teams, chuckled on well-greased axles as they rolled along their way to distant mining camps; and at its hitching-racks, ranchers drew up in their buckboards and paused under the cool, whispering cottonwoods.

In the West a by-road very commonly follows the bed of an arroyo, for its winding route is about as direct as any other among the hills, and it offers no steep grades to climb. The level of the arroyo in question, as old photographs show, was slightly below the ground level. Then there came a series of destructive floods descending from the mountains. Old-timers still recall the one which took Judge Newcomb's piano from the second story of the brick building in which he lived. In 1900, as the photographic records make clear, Main Street had become a formidable abyss, and about that time a woman walked over the edge of it one night in the darkness and fell a measured distance of twenty-one feet. Today there remains on the brink of it a section of an old brick foundation, and the merchant who owned the structure still

tells of the flood which carried away not only his store but the lot on which it stood. And the level of Main Street, as it is still called on the town plot, is below the foundations by the space of fifty-four feet!

The responsibility for these spectacular floods is placed by those who have most carefully studied the problem upon the practice of destructive overgrazing, especially in the timbered, mountainous country where the water gains its headway. Forestry officials, engineers, and grazing experts are agreed that a general cropping of the ground cover by animals denudes the soil more effectively than a mower could accomplish the same result. Grazing is always hard upon a country too arid to support turf, and particularly so in the border states where the winters are mild enough to permit practically 365 days a year for the process to continue. Constant trampling presently kills out the bunch grasses, and sharp hoofs disturb the soil as soon as it becomes bare. The first beating rain then starts it on the long downward trek to base level. Paths soon grow into deep-cut trails which in rainy season become torrents, and thus the life-sustaining moisture is dissipated within a few short hours. Farther back towards the head, the tributaries fill their beds with gravel and boulders, while in the higher country, springs dry up and the water-level of the streams subsides. The lesser ones, in fact, disappear beneath the sand, where the water is no longer available either for stock or for irrigation.

Where the carrying capacity of the ranges has been figured on the basis of favorable rainfall, the grass failure in a year of drouth upsets the equilibrium and causes the destruction of myriads of young trees and vines by famished animals which devour leaves, shoots, and bark.

And, inevitably, disappearance of animal life accompanies the destruction of the brush and grasses which provided a permanent food supply, as well as cover for the concealment of nests and dens and protection from predatory enemies, such as eagles, coyotes, and bobcats.

Over the slopes, moreover, after the soil is washed away, rainfall has little or no effect on the rocks and debris which remain, and permanent barrenness results. Farther down, as valleys widen out, the turbulent wall of water resulting from a single cloudburst may carry away not only the homesteader's crop, but the very soil on which it grew. Nor is the stock free from such danger. In the early autumn of 1932 a flood on the Gila River near Redrock drowned a herd of goats numbering five hundred animals.

The development of the San Vicente Arroyo offers a perfect example of this destructive erosion. Early in the 'seventies, the settlement later to be christened Silver

City was known by the sonorous Spanish name of *La Ciénega de San Vicente* — the Marsh of Saint Vincent, and the villagers drew their water from a spring in the Arroyo near the head of the present Spring Street. But the street name now appears to perpetuate only an idle legend, and all traces of a marsh have long since vanished. At present, except during summer floods, the watercourse is practically dry from one end to the other.

Heading back in the warm, arid canyons at the edge of the Gila National Forest, its tributaries descend like a many-branched herb until its stripes of sand unite into a single stem. All of them have "cut-banks."

The "cut-bank" is a matter deserving some notice. Though it occurs everywhere, its action can best be studied among the unforested slopes that link the final tree-dotted foothills with the bare plains. Observe any long, narrow ridge that forms the divide between two arroyos. After erosion has made some headway, it will take on, more or less, the contour of a row of beads on a string. As the side arroyos sculpture the ridge more deeply, the bead-like structure assumes greater distinctness, and there is a regular alternation of shady and sunny slopes on which the vegetation varies with great distinctness. On the one, in addition to the thin bunch grasses and prickly pear, some tufted, sedge-like beargrass (*Nolina*) and low, double-thorned catclaw will usually be able to exist on the moisture which the sun has ignored; but on the other, tilted obliquely to its rays, will flourish a stubby growth of oak bushes, juniper, cholla, and, near the mountains, mahogany, sufficient to provide a good ground cover.

The cutting continues. Between each pair of beads, there heads a stubborn little wash which incises into the soil a trench which may be no more than six feet wide, while it may be more than six feet deep. Then just where the slope levels out to meet the main valley, each iniquitous tributary comes out of its trench to spread a wasteful, fan-shaped curtain of gravel over the grassy floor, a seed bed for cockle-burs. In dissected, partially bare country, the aggregate waste of ground by such a process is very great. And as years go on, the wasting accelerates with the increasing areas of bare earth. Nature knows only one way to arrest the progress of devastation — to "hair over" the soil with grass.

Below Silver City the big arroyo has cut into the level, yucca-dotted alluvium of its bottomland a sharp trench some fifteen feet deep, fifteen miles long, and fifty feet wide — at least, it approximates such dimensions. For leagues the perpendicular banks keep up a continual crumbling after each rain, and the dark fertile loam drops upon the sands, whence it is removed and scoured away by the next deluge. And most of this immense erosive activity has been accomplished within the span of a single life.

The many-sided wastefulness of such erosion attracted more than a generation ago the attention of technical men in government service. The only remedy lay obviously in federal control. And it was clear that the place to begin conservation measures was not on the bare flats where valleys had widened out into the plain, nor yet in the Upper Sonoran foothills and canyons where only scattered oak bushes, mahoganies, and evergreens protected the soil, but far back *in the forest* at elevations where the flood waters gained their powerful momentum. The point is worth marking.

Accordingly there were set aside vast mountain tracts of New Mexico as national forests, and today every important range of the state is thus included. The immense domains are all administered from Washington, and in a manner calculated to conserve rainfall, to prevent erosion, floods, overgrazing, excessive lumbering, and other misuse, while aiding nature to restore its ancient balance. In the two states of New Mexico and Arizona, the area of such government-owned land reaches the total of 19,000,000 acres. Over the reserves generally, ground cover is increasing, and the forest reasserts its ancient sway. As man's wastefulness is reversed, floods decrease, and sky water once more in a natural way achieves its beneficent work.

The grand Gila National Forest serves as perhaps the best example of its kind. In size, since the addition of a large part of the Datil Forest, it is unequalled; and in the richness of its animal life and the opportunities for big-game hunting, it is probably unrivalled. Unlike the others, it preserves in its remote depths an expanse of one thousand square miles designated permanently as wilderness, wherein lie no settlements, where no land may be homesteaded, and into which no roads may be constructed. The only access is on foot or by pack train.

It embraces an area nearly as large as the entire state of Massachusetts. Its watersheds provide water not only for the adjacent towns and villages, but aid in supplying two great irrigation projects, the San Carlos and the Elephant Butte. The regal domain of peaks, canyons, mesas, and parks is dominated on the east by the Black Range, and on the west by the Mogollons, the center being filled with confused mountains which cradle the river Gila. To the entire mountain mass, the early Spaniards gave the musical appellation Sierra del Gila, but since their day various ranges have been given separate names, and now among the components are those known as the Pinos Altos, the Burros, the San Francisco, and the Diablos. It was into this obscure region that the Apache Indians were wont to retire for safety and recuperation through some two and a half centuries of warfare with the whites.

To secure any comprehensive picture of the region, it is necessary to pierce the forest at several points, for in range and variety it is probably surpassed by no other. Lying far in the south, it touches the fringe of the Sonoran Desert, and yet its loftiest peaks lack only a few hundred feet of reaching up to the timberline.

The Burro Mountain divide, where it descends north of the main peaks to a line of mere rolling hills, is notable for its ancient junipers. Short, thick-bodied, and silvery-grey of trunk, they are clad in bark that cracks into small squares that suggest a checkerboard, and thus give the tree its common name. But to an early botanist, the same characteristic suggested an alligator hide, and so he bestowed upon it the impossible name, *pachyphlaea*. A sign placed by the foresters states that the tree, although always short, is known to reach a diameter of eight feet and a maximum age of one thousand years. But on the dry foothills a few miles distant, such is the difference in rainfall, these little cone-shaped cedars seldom attain a diameter of more than a few inches, though each dwarfed shape concentrates in its heartwood the pinaceous fragrance of the towering evergreen family.

Beside affording ideal firewood, these junipers provide a sort of warehouse for winter supplies collected by the Mearns woodpecker. The bird selects a barkless section of the trunk or a dead branch and drills into it dozens of small holes side by side. Then into each hole a single slender acorn of the Arizona oak is snugly fitted. The completed repository resembles a board shot full of heavy-caliber bullets.

A few leagues to the north, in the Pinos Altos Range, a profound canyon, carved into the lava by the attrition of Cherry Creek, exhibits the typical blending of the dwarf desert species with the full-grown species. Along the sunny wall is found only a stunted growth of juniper, scrub oak, mahogany, and piñon, while a hundred yards distant on the shaded slope the tall pines (*pinos altos*) set in.

Around the well-known GOS ranch, which lies still deeper in the mountains, the tall pines occur in practically pure stand, although nowhere of maximum size and nowhere closely ranked. There wide parks of grass enchant the eye with sylvan beauty, and at their margin the Sapillo trickles down through romantic vistas of open forest to the deep wilderness.

But the finest epitome of the forest is found along the ride from the village of Glenwood to the top of the Mogollon Divide. The traveller approaches along the Grand Canyon Highway through the sun-baked mesas and arid little valleys, where the common plants are such frankly Lower Sonoran species as cactus, mesquite, and rabbit brush. Here rains are scanty, summers hot, and winters warm.

Out of the glen winds a rocky narrow road to Whitewater Mesa, whose flat surface is treeless, but whose bevelled, northward-looking edges support a few junipers. But above the sharp line where the tableland meets the abrupt mountain slope, an entirely different flora dominates the landscape. Mesquite disappears, and familiar key species of the Upper Zone form a dense ground cover.

As a car grinds upwards over stretches of naked stone to the next divide, the traveller notes the occurrence of no new species, but near Mogollon he comes upon the first scattered yellow pines. In approximately one-half of a vertical mile, he has topped out the Sonoran Zones. The rest is a different world.

Beyond the old, half-abandoned silver camp, a single-track road rises laboriously from the moist coolness of Mineral Creek Canyon to Willow Mountain. The way is heavily canopied by alders, wild cherries, and mountain maples—minor hardwoods which here still maintain their ground against the encroaching conifers. A little higher up, solitary Douglas firs tower in majesty from the lesser forest. Occasionally in their dense boughs one notes a rough tangle of sticks — nests of the greater hawks. Coolness becomes sharply noticeable.

Desert seems a thousand miles distant, and here the ground is mellow throughout the year with the moisture of rains and snows. White firs — true members of the *Abies* family — rise along the roadside, pointing their fat, glaucous cones at the sky. (The so-called red or Douglas fir belongs to a distinctly different breed, bearing its cones as pendulous ornaments.) Then the rising road traverses a dim, white-trunked thicket of quaking asps with which nature has healed an ancient fire scar. An antiquated but significant snow plow reddens with rust among the wayside weeds. There might be some dispute about the literal impenetrability of a forest, but if one attempted to press through the gloomy tangle of firs, aspens, and spruces on the north side of Willow Mountain, he probably would not quarrel with the word "impenetrable." No better one is at hand!

Descending from the buttresses of Willow Mountain, the road flattens out upon a mesa and is hidden in a forest of orange-barked pines which is typical of the whole region. Indeed, it is this tree, the western yellow, or, as it has been recently renamed, the ponderosa, that claims regal rank among them all, and on all the millions of acres set apart in federal reserves, it furnishes some 70 per cent of the available lumber.

Like an interminable green mantle the forest adjusts itself to the folds and curves of the land's anatomy over thousands of square miles of mountains. A worn and trampled fringe of "woodland," as the lesser growth of piñon and juniper is called by way of distinction, surrounds its hem, and here and there island peaks of Douglas fir and Engelmann spruce vary its general surface with ornaments of darker tone, but in spite of all invasions and all overlapping of alien species, it maintains throughout its favorite altitude a practically unmixed growth.

On Iron Creek Mesa, for instance, this forest is all that forest can be — green, unspoiled, silent, free. This is wilderness. Here are no roads, and rubber tires will never roll here. Here the sweet solemnity of ancient and deep-furrowed trunks that tower without branches up to the indefinite green canopy above seems to require the reverence of cathedral aisles. Myriads of dried cones lie scattered over the ground, and the strewn needles afford my horse a footing of velvet. There are stretches where his hoofs leave no print upon the soil.

Through vivid, homely sensations of touch and smell, the forest answers back to one with the earthy charm that pines have held for men since the beginning. No noise of shout or gunshot can scar the silence for more than a moment. Even the grey juncos on their inconsequential errands, and the other obscure little birds whom nobody can name, yield obedience to the overpowering stillness. Only the low tinkling of a bell declares the presence somewhere over the next rise of a sheepherder's burro. Presently we sight them — five in all, with hobbles on their feet, patient among the horseflies. Sufferance is the badge of all their tribe.

There is no path, and we are following only a "blazed trail" deeper into the wilderness — a series of gashes, one small, and another below it somewhat larger, chipped upon an occasional tree with a woodsman's axe. And though the intervals between the blazes are often pretty long and uncertain, the horses never get lost. Give them their head, and they are certain to be back at camp by suppertime.

Along the way, we note many "cat-faces." When a ground fire sweeps over the mesa, it burns through the heavy bark of the pines just above the roots. Then, in time, the tree exudes a coating of resin to protect the wound, but as the scab is highly inflammable, it readily ignites in the next fire. Repeated burnings cause the ugly marks which the rangers have named cat-faces. A mature tree can endure a surprising amount of fire and still live, but finally, after the heart is eaten away, it crashes in the first wind storm and measures its length on the ground. More eloquent still, there rise among the golden columns, stark, spectral snags of charcoal flaunting their satin luster against the neutral surfaces of the woodland — ruins wrought by lightning bolts and former conflagrations. Storm and boreal cold the forest fears not; only the red enemy it dreads. A smouldering cigarette butt will sometimes devastate a mountain side; and a clumsy, half-extinguished camp fire will produce in a government forester symptoms of frenzy.

Rarely one comes upon what is called in the old Spanish nomenclature of the Southwest a *ciénega* — a shallow open marsh in the midst of the forest, but through the summer so densely overgrown with vegetation that no water is visible. A half-mile-long expanse of wild irises, garbed in the purple blossoms of June, is a spectacle not easily forgotten.

And here the wild ducks alight in their spring migration, and here the deer come to drink in the hours of the dark. Their tracks are everywhere. This thin, heart-shaped impression was left by a doe last night, and the larger, wider one with a ridge in the middle is the track of a buck. Delicate and alert, sharply incised upon the mud, they are distinguishable at a glance from the inert footmarks of, say, calves. And trails cut by their hoofs lead out through the boundary of weeds to the deeper, colder water beyond.

And in a day's riding one seldom fails to spy a flock or two of timid wild turkeys running through the pines. Splendid creatures they! Greatest of all American game birds, the "cocks with hanging chins" were noted by the Spanish epicures of Coronado's expedition in 1540; and even before that time, as the decorated food bowls prove, they were favorites among the prehistoric men of the Southwest. They are distinctly birds of the pine forest, nesting there and never migrating.

Rarely one chances upon a flock of sheep in the wilderness, their backs high-lighted in the radiance of the low sun. Nibbling the scattered forage, they seem quite contented in the high country until rainy season comes. At once they begin to long for the sunny lowlands and grow extremely restless. Their fleece, as the sheepherders explain, gets wet in the first downpour and never has time afterwards to dry out. So they must be driven down to lower pastures, and in August, as the only indication of their sojourn, one may chance upon a "sheep-counter"— a mere V-shaped angle made of two fallen pines and left with a narrow opening at the apex, through which only one animal at a time may jump.

While it is very largely in the pine forests that the deer hunters make their kill, the trout fishermen, for the most part, seek a somewhat higher altitude, for the waters retain their pristine coldness only to the upper edge of the pines. Yet along the cold, shaded northern banks of the trout streams, the Canadian Zone is likely to invade the pines for miles.

There is one thing singularly interesting about these trout streams. Running down the Mogollon slope in an easterly direction, they thus expose one bank to the sun, while the other remains perpetually shaded. So on the one side grow the sun-loving pines and, on the other, the snow-loving spruces, and *the two do not mix*. Each creek, therefore, marks off, as by a sharp line, the zone in which aridity is the determining factor from the zone in which it does not matter.

Fishing upstream, one notes thus on his right the familiar plants of the temperate region, while on his left the same plants do not mature well, not being able to endure the long imprisonment in snows nor the deep shade. They are superseded by others which he has learned to associate with the Canadian scene — towering spruces and other pointed conifers, white quaking asps that continue in the race after every other broad-leafed tree has dropped out.

And there are other interesting things. The shaded wall of the canyon is invariably more abrupt than the other. The stream lies not in the middle of the tiny valley floor, but invariably at the bottom of the spruce cliff. And while the spruces are crowded together on their side in serried ranks, the pines on theirs are widely spaced, and very rarely cross the stream. Never do they invade the spruces and attempt to supersede them on their own terrain.

For all these things the Sky Powers have their own reasons. And it is of course with their permission that perennial streams occur on the one slope, whereas none at all occur on the other. Across the divide, the drainage courses part way down the slopes, but disappears before reaching a permanent outlet.

Following out seriatim the reasons for these matters, one discovers that the northward-sloping wall is more abrupt because it is naturally better protected from erosion. The pine slope lies just within the zone where aridity remains a paramount factor in growth, while the other lies just outside it. The pines thus stand on a hill-side inclined like a roof *towards* the sun. Its rays fall not obliquely but directly upon it, and the consequent evaporation is immense. Much different is the case of the forest on the tableland immediately above, which receives the sunshine more obliquely and, being level, suffers no heavy run-off of water. But still greater is the difference on a bank that gets scarcely more sunshine than the north side of a wall. There the incalculable drying power of the high southwestern sun ceases to figure greatly, and evaporation is limited to what the cool moist air can absorb. The significance to plant life, therefore, is extraordinary.

The warm slope, then, can never be densely covered, but must remain rather sparsely dotted with trees, and its stone ledges covered only with a thin debris of pine needles. The other, at the same time, is protected by the thickest, most luxuriant growths, both of tree and herb, which effectually retard the inroads of erosion. Where much of the precipitation occurs as snow, it comes with feathery softness; and when it rains, although it may bombard the barer side with broadsides of falling water, it falls with more of a slant against the spruces, and by their defensive canopy of needles, is reduced to a fine spray in mid-air. There the deep, porous humus, securely anchored in position by myriads of roots, drinks it up immediately, instead of allowing it to be wasted in destructive torrents.

The present difference in forestation, it is obvious, accounts for a difference in erosion. But it has done so as well for ages past. The effects are unmistakable now, and there is no reason for believing that they will not continue into the indefinite future. The crumbling of the canyon wall and the presence of rock slides, for instance, are two phenomena that belong together — indeed, are part of the same process. Now such rock slides as are found occur regularly on the sunny slope, and are rare on the other. I have examined many incipient areas of this kind from the top downward. The genesis of each is a fractured cliff above. The angular fragments lie strewn about its base and over the slope below, thinly nested in the soil and pine-needle carpet. Disturb one, and it starts rolling. If nothing impedes, its momentum will carry it down to a resting place at the foot of the hill. Eventually the rolling stones there, the gravel and other debris carried down by the rains form a bench, which fills the valley floor and crowds over the stream to the foot of the opposite cliff. So while the spruces grow to water's edge, into it, and often cross it, the pines stay completely on their own ground. An off-side adventurer immediately attracts a naturalist's attention, standing on a terrain to which it is nowise adapted.

It is apparent, then, that in their ledger the Sky Powers demand a rigid accounting for every raincloud that discharges its cargo, every snowfall that melts, and every flood that wastes its substance. Naturally, the accounting extends to the streams. On the cool, northeastern slope of the Mogollon Range, there is a perennial supply of water for six of them — the Gilita, Willow Creek, Iron Creek, the West Fork, Cub Creek, and White Creek. On the hot southwestern slope, there is not one able to maintain its flow permanently to an outlet. Call the roll — Whitewater, Big Dry, Little Dry, Sacaton, and farther down, Mogollon Creek, which reaches the Gila only as a wide, barren deposit of gravel. Dryness of the lower reaches is the common characteristic through most of the year.

And the character of the two sets of canyons is distinct. Nowhere in the Southwest has a slender mountain stream cut a wilder abyss than the Whitewater "box," though Dry Creek is a rival. Unlike the orderly walls which rise along the Gilita to the pine-forested mesa, here is no pine forest and no level mesa. Gigantic faces of bare stone now overhang, now recede a little, but the width of the gorge at the end of the foaming flood ranges from a few yards to a distance which a tall man could almost span. There is no flood plain for a valley floor, and no forest on the canyon walls. At every little interval, giant cliff-fragments, weathered loose from the bordering precipices above, have fallen to deflect and impede the tumbling waters. Here, through indefinite cycles of time, erosion has gone ahead at a different rate and with a different degree of violence. Titanic sky water has occupied itself through ages, not with widening sundry creek beds, but by sculpturing the stone of an unprotected mountain scarp.

The brief explanation of such geologic and floral divergences is found in the fact that on a range trending northwest and southeast, the left-hand slope receives the maximum effect of the ardent southwestern sunshine; the other, the minimum. Variations of other kinds, such as relate to the extent and kind of forestation — the spruces, for example, are scarcely found on the western side of the divide — to the size and number of the rock slides and the general character of the erosion, are seen to be essentially not causes but results. Sky determines!

And the basic distinctions tend to perpetuate themselves. There is no prospect that at any future date the little junipers will be dominant where the spruces now stand, or vice versa. Forests rise, mature, decay, each after its own kind. On the one side, humus is consistently removed; on the other, it accumulates to nourish future growth and so protect the ground.

And this renewing of the forest is an ever-repeated miracle. Where it stands on edge, so to speak, as along the Gilita, one may count dozens of dead spruces — trees that no disease attacked, but which in time simply passed from full age to death. Many of them finally fall upon the slope; others merely break off. In either case, contact with moist ground sets up presently incipient decay. Wood borers excavate their tiny tunnels and thus give deeper access to dampness. Decomposition in so humid an atmosphere cannot long be resisted. In a few years, toadstools, orange, crimson, or ivory-hued, ear fungi, and growths of still lower order send their sucker-roots deep into the mass to accelerate dissolution. Finally, the brown rotten wood loses its character entirely and is resolved to the inorganic stuff of earth.

Parallel and at an equal rate with the processes of decay go the processes of growth. Study of a selected area a few rods square reveals a new quota of spruces rising everywhere in ordered succession. From around the base of a hundred-foot patriarch rises a generation of sons, ranging from seedlings planted last autumn by unwitting chickarees to taller saplings and immature trees.

Among the level-ranked pines it is the same. Beside a dead trunk, ringed round twice with the serpent lightning, or a decomposing log overthrown by the wind and exposing blanched and tooth-like root-snags, a luxuriant thicket of saplings rises to reclaim the ruin. Life, forever counter-attacking, abandons no room to death.

Such is the forest, its nature, its distribution, decay, and renewal. For a glimpse at its administration, one should visit one of the ranger stations — say, on Signal Peak, on Bearwallow Peak, or on Negrito Mesa.

A ride to Bearwallow at the north end of the Mogollon Range stores up in one's memory notable treasures. . . . The horses, saddled at eight o'clock, are cropping grass among the purple asters that bend over with shivery dew. Though the sun is well up, the floor of the canyon still lies subdued in cold morning shadow. The temperature is still hanging near the forty-degree mark. And yet for a time in mid-afternoon this same nook will be a brief floral paradise for myriads of honeybees, grasshoppers, and multi-colored butterflies. And at the creek-side the fringing alders, now deserted, will be flashing with busy yellow warblers. Sunshine here, as probably everywhere else, changes the world.

Upstream along a dim path worn by fishermen we ride past the beaver colonies. Some of the dams, one notes, bend upstream according to the best engineering practice, while others, constructed possibly by apprentices, run straight. A little sleepy owl, sitting like a knot on the limb of a fir tree, gives us a yellow-eyed stare.

From behind a point of rocks the sounding Gilita pours its clean, glassy flood. Although here practically of the same size as Willow, it curiously flows three degrees warmer, for Willow Creek heads higher among the peaks and by its direction contrives to avoid the sun longer. While its temperature rises ten degrees during the daylight hours, it stands regularly in the mornings from June to September at fifty degrees.

For the next two miles we urge the horses to a trot along a by-road which here comes in from Mogollon, and their footfalls strike with an agreeable dullness on the soft dirt. Over the Canadian cliff at our left all is silent, except when a long-crested jay sounds his rattle in the distance, or an interrupted chickaree, busy with a spruce cone, chatters his annoyance from among the boughs. A few yellowing blotches along the cliff show that autumn is already working among the aspen trees.

But on the pines' slope it will be summer yet for another month. Jewel-eyed chipmunks sun themselves among the rocks, flicking graceful tails and whistling betimes. Bird notes of many qualities imply friendly if unseen companionship. Even little lizards exhibit a lusterless, reptilian emotion in the light.

Turning presently into a side canyon, we pass into a garden of wild flowers. Brilliant with paintbrush, Indian pink, and velvety cinquefoil, it furnishes the abundance of red which my eye craves. In open spaces goldenrod and many of the yellow compositae seem to have captured their radiance from the sunshine which they imbibe through long hours each day. But as suddenly as we come within the shadow of the spruces, they give way to ferns, woodland mosses, and harebells of cool purple hue. And rare pentstemons jewel the obscurity with scarlet.

After a while the trail begins to climb. The solitude grows darker, more somber. Sunlight enters only in rare golden shafts. Bird life becomes both invisible and inaudible. We pass a cold spring from which gushes a flood as large as the brook into which it falls. We have left the pines below us. The mighty Douglas firs increase in girth and altitude, while the forest grows denser with saplings that fight a motionless, impartial battle with one another for room.

Then, of a sudden, out of the somberness into the glorious light of Turkey Flat — a high, lonely mountain meadow, forest-bound and rimmed with pointed spruce tops! Though starred with myriad blossoms, its predominant growth was a broad-leafed, succulent plant which the horses ignored while eating the yellow thistles with much relish. The *ciénaga* was well named, for, riding away, we spied a large flock of half-grown turkeys sneaking through the fern brakes.

On the rim of the ridge that encloses the old bear-wallow there is an ancient burn. Many years ago fire raged up the slope through a stand of Douglas fir. It was what the foresters call a crown fire — not the grovelling kind that devours ground litter, but the majestic, terrible fire that leaps with a tiger's ferocity upon the trees and envelopes their crowns in a vast sheet of flame. Many of the massive trunks still standing were not charred but merely blackened along their deeply-furrowed, yellowish bark, yet snapped off sharply from ten to twenty feet above the ground, significantly near the point where their inflammable branches began. Now, with the lapse of time, young aspen trees were springing up, and the ground was hidden by yellowing brakes and wild red-raspberry bushes.

As we neared the ten-thousand foot level, the Englemann spruces began to come in. With them the forest was complete, for they go marching upwards, the last conspicuous tree, to the timberline. Though cousins to the blue spruces that fringe the lower streams and often dip their boughs into the water, the Englemann is a different tree — adhering less to the streams, ruddier in its flaky underbark, fonder of altitude. Mast-like, its silhouette stands out against the immaculate high snows, or on the skyline where the greater peaks crowd together. At length we reach a slope which sends us sliding backwards in the saddle — and then the tower!

From one of these fire lookouts — the one on Signal Peak which rises from the exact apex of the Continental Divide is typical — the earth spreads before one's gaze in overwhelming majesty. From a motionless point one seems suspended between land and sky. While southward the mountains sink into the featureless plain of the desert, along the gap through which passes the oldest and best of the Atlantic-Pacific highways, the peaks stretch away toward the north, where they are exalted into the snow-capped Colorado Rockies. And still northward across Wyoming and Montana they advance, to lose themselves in the Canadian Arctic, where the curvature of the globe draws the meridians together.

Upon the irregular evergreen stripe of forest that lies between treeless plains along the Great Divide, repose the silence and blithe freshness of creation morning. Wind in its freedom visits the pine tops, and while we look down upon their undulations, it fills the ear with the pleasant sound of its travelling. Free clouds sail by, intimates of the lonely peaks, whose heads they often veil in snow or rain. At this height there is no floating grit to annoy the eye, no smoke to assail the nostrils. All is primal, untrammelled like the breeze, which, having lost its staleness and dust, here moves with cool celerity, a spirit of the sky.

Through the fire season, which lasts from about the first of May to the middle of June, a forester on Signal Peak sits from morning till night in a little cabin at the summit of his tower. Before him on a table lies a map, and upon it a protractor turning upon a pivot for measuring the degrees of a circle. At his elbow is the telephone and round his neck a pair of field glasses. Fifty miles away in the northwest, beyond the intervening ridges, another man sits before a similar map and waits. Over in the Mimbres Range another man sits and waits. When a thunderclap occurs, they all get interested at once. It means that fire is hovering over the forest. But there are endless hours when the danger is scarce sufficient to keep vigilance awake. It is then that the map makes good reading. Maps, in fact, always make good reading, supplying as they do, travel, poetry, history, and, indeed, everything but fiction. Nothing can ring the bells of fancy like the names on a chart. Turkeyfeather Pass, Packsaddle Canyon, Apache Spring, Pine Ciénaga, Whitewater Baldy, Antelope Flat, Wild Horse Mesa, Montoya's Ranch, Tennessee Cabin, North Star Trail — with such words the imagination can do anything! Names are significant, and each suggests some robust saga finer than the finest imaginings of Bret Harte.

Over large areas of this country the land lines are omitted from the best of the Geological Survey maps. As the plats cannot be reconciled to the topography, only a few isolated corners are shown. In the broken region along the headwaters of the Gila River approximately six hundred thousand acres have been designated by governmental enactment as the Gila Primitive Area and set aside permanently for the preservation of unspoiled nature. Here wild life, except for the destruction of the predatory animals, goes on as it has done for unrecorded ages; and since the only trails are those laid out for fire-protection, the region will continue inaccessible except to pack outfits.

This wild solitude, one of the few areas of its kind in the United States, is preëminently the big-game country of the Southwest. In it grizzly bear still occur and black and brown bear are fairly numerous, while blacktail (mule deer) and whitetail deer abound. (According to the best information, the last grizzly bear has disappeared from the Gila Wilderness.) The game census for 1932 showed in the Gila Forest, alone, more than fifty thousand deer, of which number more than twelve hundred bucks were killed by about three thousand hunters. And the 1930 census of the neighboring Lincoln Forest showed that of two thousand hunters that season, more than half succeeded in bagging a buck. It estimated that during the year more than fifteen hundred deer had been killed by coyotes, bobcats, and mountain lions. It placed the number of mountain sheep at 175, but stated that the number of foxes, skunks, and badgers ran up into the thousands.

For centuries the forests have served man's need. To the Apache they furnished the game which was his chief sustenance; to the Mexicans, not only game but fuel. Woodcutting has gone on for three hundred years among the alligator junipers of the foothills, and to this day one frequently meets on the forest trails a Mexican driving his pack-saddled burros laden with odorous firewood. And the American has gone for three or four generations to the forest, not merely for the dressed lumber of the sawmills, but for mine props, railroad ties, and for logs to build his cabin.

Though most of the forests of New Mexico will never be cut over because of their value to the watersheds or of their inaccessibility, which makes logging too expensive, lumbering is being carried on here and there at a rate which insures a perpetually sustained yield. While in the national forests a timber crop of many millions of board feet is harvested each year by private lumbermen, cutting is done only in accordance with the regulations of a detailed government plan, and no live tree may be sawed down unless designated by a forester. The brush is then lopped and scattered to make humus and to prevent erosion, or else piled on fire lines and burned. About one-fifth of the original stand of thrifty trees is left to furnish seed for the forest of the future, and they will provide in fifty years or so a crop for another cutting.

Likewise, an account of the grazing makes another interesting page in the history of the forest. Many years ago the ranchers herded their stock into the mountain valleys, hitherto the pastures of only deer and elk. Higher and higher they kept pushing into the timbered country until they gradually overstocked the immense free ranges, which hungry animals trampled into dust and ruined. Troubles naturally followed, which took from ranching all of its profit, and caused bad blood among stockmen. As forage and permanent water diminished in a locality, the wandering herds were passed on to another, causing disastrous overgrazing in some places, while less accessible country remained untouched.

So the federal government intervened and established national forests, in which was included the best grazing land of the mountains. Since that time the whole livestock industry has been brought under supervision. A marked improvement has been the result, and under careful regulation most of the worn-out ranges have been able to clothe themselves once more in grass and brush. Allotments are made upon the carrying capacity of the land, and the number of animals permitted in any one section has been strictly limited to prevent overgrazing. Sound principles of management have secured a better distribution of the stock by improved methods of salting and the development of facilities for watering. And to each kind of stock is allotted the type of pasturage most suitable. In consequence, the quarrels between cattlemen and sheepmen, so frequently settled with Winchesters in the old days, are now a thing of the past. And while there is still many a lean old cow abroad, the Forestry Service, by continued regulation, is on the way to achieving stabilization and permanence.

Guardian of all this evergreen domain is the ranger, and he is the protector of the forest and its dwellers. Nowadays the ranger is fairly on his way to becoming a figure of romance, the personification of the free out-of-doors. He deserves the honor. Besides being game warden and fish warden, trail-maker, grazing commissioner, lookout and fireman, he marks individual trunks for the lumberman's saw, maintains the telephone lines, keeps tab on the campers and sportsmen. To his hands are entrusted the protection of from two hundred thousand to five hundred thousand acres of timber, and the grazing administration of thousands of head of stock. He surveys claims and rights of way, enforces homestead laws as they apply to his jurisdiction, assists in stocking the streams with fish from the hatchery, and administers the free use of timber. But because the price of safety for his comrade pines is eternal vigilance, his most important task is keeping a weather eye out perpetually for tell-tale smoke.

A ranger speaks: "The ground under the trees, as you see, is covered with twigs, bits of bark, and pine needles, a carpet which when it dries out in early summer is, of course, highly inflammable. Here, when a cigarette butt is carelessly thrown aside, it doesn't go out, but keeps smouldering a few minutes and then, at the first breath of wind, ignites the litter. Or a lightning flash strikes — and it often comes with little or no rain — and the result after a short time is exactly the same. The fire gets going, and then hell breaks loose. Nobody who ever saw a forest fire has ever forgotten it.

"Sometimes it runs along the ground for a distance and doesn't burn much but the grass and brush. It wastes the forage, of course, and kills the tender young saplings — the big trees of the future — and gives erosion a chance to get in its work later.

"On the ground you can often put out a fire easily with a shovel or a wet gunny sack — I've put out little ones with nothing but a green bough — but it usually won't run long until a gust of wind whips it up into the tops, and a great pine will flare up like a torch. It roars and crackles a few minutes and when the smoke clears away the tree is a corpse. The dead poles may stand for years before they rot down.

"In this business you have to report where every spark flies. You must accurately locate the area on the map; you must tell who first discovered the smoke and at what minute. The official blank asks in the next line when the fireman started and when he arrived. It asks also about the type of fire — whether on the ground or in the tree tops. It asks about the velocity of the wind and the type of terrain and the kind of trees. Finally, it wants to know the number of men engaged and the number of acres burned over; the elapsed time until the fire is put out, and the cost of fighting it. Then all facts of this kind are filed in a big atlas at the supervisor's office. Some pretty good ones are filed away in those old records. There was the Crooked Canyon fire that cleaned up four thousand acres of yellow pine, and another one, two years later, that wasn't stopped until it had spread over five thousand nine hundred acres. Ten years ago there was the Cold Springs fire that covered seven thousand acres. That one was held after burning over ninety acres, and then it broke out all over again. Shovels and axes had no effect on it. They built fire lines and backfired and used all their other tactics, but nothing could stop it until rain came to the rescue. Before it was completely put out, it had burned twenty-nine days and had cost $20,000 in money, besides the immense amount of timber burned. The big mines at Santa Rita, a hundred miles away, sent out truckloads of their men to help. In all, nearly four hundred and fifty firefighters were engaged in battling it.

"But here is an old report from the files, which gives an account of a typical big forest fire. It's an undecorated piece of routine work — just plain realism. The ranger writes:

3:00 P. M. Lookouts report fire still increasing. Wind higher. Getting together another pack outfit with lanterns, shovels, blankets and Red Cross box. Telephone for force of three hundred men to be raised at once in surrounding mining camps. Ask for equipment and horsefeed. Spare no expense. They are wrangling pack mules at near-by ranches so we can load them with tools. Ask ranchers to deny all rumors about men being lost or burned.

"Well, you can see for yourself that considerable was happening. Twenty-six hours later he wrote:

On Sunday at 5:00 P. M. the camp was moved to Kentucky cabin. At 7 P. M. the reliefs came out and just before dark, pack trains came in with supplies. I took a mule with food and water out to the main divide, as the fire had crossed over during the afternoon. The crew that had worked since noon laid off and were fed on the line, and the fresh crew continued with the line. This was slow business since it was too dark to see to work, and two men had to hold lanterns for the rest to work by. In the night I went on down the trail to the crew that was at work, and found that they had got on the wrong ridge in the darkness; brought them back and stayed with them until daylight.

On arriving at camp, about half-past five in the morning, I found that thirty-two men had just come in after an all-night trip from Greenwood. . . . Took them out on the line and divided them. I told them not to take any chances, and if they saw the fire start crowning out on the hillside below them to drop off into High Wall and come down the canyon. I left one Mexican back on the built line who was too fat and short-winded to take care of himself. I started the other crew on up and stopped to fill their canteens from the water-carrier's sacks. Had four or five filled when I heard the fire roar very close; so dropped the canteens, told the boy with the burros to get out of there. Galloped up the hill and caught this crew just as the fire topped out at the end of the fire line, and turned them back. By this time the whole of Little Fork was raging with a gale behind it. I then dropped down the canyon and the fire fell all around my horse before I got half-way down. There were nineteen men caught behind this fire, and I rode up the main canyon trying to get some trace of them, and then dropped down to camp. Two Mexicans came in who had been with the first fifteen, but were too badly scared to give any information. I scouted round in High Wall again, and out to Rock Springs. By this time there was so much smoke in the canyon one could not tell where the fire really was. It had topped out in Aspen Creek, Wolf Creek and Little Fork at the same time, and crossed High Wall."

Our ranger laid aside his pipe and continued. "There's a picture for you — that great sickle of flame stripping the forest from the mountain slopes for five days. It left the hills black — the hills that had been green. The smoke cloud was a horrible grey-and-buff thing that rose thousands of feet into the air before it thinned out. Underneath there was a sickly twilight, and the sun was just a little red disk that you could look at with the naked eye. The wind kept blowing a gale all day, and only went down at night. There's always a high wind anyway in a big fire, or else the enormous air currents seem to make one.

"The noise drowns out all signals and commands. You can't hear anything but the flames and a lot of confused shouting. The heat burns your face, the smoke ruins your eyes. Big blazing pieces of bark go sailing overhead and keep setting new fires in front of the main line. And the flames leap across an open space and throw themselves on a tree like a mountain lion attacking a sheep. But the most dangerous thing about a forest fire is one that a tenderfoot never realizes — the speed of it. You can't escape it by running. It will outrun a fast horse, and it never tires like a horse.

"Of all the places I don't hanker to see again, one is a little narrow divide between two canyons that run down into Ice Canyon. There was a fire in each one and it was eating in behind us. And it was travelling, as I say, for a fire races up a hillside as if the devil was behind it. Well, here it comes. There were three of us. And it was closing in on us like a pair of sheepshears. . . . But they got us out of there on horses — finally. Burns? Well, none of us died.

"But here's the end of this report:

8:40 A. M. Lookouts say not so smoky. Raining. No wind. 10:40 Fire under control. Send no more men. 11:00 Went home — dog-tired.

"And this was on May 23, five days after he left his cabin. In fire season, a ranger sure has a life of ease." (In the drouth summer of 1946 nearly fifty fires — four of them serious — occurred in the Gila National Forest before the middle of June.)

CHAPTER SIX

FORGOTTEN PEOPLES

A LOCAL "POT HUNTER" SOME
years back had the extraordinary luck to happen upon a
sacred spring in the Mogollon Mountains, and in it he
discovered nearly two hundred obsidian arrowheads. Of
the total number more than half were perfect, and all
but one were black. Now, obsidian is a volcanic glass of
varying degrees of transparency and capable of being
chipped accurately into shapes of delicacy and beauty.
When the points were graded according to size and
mounted upon a card, not one was found to be less than
half an inch nor more than an inch and a half in length.
In beauty of material and symmetry of design, the whole
collection viewed as a unit suggested less the work of a
weapon-maker than of a prehistoric jeweller. Such votive
offerings constitute the most primitive form of ritual
veneration of water, which in the Southwest is the well-
spring of life. In a semi-desert country, if there was no
actual worship of water, it would at least be regarded

with religious reverence, and a cultus of the Sky Water would develop inevitably in an aboriginal priesthood.

In such a find archaeology touches poetry and gives wings to the imagination. The prehistoric redmen, no less than the early Greeks, are thus seen to have had their idyllic emotion in which sacrifice was offered to the spirits who dwelt in friendly fountains.

With such votive springs, rich in arrowheads and beads, with myriads of pottery sherds, and with house ruins, the Southwest is everywhere reminiscent of the Forgotten Ones. Here their culture reached one of its supreme peaks, and an arid climate has favored to a remarkable extent the preservation of their antiquities. Thus throughout the Land of Desert, Mesa, and Mountain, their presence is felt as a wistful, elegiac enrichment, and to this day they have not been entirely dispossessed. Yet the feeling is not perceptible in all localities. In the out-and-out desert, for instance, it is lacking. There the gentle ghosts own no abode of peace, for the acute realism of existence in the form of heat and thorn subdues all subtler things. Nor are the high mountain slopes richer in associations, for the culture of man, whether red or white, is bound up with the ploughlands, the valleys, and the running water. Where grain will not grow, life remains uncertain, squalid, nomadic; and it has been well said that the rise of civilization has been contingent upon the cultivation of cereals.

Accordingly, the Ancients left their material remains and their spiritual intimacy beside the waters. Along the upper course of the Rio Grande, and upon the giant benches which slant down from its bordering mountains; through the basins drained by the San Juan and the Little Colorado, far in the northwest section; and finally down in the Gila country and over the valley plain of the

Mimbres — everywhere in these regions the excavator's spade turns up reminders of them. And the spade demonstrates, above all minor facts, the fact that they lived in community strongholds by which they were able to maintain possession of their farm lands. Since life was precarious or impossible on the inhospitable desert, they chose — as the sky determined — the choice valleys, settled, and established themselves in frowning fortresses which warned off all trespassers. (To this, the Mimbreños were in part an exception, but there was, as we shall see, a reason.)

Climatic conditions thus anchored them to one spot, and from this permanence grew many notable consequences. They studied out, for instance, a science of architecture which produced eventually a type of home that was half castle and half apartment house, and nearly impervious to extremes of heat and cold. They raised agriculture to the point where it provided for them a sure living, utilizing a rudimentary form of irrigation, and perhaps beginning the domestication of wild animals. There is evidence, furthermore, that in pre-Spanish times they tended cotton and practiced weaving. They developed a social system according to their need, and a complicated religious system of which the subterranean kiva was the sanctuary. In the realm of art they created a pottery which was equalled nowhere else on the continent. This progress in comfortable and secure living began in prehistoric times and continues to the present. It is the direct result of climatic environment.

In the ages that such a civilization was evolving in the valleys of the Southwest, the plains Indians arrived at no higher state than that of nomadic savages dwelling in skin tepees.

One thousand years before the coming of white men

in 1540, a type of culture generally similar had arisen in the Southwest and spread over five different areas. A brief consideration of two of them, however — those along the Rio Mimbres and those on the Pajarito Plateau in northern New Mexico — will suffice to show how climate determined the essentials of their mode of life.

Before one, facing north from the Tesuque Divide, a short distance above Santa Fe, there spreads a panorama in which the Forgotten Peoples, the Pueblos, the Spaniards, and the Americans have all acted their part. The Americans have striped the country with thin lines of highways; the Mexican villagers have done a little tilling in the hidden valleys; and the Indians have here and there during past centuries erected a few neutral-toned pueblos, as unobtrusive as a robin's nest in an apple tree. So far as a preliminary glance can tell, the land is still in its virgin state.

Through the middle of the prospect flows the Rio Grande. At the right, towering in green majesty, the Sangre de Cristo Range slants grandly upwards past the timberline, while far in the west frowns the Jemez Range whose lower slopes merge into a vast level, though deeply eroded, blanket of volcanic tuff which reaches down to the river — the Pajarito Plateau. The foreground is occupied by a pinkish deposit of clay, gravel, and loam, which is known among geologists as Santa Fe marl. Sculptured by the chisel of erosion, this formation assumes in many places a badland character, and when studded thinly by small round evergreens, it presents a half fantastic beauty.

Here is a land which to professional students of man and of human progress is as interesting as any on this continent. At Puyé and along El Rito de los Frijoles there are cliff dwellings whose walls are still black with the smoke of primeval camp fires, and where the presence of stone-age peoples is very vividly felt by the imagination of anyone who has an imagination at all.

Frijoles Canyon, cut into the level mesa of volcanic ash, has for its northern wall a vertical escarpment for some two-thirds of the way to the bottom. There it meets the sharply descending talus slope, and along this level, protected completely from above and only a little less so from the front, runs the line of many primitive rock dwellings.

In fact, so complete is the protection that they are invisible from the rim rock above, and the gaze is occupied as one descends only with the rudely circular ruins of the great communal house or pueblo of Tyuonyi on the canyon floor. The ruins are of tufa, and the indications are that the structure was three stories in height and of the terraced shape found in modern pueblos. Seen from half-way down the trail, it is spread out like a map, and the low sun of late afternoon throws the walls into sharp relief. The plan is that of a circle flattened on one side, and the curved design surrounding a court — like that of a college stadium bowl — suggests not merely a place of residence but a fortress. Access to the interior could be gained only by one entrance, and as in other pueblos until recent times, the occupants entered their apartments from above and by means of ladders. The court was thus surrounded by a ring of masonry from three to six rooms in thickness. As a "strong rock and house of defense," it suggests by its guardianship of the valley floor, with its flow of living water, the possession of something keenly precious, a prize that any would be glad to wrest away.

From the level of the stream one gazes upwards at a length of curiously weathered cliff which resembles nothing so much as a piece of timber badly corroded by gigantic wormholes; and from here also, one gains a view of the rock houses in their true perspective.

At the foot of the cliff one walks along the narrow terrace of talus, trying to reconstruct the life of the inhabitants. From the ground one picks up a fragment of beautiful cherry-colored pottery. It is hard, close-grained, and on the black lines which once formed part of the pattern is a vitreous glaze. It is, therefore, a genuine antique, for modern pueblo pottery is unglazed. Embedded in the soil hereabouts also lie shining bits of obsidian, material for the jewel-like arrowheads. On the cliff above, carved deeply with some intention no longer discoverable, are pictographs — circles, crosses, mythic monsters. With notebook and camera one makes records industriously, yet with a sense of bafflement.

A walk along the Rito propounds the ultimate enigma: "Why did they leave this green valley?" One stoops for a drink to find that the water is sparkling and icy cold. Along the banks flourish violets, wild strawberries, woodbine, and other such plants of the well-watered East. Almost the only plant which reminds one of the desert is a small, prostrate prickly pear (*Opuntia tricophora*). The query keeps recurring.

At Puyé, the other center of ancient population on the Plateau, the same intention of building a stronghold is evident. While it is the row of cliff dwellings which has caused the place to be well-known to tourists, the great 1,600-room pueblo on the mesa above it, surrounding a plaza with a thick rectangle of masonry, must have been to the inhabitants themselves the important thing. In the nature of the case, it was another fortress. Here, too, the ancients felt that when a base of supplies had been selected, it was to be defended against all comers. A country as poor as theirs in nature's provender was not one to dare with impunity.

Thus the significant fact about the Pajaritans is not that they lived in cliffs, but that they lived in strong communities. The cliff, offering as it did weather-proof and easily defended houses at the cost of small labor, may have been an afterthought; but it was not an afterthought that when the people had once selected a valley or other place where water was obtainable, there they concentrated their might. While it is true that the Apaches and other harrier tribes devised an exactly opposite technique in meeting arid conditions, the Pueblo answer was older, more permanent, and more human.

Simply as a spectacle of ancient life, the row of cliff dwellings, which honeycomb the pink tufa, is of great interest. The escarpment itself is smooth and sheer like a wall of masonry. Looking into the domed, smoke-blackened cells cut from its substance and noting even the plaster adhering in places, one feels the people of the Stone Age curiously near. They lived on the line where the last junipers reach up to meet the first tall pines. Along their deep-worn paths flame up from the grass Indian paint brush and rare scarlet gilias. Below them, down in the Rio Grande basin, sunset fills the badlands of clay and shale with a light which is indescribably rose-tinted. And seen from their mesa, farther down, the Sangre de Cristos rise with four majestic mountain masses in four equal arcs upon a sky of turquoise. They must have been a race of poets, these Ancients, or else poets they became from contemplation.

But one turns from the wild magnificence of the setting to the human scene. All lies in silence and mystery. What caused the disappearance of this people? The ordinary blights, like pestilence and war, that bear so heavily upon savage life, appear to archaeologists to have been absent here. So for lack of any other, some students have felt impelled to assign a climatic cause, and the progressive desiccation of a once favorable climate is now among the best-known theories.

But the evidence that failure of irrigation water due to changing climate on the Pajarito Plateau caused its depopulation is not after all much more impressive than some other guesses. In the first place, the Plateau could never have been the scene of extensive farming by a large population. The soil is entirely too poor. The hypothesis fails to consider that not only water but soil is a condition of agriculture. The thin mantle overlying the rocks there could never have been fertile, and the early dwellers in the vicinity of Puyé probably did very little of their farming on the mesa top, and, at the cost of much toilsome journeying, must have tilled the alluvium on adjacent valley floors. Whatever the motive that led to the building of the great Puyé pueblo on the height, whether for defense or for some other reason, it was not an agricultural one.

Incidentally, there's the probability that the inhabitants, like some of the modern puebleños, eked out their larder with game. Puyé means Place of Cottontails.

And in the second place, if the assumption of crop failure on the Plateau turns out to be improbable, the assumption of a cause for it shares in the improbability. There is, in fact, an entire lack of concrete evidence that a permanent desiccation has taken place at all, and the supposition looks like an invention of baffled and hard-pressed archaeologists. So great a change in the climate is elsewhere unknown, and it leaves a vast cause to be explained. Thus far none has been discovered or suggested for the transformation, within the relatively short space required, of a humid country into an arid one. And on the other side, evidence in the shape of yucca sandals and juniper house timbers among aboriginal remains proves clearly that two of the most typical of arid-region plants flourished here then as now. Add to that fact the total absence of woods and other vegetal substances characteristic of the hypothecated Carolinian (Gulf States) flora, and the richly detailed testimony of the Mimbres ceramic paintings about the contemporary fauna, which was identical in all respects with that of the present — and the "progressive desiccation" theory may be dismissed.

The existence of an essentially arid-region flora in ancient times may then be accepted as a fact. And another condition that may be equally accepted as a fact is that a thousand years ago the canyon floors, then as now, received inevitably the drainage of the higher lands adjacent. We are faced by the additional fact that the scourge, whatever it may have been, swept bare not only the mesas, but reached down with the same thoroughness into the stream-nourished bottomlands. It depopulated not alone the pueblo on the mesa rim at Puyé, but also the pueblo on the floor of Frijoles Canyon. Can we still believe in the responsibility of the Sky Powers?

Conscious that the offered solution may not exceed in probability other guesses on the same subject, the present writer is reluctant to leave the fascinating problem untouched. The reluctance is based upon some knowledge of the Sky Powers and their consistent and all-pervasive influence upon this southwestern land. They have a finger in everything. Future research may demonstrate the truth of that dictum in the present case.

There remains a possibility of desiccation, but intermittently in drastic pulsations, and with terrific effectiveness. If the region was arid then as now, it is possible that there were years on end of withering, starving drouth, when practically all rainfall was lacking for the crops, when the meager irrigation failed, when the puny streams dried up and springs, as nowadays, dwindled to a trickle, and when game itself was thinned out to the vanishing point. The tree rings, as Dr. A. E. Douglass finds, give evidence of a great drouth in the Southwest which lasted from the year 1276 to the end of the century. Lesser ones have occurred many times since. Now, a primitive people, with few facilities for storage, having no commerce and living at best practically a hand-to-mouth existence, would soon be reduced by a series of such seasons to actual starvation. And making all allowances, the Plateau must have been, for an Indian country, rather densely populated; but so long as the streams maintained their accustomed flow, provision was assured and sufficient, yet it became precarious at once with the diminution of the water supply. When the shrinkage reached a certain deadline, catastrophe fell upon the people. With the failure of both hunt and harvest, depopulation could not have been long postponed; and with the perennial rivulets reduced to a trickle and the bed of the Rio Grande itself dry gravel, both the populous Plateau and its once well-watered valleys must have witnessed tragic scenes. . . . And the remnant, if remnant there was, wandering away, joined themselves to alien peoples and were thus absorbed.

When the Sky Powers were finally placated and the rains came once more, there was no reason to go back. Houses had fallen to ruin, and the fields, lacking for so long their annual replenishment by rotting plant life, became sterile as such fields still do. Thus the place became an ill-omened solitude, a haunting place of embittered tragic ghosts.

The Rio Mimbres is a small watercourse, but the only perennial one in the lower southwest corner of New Mexico that flows down the Atlantic slope. It succeeds in arriving nowhere. For some forty or fifty miles it trickles in a southeasterly direction and then subsides quietly into the sands. Yet from end to end it possesses altogether uncommon interest. As a clear mountain stream, it emerges from the wilderness and ripples south along the buttresses of the mighty Mimbres Range. For some thirty miles it traverses a ruin-dotted valley of rich farm lands, which is nowhere in the Southwest excelled in antiquarian interest; then it leaves the mountains to traverse a region which is *par excellence* the Land of Desert, Mesa, and Mountain. Up from the winding strip of cottonwoods the valley ascends into a wide plain, but on the plain, standing so thickly as almost to disguise its presence, rises an archipelago of buff-hued, lava-capped mesas and buttes whose feet coalesce at the bottom to form a continuous series of fan-like slopes. Through most of the months a cover of ripened grasses mantles the open, treeless hills as with velvet piling and reflects the sunlight like snow. In late afternoon the strangest purples linger in the shadows of these golden hills, and in the dawn, air like the indescribable blue of the spectrum floods enchantment among their valleys.

Here among the volcanic mesas bubble forth mysterious hot springs, impregnated with chemicals and warmed to the steaming point by unknown fires beneath. And on the rim rocks above the plain prehistoric tools have etched pictographs of many shapes. But in the mistiness of time only the bends and convolutions of the serpent continue intelligible. For ages it has been a place of rattlesnakes, and such it continues to this day. And for the present writer, that dry, blood-chilling alarm there of a coiled snake beside his foot remains a memorable experience of horror. On the east Cook's Peak rears its abrupt porphyry horn eight thousand feet into the sky — the noblest landmark of the region. (Both the spring and the imposing peak near Deming, N. M., were named for Col. Philip St. George Cooke. Yet for some undiscoverable reason, the name is spelled on maps without the final "e.") Then presently the Rio leaves the hills behind and strikes forth across a flat, arid, red-earth country sparsely clothed with yuccas and the green, leafless shrub called by the Mexicans *popotillo*.

Once beyond the drainage of the slopes its flow diminishes rapidly to a thin ribbon which scarce suffices to slake the thirst of the few wandering Herefords, and east of the sable island of basalt named Black Mountain, it has degenerated to a strip of gravel lying at the bottom of a winding trough. Finally, at the north end of the Florida Range it disappears in an alkali flat, mourned only by some forlorn, bushlike willows of the desert. Within fifteen or twenty leagues it has passed from a living stream chilled by mountain snows to a treeless, lonely arroyo whose sands are whipped by the burning wind. It has no rushes to hide a green frog nor entice a killdeer to tarry on its northward way.

When the Spaniards first saw the Rio, its valley was uninhabited, and until about twenty years ago it was supposed to be lacking in aboriginal remains. Then one day a homesteader sent his hired man with a wagon to gather material for adobes to build a house. The hired man returned with a curious sherd. It was the first piece of Mimbres pottery beheld by a white man. Mr. Deloss Osborn of Deming investigated, and in a short time reported his finds to Washington. In a month or so the eminent archaeologist, J. W. Fewkes, of the Smithsonian Institution, came in person to conduct a search.

The sequel is well known. Since then the light of intensive research has been directed upon every phase of the Mimbres remains. Recent excavations have shown that the houses were of three types according to age, the most ancient being pit rooms, the next, semi-subterranean, and the latest being surface rooms. In the earliest period the dead were buried beneath the floor, and the pottery was mostly plain or corrugated. In the next period the tribesmen had emerged from the pit-dweller stage, and walls stood some distance above the ground level. The custom of house burial still prevailed. Plain bowls continued, but naturalistic bowls had become commoner. This is the time of the superb bowls of geometric design. In the third stage red-on-white pottery grew common, while black-on-white declined in popularity. Such, says Nesbitt, is the sequence.

Of all the domestic utensils found in the ruins, the *metates,* or corn-grinding stones, are the commonest. In general they are nothing more than slabs of lava with a shallow depression hollowed out of one side. Since the friction of the *mano* (pestle) was heavy and constant, a frequent roughening of the surface of the *metate* was needful for effective grinding, and for this reason a coarse lava of vesicular or honeycomb structure was preferred, since no amount of abrasion would render it smooth.

Other stone objects, such as axes, scrapers, hoes, and arrowheads occur commonly in the debris of houses. The axes are usually fashioned with great accuracy from a heavy, resistant rock called diorite. Arrowheads of several styles are found, the larger ones being of flint, the smaller of obsidian. Seen in a museum case beside others gathered from all over the American continent, these delicate glassy ones are seen to be the triumph of the primitive stoneworker's art. For fineness of line and perfection in fashioning, they are unequalled.

Personal ornaments are abundant. The shining, translucent crystals of quartz had probably a magic significance, but their brilliancy may well have caused them to be prized as jewelry. And pendants of turquoise, beads, and amulets all show traces of an emotion which could not be satisfied merely in eating and begetting. Turquoise, the sky gem, has for ages possessed the imagined power of warding off evil from its wearer, and some such belief here explains the great care taken in its manufacture. Seashell, enjoying the rarity that came from being traded a thousand miles inland from the Pacific, was another prized adornment. A clam shell was readily shaped into a bracelet by the simple process of grinding on the convex side, and when worn down to a thin ring it could slip over the hand. Many of these bracelets are discovered in burials, some of them shining and smooth to this day, while others are corroded and stained by acids which formed by disintegration of the wearer's arm. Charms and trinkets of shell, carved into the shape of lizards, birds, and butterflies, all show a love of shining surfaces. The pottery must be treated by itself.

To the general pueblo formula — a community stronghold beside the water — the Mimbres culture offers in part an exception. True, they lived in settled communities, but their settlements appear to have been practically without defenses. At first glance the fact would seem to run counter to the thesis of armed possession. But in reality it proves only that since they lived before the introduction of horses, which made long raids practicable, they had no interlopers to fear at the time.

There is also another marked difference between the Mimbres, which is the southernmost, and the northern cultures — the marvellous advance which the former made upon already excellent pottery. Both call for an attempt at elucidation, and both appear to the present writer connected with climatic conditions. The starting point is the fact that the Mimbreños alone among New Mexico pueblo peoples lived in the Lower Sonoran or desert zone. The others lived in the Upper Sonoran.

The distribution of sherds indicates to archaeologists that the Mimbres culture covered a considerable expanse in southwestern New Mexico, extending over the Arizona line down as far as the Chiricahua Mountains, eastward across the wastes of Chihuahua, and then northward along the Florida Mountains and up the valley of the Rio Mimbres itself. Though their range included the well-watered Sierra del Gila, their important ruins all lie to the south of it in a gaunt, close-picked, sun-parched region, the most desert part of the state. In later times it was to become the haunt of the Apaches, whose distinctive mark was a supreme, coyote-like adaptiveness to the arid environment. But as yet the Apaches had not come. In fact, there is evidence which tends to show that their coming was well down towards historic times.

The Mimbreños were scattered over a region in the main unforested and so much poorer in food resources than that of the surrounding peoples that they were in small danger of being dispossessed. There is no competition for the place at the foot of the class. In short, the absence of fortresses is explainable by the general poverty of the country. Marauders, travelling in those days on foot, probably avoided it as much as possible. The chief prize, the upper valley of the Mimbres itself, was protected on three sides by mountains and on the fourth by desert. And these facts, supported by the marked absence of weapons of war and of evidence of violent deaths, point very strongly to the probability of a peaceful, un-warlike existence.

Then the insistent aridity seems to have worked an-other modification in the general pueblo scheme by developing still further the veneration of water. Only thus does their extraordinary proficiency in ceramics be-come intelligible. The Mimbreños were not a race of artists like the Greeks, who with universal genius ex-celled in all of the arts. Their personal ornaments, of which great numbers have survived, show no especial advance beyond those of other savages. It is only by their pottery that they have astonished critics, both American and foreign.

In *Art and Archaeology,* the eminent French critic, Dr. Salomon Reinach, was recently quoted by Professor Jenks as saying that in abstract geometric design even the Greeks were inferior to the Mimbreños. Edgar L. Hewett in his late book says that nowadays the museums of the world are scrambling for Mimbres pottery — and the word he uses is "scrambling." Since 1930 three im-portant scholarly books on the culture have appeared, and within recent years excavations have been made by the Peabody Museum of Harvard, the Logan Museum of Beloit College, the Southwestern Museum of San Diego, the University of Minnesota, the Smithsonian Institu-tion, and others. From all this it would appear that these prehistoric artists bequeathed to the world something worth noting.

The simplest pottery is the corrugated, made like the other kinds by winding a continuous coil of clay upon itself. Beyond this there is a smooth ware made in the same manner, but having the indentations removed by the use of a polishing stone. Though often of red paste this kind was more often of black, and its ornamental feature is the luster which it gained from much smoking and polishing. Both types were utilitarian. It was only in the painted ware that the creative impulse soared away into the realm of pure beauty.

Although the decorated pottery is divided into so-called "realistic" and geometric types, the former is somewhat of a misnomer. Perhaps a majority of the "realistic" designs are not realistic at all, nor meant to be so. Rather than accurate representations, they are more likely to be impressionistic designs in the mood of modernism — our present day modernism — or fanciful mythologic creations. The thin jack rabbit, for instance, is attenuated still further into a graceful rainbow arch. Again, a bird may be represented with the pincers of a beetle, or a turtle may be designed with wings; and the butterfly is usually conventionalized into a series of triangles. Human figures are merely the crudest of caricatures. Yet the same burial may contain a bowl decorated with figures of bird, fish, or reptile executed with perfect mastery.

By far the finest craftsmanship is shown, so the present writer feels, in the geometric bowls. Says A. V. Kidder, "No ware of the Southwest can approach that of the Mimbres either in technical perfection of brushwork, or in the variety, freedom and sheer boldness of its decorative conception. It is amazing stuff."

Though at first sight the austere black and white of a Mimbres bowl leaves one as unmoved as the equally austere Greek vases of the 4th century B.C., a longer contemplation of the finer ones produces the most striking impression of a kind that I can imagine. The extraordinary intricacy and inventiveness of line; the dexterity of hand evidenced in the decoration of curved interior surfaces; the supreme gracefulness and delicacy of the painting achieved with a clumsy yucca-leaf brush; the inerrant sense of proportion shown in covering the available space with the bewildering yet thoroughly integrated pattern — these are some of the features of a technique possessed by the Mimbres artists, and shared in only by the sensitive and accomplished artists of any age or clime.

The astonishing inventiveness of the potters and the sheer inimitableness of their designs may be inferred from the fact that among all the thousands of bowls thus far unearthed, no two have been decorated alike.

But how to account for so strange an artistic freak — it is a puzzle. Cosgrove points to the leisure enjoyed by an unwarlike people; Fewkes to the rich fauna along the upper Rio; Kidder suspects one supremely gifted individual. In all of these opinions there is doubtless truth, yet all seem inadequate.

There must have been leisure, and subjects, and leaders. But there must have been also a background of deep-lying need to motivate that ever-refining craftsmanship. And it must have been an impulse which animated the whole people and stirred them profoundly. As has been said in explanation of the rise of balladry among Germanic peoples, "The folk made verse," so here the folk made pottery. One suspects some rich tradition, a cherished possession of the whole people, a part of the everyday experience in which they lived.

In such an environment as theirs, the fertile, art-producing strain must have been the veneration of life-sustaining water. Pottery has to do with water. It cannot be dissociated from water. When the earliest Basket-Maker learned the convenience of a vessel in which he could carry it and store it for future use, he ceased to be a Basket-Maker and moved forward his cultural frontiers. The ever present need of water mothered his ingenuity.

Recently I stood on the cliff at Oldtown, where Doctor Fewkes made the first scientific investigation of Mimbres culture. The trickling thread of the Rio lay some hundreds of yards distant. Furthermore, I was on the top of a bluff. And it was a hot day. To be running down to the stream for a drink every hour or so would have been most inconvenient. Especially so on a rough stony path at night, or in time of siege. In short, water had to be stored, and pottery thus answers to an elemental need — thirst. It is easy nowadays to be facetious; but real thirst is not funny — not in fever, or in battle.

At my feet, as I glanced down, there lay the sherd of a prehistoric *olla* (water jar). Baked in the fire of a thousand years ago, it told of man's need of water as freshly as though it had come from the kiln only yesterday. It was no accident that here the ancients were conspicuously expert potters, and that the early Pennsylvanians, for example, were not.

But the impulse did not dry up with mere necessity. In the well-watered country along the Monongahela I have picked up the crudest sort of thick, burned clay tempered with mussel shell, where, no doubt, it sufficed for primitive need and satisfied a primitive soul. But along the Mimbres, I have found delicate, beautiful ware that differed from the other as a flower vase differs from a milk crock, or better, as a sacred chalice differs from a teacup — for the religious intent was there.

The explanation is at hand. No one will ever be able to arrive at a very accurate estimate of ancient life without allowing several times the weight to religion that he thinks it ought to possess. Pre-scientific peoples constantly felt themselves in the power of the gods, and this consciousness pervaded all of their thoughts and actions. Propitiation was one of their commonest conceptions, and with the dance, with charms, exorcisms, chants, and symbols, their seasons were a constant round of placations and deprecations. While the remains permit no reconstruction of the Mimbres religious system, their pottery preserves for folklore students a vast amount of symbolism more or less religious in character. A little of it has been deciphered.

Now, symbolism is a kind of prayer, especially in primitive life, for it is the only language which the worshipper and his god have in common. Man makes the sound of showers with a gourd rattle to tell the Sky Powers that he needs rain. He draws the lightning symbol on his *olla* to convey the same message.

The greatest of all rain-bringers was the Thunder Bird. And then there was, very rarely, the Plumed Serpent. Both were religious symbols of the highest efficacy.

On the surface of the *ollas* and bowls the devotee could readily record in lasting form for his gods, as he could not do in laborious pictographs, his (or, more especially, her) significant prayer symbols for rain, fertility, success in war and the chase. (Among the modern Pueblos, it is the women who make the pottery. It should be clear that the writer is not assuming a different practice in prehistoric times.) Moreover, while stone and bone and seashell were too obdurate, too unyielding for his freest self-expression, the clay was pliant. In his hand he could easily mould it to fit his finest ideals of the useful and beautiful, and thus, with its two-fold responsiveness, pottery became the unrivalled medium for his artistic and religious aspiration.

But the petitions, charms, and vows embodied in the baffling symbolism, archaeologists classify now only as scrolls, checkerwork, hachure, etc., neglecting the obvious fact that they were drawn not for future scholars but for the spirits.

Our knowledge of the modern puebleño as a religious being can direct our hypothesis a little way towards probability. While the practices of the kiva are guarded with jealous care to this day, it is known that they have to do with the blessing of the crops and the increase of life — in short, with the principle of fecundity, a form of nature worship which is world-wide. Whatever fertility of seed, therefore, in man and beast as well as in scattered grain which the spirits of the region could insure; whatever coöperation they could supply in the shape of fructifying rain and sunshine; and whatever of beneficent influence in herb or stone they could exert to charm away sickness, to cast a spell upon a foe or thwart an enemy magic; and finally, whatever consort or protection they might vouchsafe to travellers in the realm of shades — all these, we may surmise, were the object of supplications performed in the kiva and inscribed upon the pottery's curved surfaces.

Although it must be said that a majority of the angles, curves, and dots have at present no discoverable significance beyond abstract design, numerous others appear to be highly meaningful.

On a rare bowl unearthed by Mr. Osburn near Deming and pictured in a bulletin of the Smithsonian Institution (*Designs on Mimbres Pottery*, p. 33), there is a beautifully decorated figure of the Plumed Serpent, water deity of the cloud world. The fact and peculiar significance is that the monster has the fins and tail of a fish. Thus the artist's intention is almost as clear as though expressed in print. He was not drawing merely a serpent. In order that there might be no possibility of confusion of identity between the Water God and a lowly reptile, he added not only a crest, but also a fish-tail to show unmistakably its connection with aquatic phenomena of sky and earth.

On a large sherd in my possession, which must have belonged, if one may judge by the superior accuracy of the drawing, to a remarkably fine bowl, there is a rainbow and lightning design. The bow has the four lines to designate the four colors — red, yellow, green, and violet, which are all that the naked eye can recognize; and of these the widest is the outside red band, as it appears in nature. The lightning is drawn in negative — a pure white jagged line outlined by pure black paint.

On the ancient pottery there is, as well as on the modern pueblo ware, a geometrical figure made up of triangles and called the butterfly symbol. It is a symbol nowadays of happiness and fertility. The corn nowhere appears as a growing plant, for the Mimbreños very rarely employed leaves as decorative motifs, but a cross section of the ear is not uncommon on the bottom of a bowl. Then drawn on the side of game animals there is a curious diamond-shaped figure which seems to have a discoverable meaning. It is in modern designs called the "medicine man's eye," and here it would suggest some sort of spell put upon the animal to make escape from the hunter impossible — a form of animistic belief common among savages in many parts of the world.

Commonest of all are the designs based upon bird and feather motifs, for birds, according to Dr. Fewkes, excel in variety and numbers all other animals depicted upon Mimbres ware. He says: "From their mysterious power of flight, and other unusual characteristics, birds have always been considered by the pueblos to be important supernatural beings and are ordinarily associated with the sky. We find them often with star symbols and figures of lightning and rain clouds. There is something mysterious in the life of a bird and consequently there must be some intimate connection between it and those great mysteries of climate, upon which so largely depends the production of food by an agricultural people." (*Designs on Mimbres Pottery,* p. 13.) The wild turkey, associated by the Hopi with the sun and the rain, is, he notes, common on Mimbres pottery, and, what is particularly important, unattached wings (so he calls them) appear as decorative patterns. While the identification is somewhat doubtful, it looks plausible, and Dr. Jenks, in discussing a design recently, speaks of a "winged" line. (*Art and Archaeology,* June, 1932.)

Wings, Thunder Bird, Sky Powers — all are inextricably bound together in Indian superstition. The Mimbreño artist had sufficient draughtsmanship to make his bird recognizable when he chose to do so, and when he did not, one may infer that it was because he had no model or else no clear notion of his subject. This, I believe, will account for the strange, archaic-looking birds made up of triangles which are frequently found. Likewise, the very carefully executed birds, covered with ornamentation but not referable to any known species, are also probably Thunder Birds. But far more prevalent than they are the tapering, serrated wing figures. They are everywhere. At times a bowl will be covered with them, and the composition will suggest more vividly than a modernistic poem the power of dynamic flight. Nothing could symbolize so well the swift, free-motioned Powers of the Sky.

It is in the Mimbreño cult of the dead that beauty touches us most with its poignant surprise. As if to assure the wistful ghost of a continuing place in the hearth-fire circle, the dead were buried underneath the floor of the dwellings. Flexed or in a sitting posture, the body was interred with its turquoise beads or bracelets of seashell or other dear but ineffectual finery for the spirit's long journey, and then over the face or upon the head was laid, like a flower of farewell, the mortuary bowl. And in each, chipped from its bottom at the center, was a round small hole which "killed" the bowl and gave escape to its spirit, which then fared forth with the master. The honor accorded to the head suggests that fine Horatian ode in which the poet laments beside the body of his friend the futility of tears, which

Thaw not the frost which binds so dear a head.

Occasionally there is discovered a bowl which covers the burial of an infant and stirs even in dusty archaeology a timeless pathos. And one recalls a relic of the antique native symbolism which is said to linger still among some of the Pueblos: when a child dies, a thread is laid from the grave to its home to point the little spirit back to its mother.

Indeed, it is only from the mournful and sacrificial function of the Mimbres bowl that we come at length to understand the uniqueness of its perfection. There is no other explanation. The finest bowls are not scraped on the bottom and show scarce a sign of use. Naught but the ultimate memorial purpose for which his masterpiece was destined constrained the potter and gave him his supreme incentive. It availed at the same time for statuary, urn, and elegiac inscription. Few of the bowls are found apart from burials and "unkilled," and this fact leads to the surmise that if the finer specimens were used at all by the living, their higher intention was purely funereal. One can hardly doubt that religious emotion sustained the craftsman's hand, and that here, too, noble art was animated by a noble purpose. Apart from medieval faith medieval cathedrals are unintelligible — the faith of folk who built for the glory of God and intended a habitation for His Presence. And, similarly, in this remote valley the aim was in a unique way to glorify sorrow, and in this aim the soul of a people flowered. To grief there are no ethnic bounds. And for the departed, white or red, no tokens are too precious.

Over the fate of these primitive artists the curiosity of the anthropologist has busied itself with intriguing but barren suppositions, and at present any attempt to explain their disappearance is based upon hypothesis.

Perhaps they were annihilated in war — the fate that overshadows so much of primitive life. Yet on this theory Nesbitt remarks, "Every ruin on which there is literature shows, moreover, that the abandonment of the pueblos was not due to internal warfare nor the attacks of outside enemies. This is evidenced by the dearth of implements or weapons of war." Or perhaps the population was exterminated by pestilence or disease — in fact, malaria has been rather rashly suggested. Or the land may have been abandoned on account of some portentous aboriginal fear — volcanic convulsions, earthquakes, meteoric disturbances. Cosgrove believes the abandonment to have been peaceful and voluntary.

Possibly there may have occurred one of those great and long-continued drouths, as we surmised on the Pajarito Plateau, which have scourged the Southwest in an irregular and tragic rhythm. Like Israel and his sons going down into the land of Egypt during a similar visitation, the survivors may have left their homeland to buy grain. When the drouth had at last ended there was no returning, for the broken tribesmen were either enslaved like the Israelites, or else exterminated. ¿Quién sabe?

In all of these there is possibility, but only the last appears to the writer to go a little beyond mere possibility. Evidence gleaned from the designs of the Casas Grandes pottery in Old Mexico seems to indicate a decided Mimbreño influence, and one may surmise that they migrated southward, down into the province of Chihuahua, and left there among their kindred potters an inheritance of their genius.

But the folk migration — what was it like? Imagination, not freed from the sober facts of archaeology, but rather guided by them, re-creates the scene of their departure. Over the ancestral valley of the Mimbreños a scanty band, the remnant of their people, look down from the rimrock of the mesa. Secluded between the protecting hills, and over-canopied by its frosted, autumnal cottonwoods, the Rio shines in the sunlight like a golden serpent. The narrow cornfields lie asleep in the mellow, transparent air, while over them the ravens make noisy holiday; yet no squaw is there to affright them or gather the scragged, worm-bored ears for her *metate*. Among the pine trunks browse the timid deer, and no more a feathered arrow flies hissing to sting them.

The spirits are inexorable. No point of ritual has been left unperformed in the incantations and prayers, yet all have been unavailing. Famine presses sore upon them. The luck-bearing amulets of seashell and the powerful fetishes of stone have failed. Even the turquoise is ineffectual. Now even the resistless ceremonial magic of the dance itself has failed — failed with its entreaty of measured footbeats falling in perfect tempo with the drumbeat, and its gestures and sacred miming that no god nor devil could misunderstand; failed with its rain-bringing rattle of gourd seeds and tortoise shells, its glory of eagle feathers, its tinkle of copper bells. No propitiation availed to bring back the harmony between man and sky and soil. All had failed, and in the failure the old men and the priests, interpreters of the wisdom of the Ancients, read the signal to depart. And so with aboriginal dirges on their lips and aboriginal *Weltschmerz* sleepless in their hearts, they set forth. Each bears a few scanty treasures, his weapons and a mortuary bowl. Far from their native fields they will preserve to the last the hallowed burial custom of their fathers. Down the bends of the valley they vanish, and the afternoon wind rising in its strength confuses the sound of lamentation and the tinkling of little copper bells.

P.H.

CHAPTER SEVEN

CONQUISTADORES

I<small>T WAS A SINGLE ERRAND WHICH</small> brought the Conquistadores into New Mexico — the search for precious metals. And yet they were motivated by no more than ordinary cupidity, for in a land so worthless, according to their view, it was gold or nothing. And thus Sky Determined the object of their quest, and, consequently, the uneconomic nature of their general policy. By a momentous chance, the Sky Powers laid out for them a trail beside the waters down in the canyon instead of over the mesa and along the mountains. So they passed the gold and silver only a few leagues distant — and they never knew. The epic in its first canto bent away to the left, so to speak, and the flame-colored banners of Spain conducted the mailed cavalcade and the brown-robed priests down the other path to obscurity, while the treasure waited in the earth for men of a different breed.

The three hundred years of Spanish history in New

Mexico were enacted, with the exception of sundry incidents along the Zuñi-Albuquerque trail, in the narrow theater which the Sky Powers prepared and designated for the purpose — the north-and-south trending valley of the Rio Grande. The Conquistadores kept close to the waters, and that fact was fraught with the most striking consequences. Along with the history which we accept as authentic there could be written a far more dramatic history of might-have-beens, but historians, occupied with actualities, have never lifted up their eyes to see how close to the surface runs a substratum of almost fact.

Yet history came within an ace of being splendidly blazoned in golden characters, for the missed road led to opportunities that really were stupendous. Suppose, for instance, that Oñate, who was a practical miner, had come marching up the Gila instead of the Rio Grande, and had founded his settlement not at Santa Fe but at Silver City. The names tell the tale. At the edge of Silver City lies a thread of valley in the hills which back in the 'seventies yielded white metal — as fast, they say, as it could be taken from the ground — to the amount of five million dollars. What would it not have done for the perpetually bankrupt little colony at Santa Fe! It was precisely the kind of bonanza that the Conquerors sought. The total wealth of their colony through its whole history could not hold a candle to it and the others discovered near by. Instead of poverty, isolation, and peonage, there would have been wealth, progress, growth, and the flowering of a native culture. It is all a simple equation in economics. For instead of some scrubby sheep and longhorn steers, the only export of a people whom a hostile balance of trade left to grow perennially poorer, a few mule-loads of silver from Chloride Flat and some of the gold from Pinos Altos, would have set up a balance in their favor and given them in rich measure the commodities of civilization — tools, clothing, furniture, equipment. Precious metals could have saved the day — and they alone.

And as no far-fetched corollary, the general worthlessness of the country was destined to affect particularly the nature of the impact of white culture upon red, and to concentrate the attention of both sides upon the contact-zone of religion. Whatever importance the little settlement was to possess, as the Spanish authorities soon perceived, would not be commercial; and as the dearth of economic advantages became more and more obvious, they devoted more and more of their attention to maintaining their northernmost outpost as an effective base for the conversion of the Indians. But the Indians, it has already been noted, had since time immemorial been developing a nature religion of their own peculiarly appropriate to the desert. The result was to be that in the entire history of Catholic missions no citadel of heathenism ever put up a resistance so stubborn and so long-drawn.

The original lure for the men of Spain was that mirage of the mysterious Seven Cities of Cíbola, which wavered in a golden haze across the sands of the north. Almost from the start, that magnificent myth of an Eldorado wrought out of the substance of dreams, fascinated the imagination of every Spanish soldier and adventurer.

The story was first told about 1538, it seems, by some Indians to the avaricious Nuño de Guzmán, Viceroy of New Spain. He sent out a searching expedition. Although no gold was found, his failure had little effect on the over-exuberant imagination of his countrymen. Then into the saga come the Franciscan Friar, Marcos de Niza, and the magnificent, fanciful figure, Estévan, the blackamoor slave from Morocco. Like an extravagant personage out of an Elizabethan romance at its most fantastic, this "black man with a beard, wearing things that sounded, rattles, bells, and plumes on his feet and arms," had passed into Indian legend almost by the time his body was cold. With his master and Cabeza de Vaca and another Spaniard, he had been with the ill-fated de Narváez expedition to Florida some years before, and after being shipwrecked, they had actually made their way, after one of the most remarkable journeys that history records, across the American continent to the town of Culiacán, near the west coast of Mexico. Captured and enslaved by the Indians, they had consumed years on the way, but had finally arrived among civilized men to tell their story.

Although Estévan, it seems clear, had probably not touched any soil of New Mexico on his wanderings with de Vaca, he was selected as guide and companion for

Marcos de Niza, who was then being sent by the new viceroy, Mendoza, on a northern tour of exploration, "for the service of Our Lord, and the good of the people."

With Indian guides and with another friar who presently fell ill and was left behind, the two strangely assorted comrades set out from Culiacán early in March of the year 1539. When Holy Week arrived the Padre paused at a place called Vacapa, and sent the Negro ahead with the famous directions about sending back a cross. If nothing of note was found, the cross was to be the length of a man's hand; if any great matter were discovered, one twice as long. But if the country were as fine as New Spain, a large cross was to be sent back. Four days after the Negro's departure the Padre received a cross as tall as a man! And with the messenger came an Indian from Estévan, who furnished full particulars of the wonderland which they were seeking. Cíbola was not merely a city but a province of Seven Cities ruled by a single potentate. The inhabitants wore jewels of turquoise in their ears and about their garments; and their houses, which were of stone three or four stories in height, had on their chief portals ceremonial designs executed in the same gem.

The turquoise, bright stone of the sky color, runs like a blue pattern henceforth through the Indian story. It was for them not an ornament merely, but an amulet, a protector freighted with sky magic, the logical and inevitable talisman for conjuring the supernal spirits which guard men against sickness and other machinations of the infernal ones — ghosts, perhaps, of the human dead. Possession of it offered to the Sky Powers witness of the wearer's devotion to their cult, and gave to him basis of irresistible appeal for their protection. Holding the sky gem in hand, he had in some irrational, transferred sense, a power of command over the spirits which it symbolized; and so among primitive animists who held the sky in veneration, turquoise could hardly fail to become an adjunct of its worship. Prized among the aboriginal tribes of the Mimbres Valley, it is found among their burials wrought into the form of pendants, charms, and necklaces; and it has thus a history in the Southwest which reaches from immemorial antiquity to the modern Zuñis and Navahos.

The slave's description, fantastic as the adventures of Marco Polo in Cathay, was what might have been expected from the glamorous Estévan. Yet his romantic imaginings deceived the good Friar, and were to inspire adventurers and determine Spanish policy for some three generations. So pushing with haste across the desert of what was later to become southern Arizona, the Franciscan reached at length a large river which would appear to have been the Gila, subsequently a well-known link in the New Mexico-Pacific trail. Up this stream he journeyed five days, when he reached, early in May, a range of bold, snow-capped mountains. Then as he was proceeding along their flank, he received almost alarming tidings — Estévan was dead! He had reached Cíbola, and there the inhabitants had murdered him along with many of his attendants.

The Moor, it appears from the account of Twitchell, who gleaned it from the old chronicles, had proceeded in regal and barbaric state.

"Carrying with him a gourd," says the historian (*Leading Facts*, vol. I, p. 157), "decorated with two bells and feathers, one white and one red, he sent messengers ahead, displaying the gourd as a symbol of his authority. . . . He was also attended by a large number of handsome women, whom he had attached to his party along the route. He also carried turquoises, and the Indians who accompanied him were fully convinced that while in his company and under his protection, no danger or ill could befall them."

When near Cíbola, he had dispatched messengers ahead with his gourd, stating that he had come to seek peace and heal the sick. Reaching the town with a retinue of three hundred, he had been denied entrance, and later was killed; his black body, as reported by the explorer, Alarcón, was cut in pieces and distributed among the chiefs of Cíbola. Thus passes from the stage of history the discoverer of New Mexico, than whom none was more strange; and the great traveller, than whom few of the race of mortals since the days of the "much-enduring" Ulysses, have more endured.

The Friar, strengthening himself by prayers, continued to Cíbola. Ascending a mountain to view the now ruined Zuñi pueblo of Hawaikuh — for such it was — he gazed upon it from a distance. Then, in the sweetness of the desert springtime, raising a cross upon a mound of stones, he took possession of the land for Spain, calling it "The Kingdom of Saint Francis."

Making his way back to the southern provinces at once, he gave his report, based upon the veracity of Estévan. Instantly every adventurer was inspired with fierce desire. The Viceroy lost no time in organizing an expedition. For captain-general, he named his friend, Francisco Vásquez de Coronado, the governor of New Galicia, and designated the town of Compostella as the point of mobilization.

The roster of romantic names perpetuates the pageantry of a splendid but declining chivalry, while the whole project has the sound of a blank-verse tragedy of the sixteenth century. The first of the captains, next in command to the general, was Don Tristán de Arellano; then followed among others, Don García López de Cárdenas, and Don Rodrigo Maldonado, whose brother-in-law was a duke. In command of the artillery, which was then coming into picturesque though rather ineffectual use, was Hernando de Alvarado, while the standard bearer was Don Pedro de Tovar, whose father had been a member of the Emperor's household.

The army was accompanied by its own historian, Pedro de Castañeda, who calls it "the most brilliant company ever collected in the Indies to go in search of new lands." The commander had already attained the eminence of a governorship, and had married not merely a noblewoman, but Doña Beatriz, cousin of the Emperor. The *caballeros* wore the Spanish armor of the period, while the General, more resplendent than they, was literally, El Dorado, the Gilded Man, on account of the splendor of his suit of mail.

The horsemen carried lances but no firearms — and swords of the famed Toledo steel, one may be certain. One such ancient Spanish blade was picked up not long ago in the Mimbres Range, broken and rust-coated, but just below the hilt was still visible an arabesque design of extremely fine workmanship inlaid in gold. In addition, there was a company of seventy footmen armed with either crossbows or with the primitive and cumbersome musket called arquebus. Four chaplains, the vanguard of the indomitable train of Franciscans, went along to care for the spiritual needs of the army and to study the country as a field for future missionary labors. Finally, the rear was brought up by some hundreds of Indians and miscellaneous camp followers, who attended the herds brought to provide sustenance on the desert marches.

Naturally, the march was slow, but by Easter of the year 1540 the host arrived at Culiacán, and reached at length, some time in July, the pueblo of Hawaikuh, the first city in the Province of Cíbola, which Friar Marcos had beheld from a distance. Raising their famous war cry, *Santiago,* they assaulted the walls. Coronado, shining in his golden armor, led the attack in person. Though twice felled by stones hurled down by the defenders, he led his desert-worn forces to victory and the village surrendered, turning over to the famished army an abundance of food. Renaming the fallen stronghold Granada, in honor of the Viceroy, the triumphant Spaniards took possession, while the defeated tribesmen with their women and children withdrew appropriately to Thunder Mountain, the abode of their protecting sky spirits.

Settling for a time, Coronado sent out exploring parties. Captain Tovar penetrated the northwest to the country of the Hopis. On his return a second party under Captain Cárdenas was sent out to seek a fabled stream "whose banks were three or four leagues in air." Proceeding eighty leagues west of Cíbola, they discovered a gigantic chasm into which, after long search, they found a place of descent. It was the Grand Canyon of the Colorado, whose abyss they were the first civilized men to behold. From the rim, thousands of feet above, the mighty stream appeared but a brook, but on descending they found that rocks which at first looked small were as tall "as the tower of the cathedral in Seville." Unable to reach the bottom of the vast gorge, they were finally driven back by thirst.

In the interim the fame of the Spaniards was spreading, and a deputation headed by Chief Bigotes came all the way from the pueblo of Cicuye on the Pecos River to visit them. Coronado exchanged presents with them and listened to their stories of buffalo herds on the plains far to the east. Then in August he dispatched Captain Alvarado with twenty soldiers to investigate. Their trail led them past Acoma, the Sky City, said to be the oldest in the United States, and there the Acomas drew a line of sacred corn meal on the sand, which they forbade the white men to cross; but as an assault was about to begin they weakened and brought out presents of piñon nuts, turkeys, deerskins, and corn.

Continuing eastward, Alvarado discovered the famous stream which was henceforth to figure so prominently in the history of the region. He saw it first a little north of the present Albuquerque at a pueblo named Tiguex, and as the day was September 7, the eve of the Blessed Virgin's birthday, he piously christened it the River of Our Lady. Later generations have known it as the Rio Grande.

In a document which he calls the "Search for the South Sea," Alvarado draws back the curtain upon the Indian scene of four hundred years ago.

This River of Our Lady, he states, flows through a very wide open plain sowed with corn plants; there are several groves and there are twelve villages. The houses are of earth two stories high; the people have a good appearance, more like laborers than a warlike race; they have a large supply of corn, beans, melons, and fowl in great plenty; they clothe themselves with cotton and the skins of cows and dresses of the feathers of birds; they wear their hair short. Those who have most authority among them are the old men; we regarded them as witches because they say they go up into the sky and other things of the same sort . . . they [the pueblo people] worship the sun and water.

Then, as later, it is clear, the Sky Powers exercised dominion over the land and its inhabitants. And it was easy for the Spaniards to see the reasonableness of such worship, for in the hundreds of weary miles they had traversed since crossing the Gila, it was the first considerable stream bordered by valley cornfields.

Proceeding eastward, Alvarado and his party reached Cicuye, where they were greeted with drums and the music of barbaric flutes. The chronicler Castañeda says that there, also, turquoises were presented to them, and then goes on to describe the four-story houses. The pueblo was a square structure built around a court. In it there were no doors, for ladders instead were employed as a means of access to the interior. The fighting strength of the village, he estimates, was about five hundred warriors. It was a perfect example of the pueblo formula — half domicile, half stronghold.

At this point enters a plains Indian, El Turco, so named by the Spaniards from the oriental cast of his countenance. Held as a slave in the village, he seems to have been compelled by his masters to aid them in getting rid of guests that very shortly became unwelcome. At any rate, he began entrancing the Spaniards with tales of exactly what they were looking for — shining cities and treasures of gold. Far to the northeast on the buffalo plains, so ran the account, dwelt the grand chieftain of the Quivira country, who napped every afternoon in the shade of a tree which was hung with little golden bells, whose music lulled him into slumber. Thus with properties generously selected, as it might be from a voluptuous eastern romance, the Turk wove a renewed spell for the imagination of the treasure seekers. After the dire disillusionment at Cíbola they might have discounted such narratives, one would expect; but again they listened eager-eyed. The real purpose of the inventions was to rid the country of its invaders by luring them forth away from the waters, where the friendly Sky

Powers of the red men could take revenge in their own way. Coronado took the stories with considerable salt, but nonetheless set out eastward.

The remainder of the extraordinary tour of exploration is obscure, but with one man charged with the responsibility of counting the steps, they estimated that at the end of thirty-seven days' march from Tiguex they had traversed 250 leagues. Bandelier surmises that this was not in an air line, however, believing that the party had lost their reckoning on the plains and travelled along the arc of a circle, first northeast and later southeast, and he cites in proof a remark of Castañeda that the guides led the army "too near Florida." Finally, the commander ordered the return of the main body under Captain Arellano, while he himself, with thirty picked horsemen, continued the search for Quivira. Taking with them Friar Juan de Padilla and El Turco, they then rode sixty-seven days longer. While the meager data have been variously interpreted, the accepted conclusion is that Quivira, which Coronado says he reached in latitude 40 degrees, lay somewhere in the present state of Kansas, probably north of the Arkansas River. But whatever its location, they found no metal of any kind, except some little copper bells. At the farthest point, they went — rather sadly, one might imagine — through the usual and empty formality of raising a cross and making the act of possession in the name of the crown. On the cross they left an inscription saying only that Francisco Vásquez de Coronado had "reached this place." They then strangled El Turco in his sleep, and shortly after the middle of August, 1541, began their return. They reached their starting point after forty days more of toil and privation.

Meanwhile the main army, under Arellano, had returned from a point on the Great Plains along the course of the River Colorado. The Indian guides, in order to keep accurately on the course, would shoot an arrow at sunrise each morning in the direction of the line of march, and by the simple expedient of shooting others in the line which it determined, would go forward through the day without error. At the rendezvous Arellano waited in vain many weary weeks for his commander, who returned with his troop only after a relief party had gone as far as Cicuye in search of them.

After a second winter of inactivity and internal dissension in the army, Coronado started in April, 1542, to lead his army southward. The Gilded Man reached Mexico "very sad and very weary." He had discovered no gold and the return marks his exit from the illumination of glory. . . . Cíbola and Quivira — twin mirages of that cruel and beautiful Eldorado which enticed brave men across the wastes with a siren lure that was stronger than the certainty of travail and the fear of death!

Illumination of a very different quality rests upon the names of the two Franciscan friars who remained behind when the army marched away under the banners of the Emperor. Father Luis de Escalona and Father Juan de Padilla stayed behind to undo, as far as lay in their power, some of the hideous wrongs inflicted by their countrymen. Friar Luis cast his lot with the pueblo of Tiguex, "where the old men say they go up into the sky," among the heathen folk who "worship the sun and water." There presently an arrow pierced his dark robe, and he fell a sacrifice to the ancestral deities and the religion of the rain. But Friar Juan, who had been a soldier in his younger days, returned across the pathless plains with a small escort to Quivira. There, on his return, he found a cross which he had set up, "and all around it clean, as he had charged them to keep it."

Prostrating himself before it, he began the duties of an apostle and teacher of the people. But only a little later he, too, as the chronicler relates, "attained the felicity of being killed by the arrows of the barbarous Indians, who threw him into a pit and covered his body with innumerable stones." Before generalizing on the soldiers of Spain, it were well to consider these soldiers of the Cross.

It was only as a treasure seeker that Coronado failed. As an explorer and trail-maker, he easily marches with his countryman, De Soto, and the French La Salle, at the head of all that indomitable company who conquered the upper half of the New World for posterity.

The ethnologist and historian, Frederick W. Hodge, boldly makes the challenge that Coronado's feat was "the most remarkable expedition that ever traversed American soil" and calls attention to its immense scientific importance in giving, along with the narrative of De Soto, the first insight into the vast, unknown interior of North America. The magnitude of his explorations must indeed be reckoned on a continental scale, for from the starting point at Compostella, which lies inside the Tropics, his journey stretched well up towards the Great Lakes, and traversed Sinaloa, Sonora, Arizona, New Mexico, Texas, Oklahoma, and Kansas. His captains discovered the Grand Canyon of the Colorado and described the lower reaches of the stream. They explored the valley of the Rio Grande and gave to the outside world the earliest information about its sedentary pueblo tribes, as well as of the hunting tribes of the Great Plains. Coronado added to the sway of his Emperor more territory than any man of his time, and added to geography a whole new realm — the American Southwest.

And here is suggested the final valorous note of the man's achievement. Geographically, the *amount* of country matters less than the *kind* of country which he conquered in his superhuman travail. What other explorers endured, he endured, plus the desert. Through the most arid regions of the Southwest in burning sunshine and across sandy waste — Sonora, Arizona, New Mexico — we see in far memory this iron Spaniard and his armored horsemen toiling forward, sometimes with water enough, sometimes with no water at all, through the endless leagues toward Quivira, dumbly, mechanically counting paces . . . "ninety-seven, ninety-eight, ninety-nine." And all the time inimical Sky Gods look on with avid eyes.

As it were through some mighty enchantment, the land was held under their domination and it never acknowledged the King of Spain. Indeed, that monarch profited from it little then or later. Discoveries which might have afforded claim to a new empire north of his Mexican realm added to the Crown nothing but barren glory, and an expanse of still more barren country. So the Conquistador was foiled. Beside his, the march of Xenophon and his Greek immortals was perhaps no more than child's play—for, after all, what is valor against the desert?

For two generations after the disillusionment of 1542, treasure hunters turned their attention to the south, where they were better rewarded, and thought no more of Cíbola. But at length, in the year 1581, three more Franciscans responded to the appeal of the Cross with another attempt to carry the Faith to the pueblos of Tiguex. Their names were Agustín Rodríguez, Juan de Santa María, and Francisco López, and although they disappeared almost as promptly as lost ocean fliers, they achieved in death the splendor of heroic failure. More especially, their fate affords some illuminating implications as to what the future reaction of the native religion would be to the Catholic evangel.

Considerable attention has been given by historians to the determining of the place where the friars met death. But the really important question is not where they were killed, but why. One of the early reports alleges that after the departure of the military escort the Indians killed them to gain possession of their horses and supplies. Perhaps so. But theft would have been a simpler course than murder.

The manner of death suggests a further and weightier motive. It must be remembered that the one purpose of the friars was not domination or plunder, but the conversion of the "gentiles" by peaceable means and with the works of mercy. Now the village of Puaray, in which they established themselves, was the identical Tiguex of Coronado's expedition, in which Father de Escalona had been martyred and where, as Alvarado stated, witch men claimed to go up into the sky. In an atmosphere so charged with heathenism, the progress of Christianity depended entirely upon discrediting and supplanting the native witchcraft. As in a greater contest long before, denunciation of the existing priesthood brought promptly a bloody retaliation, where the scribes and Pharisees uniting their power brought the offending one before their Sanhedrin and pronounced Him "guilty of death."

With peculiar aptness, death came upon Father López at a moment when he was in prayer. Father Rodríguez was permitted to give him Christian burial. It may have been murder with robbery for the motive; it looks more like judicial execution. A few days later, Father Rodríguez himself was martyred. The savages threw his body into the waters of the Rio Grande — on which, even to the present time, neighboring Tewa people lay their offerings, so that the sacred stream may bear them away to the great Sun Father. Friar Juan was overtaken by red assassins while on a journey.

In addition to earthly fame, which they scorned, the friars achieved the blazing of a new and greater trail into the north. Henceforth, men trekking up from the south would no longer follow the circuit of Friar Marcos and Coronado; they would march directly up the Rio Grande. A new route had been blazed, and it lay for hundreds of miles along the water, but far from the deposits of gold and silver. In Nueva Viscaya the spread of the Spanish population had been northeastward towards the rich mining district of Santa Barbara, whence there was a water route along the tributary Conchos to the present Rio Grande. This, of course, would be the path of the future, for being near water, it would have incalculable advantages for both men and beasts.

When the fate of the friars became known in New Spain, the Franciscans at once organized a rescue party. As a testimony of devotion to the Church a wealthy mineowner at Santa Barbara, Antonio de Espejo by name, volunteered to accompany them and furnish an armed escort. Espejo, being not a mere gold-seeker but a miner, made extensive explorations in New Mexico and returned home reporting it a country of great mineral wealth and announcing his intention to seek authority for colonization.

Nothing came of his plans. More than a decade passed, and then another miner, Juan de Oñate, owner of some of the richest ore deposits in New Spain, experienced the northward urge. But this time, the adventurers were not treasure-hunters, but colonists. The Eldorado legend had been exploded. As the provincial exchequer was empty, he fitted out a great expedition at his own expense. There were 130 soldiers besides many women and children. Ten of the brown-robed Franciscans were again in the spear point of adventure. Eighty-three of the primitive heavy-wheeled Spanish ox-carts comprised the supply train, and a herd of several thousand head of stock was driven in the rear.

On May 4, 1598, just below the modern international boundary, they reached the Rio Grande, and a few miles upstream crossed to the east bank, called the ford "El Paso del Norte, The Pass of the North, a name which henceforth was to hold an honored prominence in the annals of the Southwest.

The commander himself, with a small party, soon left the slow-moving train to press on ahead. Famine, as might have been expected in the inhospitable region, soon broke upon them. Their way lay across the desert, later to be called, ominously, "Jornada del Muerto" — Dead Man's Journey. Ox-carts stalled in sand-choked arroyos, famishing children, thirst-crazed animals, shade-less heat across the gravel mesas — such were the details of their crossing. Then down from an Indian village in the north, says an old tradition, help came generously in the shape of a great gift of corn. And they named the place "Socorro" (succor), a memorial which survives to the present time.

Directly up the Rio Grande dragged the great caravan. There was nowhere else to go. At Santo Domingo the commander held a great council with the chieftains of thirty-four pueblos and received the allegiance of all of them to the Crown of Spain. Then past the black, basalt-capped mesas he rode northward to the pueblo of San Juan, where he halted. The valley of the river was fertile, and there was enough land for cultivation. The climate was ideal, and the Indians were friendly. It seemed the spot for making history. The day was the eleventh of July, 1598. By mid-August his belated colonists had arrived. They found the choice made, and a new commonwealth, the second permanent one in the country which we now call America, in existence. The town was regularly placed under the protection of San Gabriel, and named in his honor. A full generation was to pass before the world heard of a boulder on the eastern coast called Plymouth Rock.

Oñate was an executive, and within a few days he had his men and fifteen hundred natives at work on irrigation and supply ditches. The first necessity, as he well knew, was water, and he continued the work until the supply was adequate. Then by the time his colonists had been two weeks in camp, he had ready for them a fine new chapel, which was dedicated with appropriate ceremonies on September 8. The festal occasion included as we learn from the poet, Captain Villagrá, who recorded the earliest New Mexico history in an epic — a famous sham battle between the Moors and the Christians, which greatly delighted the Indian spectators. On the next day, Oñate assembled all the native chiefs and bade the Franciscan *comisario,* Friar Martínez, apportion the pueblos into working districts and assign a padre to each. The villages in the Tigua province alone, as shown by the historian Bancroft, were sixty in number. But unhesitatingly, without knowledge of the language, without money, without equipment, the seven friars went forth alone to take their posts. Soldiers of the Cross — soldiers, indeed!

Within a month the dynamic governor had turned to exploration. He ordered Captain Zaldívar to take sixty men and strike out eastward by way of the famous gorge later to be known as Apache Canyon. Without waiting for their return, he himself set out after them for the Pecos and returned from the south after a roundabout journey across the Manzano Mountains. Hardly pausing to rest, he set his face westward on the long trail to Acoma, whose formal submission he received; and then from the Hopi villages beyond, sent forward one of his captains still deeper into the west to look for some famous mines. After water, then religion and gold! The future of New Mexico looked extremely bright. But the Sky Powers were biding their time.

But while the indefatigable governor had grown accustomed to living at concert pitch, the energy of his people was fast burning out. Paying no heed to them, he sent to the viceroy at Mexico City a request for heavy reinforcements, and to the Franciscans an invitation to send more friars. Then in June, 1601, with eighty men he struck out across the Great Plains for that fatal destination which had ruined the Gilded Man before him — Quivira. Again, when he came near the place, was raised the lying cry of "Gold," which led him farther and farther like an *ignis fatuus* across a morass. And again nothing was found — no precious metal, no cities, nothing but some miserable savages.

In his absence the colonists, who had grown tired of living on glory, thought things over. Weary of empty fighting and still emptier wandering, they had been unable to reserve time from their other occupations for the indispensable tasks of sowing and reaping. The little planting which a few had done was ruined by a great drouth. The Indians were already living on wild seeds. The Sky Gods were tightening down. And autumn was upon them. They acted quickly.

"When Oñate arrived," says Twitchell, "he found the

place almost deserted. Everybody almost, including colonists and friars, had returned to Nueva Vizcaya." In the springtime the governor had been an enthusiast, intoxicated with his own achievements. Before the winter he was a defeated man. In his plans he had reckoned without the mocking Sky Powers.

Meanwhile the destiny of his colony lay upon their knees. Could he have looked into the future to see the extent of their sway upon a retrograding posterity, the vision would have saddened and broken his great heart; for he and his hero Conquistadores, whose strength was that of Hercules and whose travail that of Odysseus, availed only to found a few adobe villages at the back of the desert and make some fruitless journeys before their impulse reached substantial exhaustion.

After all, little San Gabriel was not completely abandoned in 1608, but a new settlement was begun about that time by Oñate or another which at once cast it into dark eclipse. The other town, some thirty miles farther south, founded none knows precisely when, at once became the capital, and on account of that preëminence, its history for the next hundred years or so becomes the history of New Mexico. Though later the immigrants were scattered for many leagues along the Rio Grande Valley in thin *poblaciones* (settlements), the fringes were left in obscurity and the tiny capital occupies the spotlight alone. And until the Reconquest in 1692, it was the single villa, or incorporated town.

Thus, uniquely old among American cities, Santa Fe, the Villa Real de la Santa Fé de San Francisco, is also uniquely small among them. She beheld New Amsterdam in the days when that Dutch village squatted on a lowly spread of bayside land, which was worth no more than $24.00 to the original owners, and has ever since continued to gaze upon her, striding goddess-like down the years until her shining towers are the wonder of the world. Manhattan, Boston, Philadelphia, and Baltimore in their pride are all her younger sisters. And nowadays she is watching the upstart towns of Detroit and Los Angeles grow from insignificance into huge, million-peopled cities. Most phenomenal of all, indeed, is this other Spanish city of the equally sonorous name — Nuestra Señora de los Angeles. In 1931 Our Lady of the Angels celebrated the one hundred and fiftieth anniversary of her founding. At the time of that event, the Royal City of the Holy Faith of St. Francis was not far from the two hundredth milestone and was boasting a population in the neighborhood of twelve thousand inhabitants; today it has thirty-four thousand, while the other has two and a half million. (See page 7.) What is the reason? Why should this city, the Mother of the West, first of a thousand commonwealths and so uniquely old, remain so uniquely small? Did Juan de Oñate and Pedro de Peralta make a mistake? And was there some inherent handicap which human resources could not overcome? And was the game, after all, worth the candle? The answer to these questions lay with the Sky Powers, and is summed up in the one word, aridity.

In the first place, the sky determined that New Mexico should have no waterways. The reader will at once remember that in the East, the colonists thrusting westward invariably built their cities along the water's edge. Pittsburgh, Cincinnati, Detroit, Chicago, St. Louis, and Kansas City are cases in point. Because they offered a route with no mountains to climb, no valleys to bridge, no ambuscades to guard against, the greater rivers were always the chosen arteries of travel. The superiority of a flat-boat to a covered wagon is easily apparent; and a pack train, weighted down with its water supply, crawling across burning sands, offers no comparison at all.

Furthermore, Oñate's colony, considered from every point of view, was the deepest penetration of civilized man into North America. Colonies on both coasts could be reached after a long but comparatively safe sea voyage, and the French outposts in the far interior were accessible by means of the Mississippi and its navigable tributaries, or, after a portage past Niagara Falls, by a fairly calm water route by way of the Great Lakes. New Mexico, which had been reached originally from the southwest by an enormously difficult journey across the Sonoran desert, came soon to use the Rio Grande trail exclusively. But every article of European manufacture that reached the consumer still had to be shipped across the wider part of the Atlantic to the port of Vera Cruz, freighted by pack horse or in snail-slow ox-carts to Mexico City, and thence northward past Durango, Chihuahua, and El Paso del Norte for two thousand perilous, Indian-haunted miles to remote Santa Fe. Naturally commerce was out of question, and trade would be limited to barter among neighbors. Though ocean freight rates were high to New England, and still higher to Mexico, the overland tariff was prohibitive. In this inaccessible valley beyond the desert, goods could neither come in nor go out, and thus there was not one gainful occupation to attract settlers.

Transportation was thus impossible; there were no goods anyway to transport — such seems to sum up the conviction of the administrators in Mexico. So almost from the start it was natural and, in fact, inevitable that they should consider abandoning the venture. The same lack of rain that had denied waterways had made agriculture impossible without the added expense of irrigation.

And there was no gold. So for the better part of its first century the colony, of which Santa Fe was the head, retained only the most precarious hold on existence. It was begun in a year of drouth-caused scarcity, and continued through years when drouth and food shortage threatened many times an abrupt terminus. There was frequent dearth not only of food, but of military supplies and necessary equipment of all kinds. Then, at inconvenient times, the Apaches would descend upon the settlers; the Comanches would steal their horses, or the Pueblos would murder a friar. There was no money in the province, and little wealth of any other kind. Not surely an attractive opportunity for immigrants with the economic point of view! In brief, there was no way to get to New Mexico, and when one got there it was not worth the trip. The reasoning seemed cogent and final.

The result was that the administrators of New Spain soon began to think of their northern colony only as a base for explorations and an outpost against the "gentile" tribes who had the habit of raiding from time to time the superlatively rich silver mines of Chihuahua. Later, it was to serve as a lookout from which a watch could be kept on the French encroachments upon the Great Plains. The sum of the early Spanish explorations is like their other achievements — a romance rather than a prosaic record of development. They penetrated to the lower reaches of the Colorado and visited the Grand Canyon; they went once more in 1629 to seek the mirage city of Quivira; they explored the country of the Brazos in Texas, and they made a long beginning on the trade route along the Gila, upon which traffic was to flow more than a century later to California.

Yet Santa Fe never became the hub of a great wheel of trade routes. And owing to the unconquerable practical difficulties, serious attempts at colonization were early abandoned, and the town was suffered to survive chiefly by its own efforts as a military outpost and a focus of missionary endeavor. And as these were both enterprises that demanded the service of few men and still fewer women, the colony grew neither by immigration nor by natural increase. So during the Spanish regime the Royal Villa bulked no larger in the general strategy of the empire than an insignificant presidio in the hinterland garrisoned by a few picturesque but ragged and badly officered dragoons.

The Church alone took the colony seriously. When at length the Spanish authorities found the gold of Quivira a myth and the expanse of land a worthless waste, why did they not abandon the enterprise? It was the Franciscans, aflame with ardor born of the Catholic Counter Reformation, who kept holding up a great and sacrificial missionary ideal. "You came," said they, "not to wrest away the Indian's land nor anything that is his. You came not to obtain, but to bestow — to bestow the Faith of the Cross." So far as any such challenge can ever be accepted, it was accepted here; the profit motive yielded to the inspiration of religious zeal, and the colony went ahead and became the one great missionary base of the north. And here even the high government officials coöperated, so that the Franciscan Order was able to obtain from the government a triennial grant or subsidy of approximately fifty thousand pesos for the prosecution of their work among the native tribes. Here, again, appears the astonishing emphasis on religion which characterized seventeenth-century Spaniards. At the foundation of the colony in 1598 eight Franciscans had been brought in; and ten years later, while the field force consisted of only the *comisario* and nine friars, thousands of Indians had been instructed in the Faith and baptised. By 1617 eleven churches had been built, and during the years following, both building and teaching went on apace, for soon the country was raised to the dignity of a province, named the Custodia de la Conversión de San Pablo, and was receiving the ministrations of fifty friars. So in the general absence of other satisfactory motives for maintaining the colony in what long seemed a losing venture, one is compelled to put some trust in the professed motive of the Spaniards themselves — their desire to evangelize the Indians and extend the Catholic Faith in the new world.

In the year 1630 the *custodio,* Father Alonso de Benavides, went to Spain with his famous *Memorial on New Mexico,* a treatise which he presented to the King in person and which within a few years had been translated from the Spanish into French, Dutch, Latin, and German, and was glowingly disseminating throughout Europe information on the Franciscan missions in the American Southwest. The figures given in this report, as in many of the other early ones, seemed to show that the devils were being driven out of the aborigines at a great rate. But the Sky Gods were not giving up their devotees without a struggle, and now after three hundred years they are still receiving a fair share of Indian homage. The natives, in spite of the statistics, probably did not always take their conversion with extreme seriousness. They were merely nature worshippers, and did not object to having another sky god in their pantheon to whom they could address rain prayers.

As an aside one may remark that it is not impossible that the Padres may have felt at times compelled to trade upon this very superstition and pose as rain-makers. There was, for instance, at Acoma (and still is) a very famous picture of St. Joseph reputed to have miraculous virtue as a bringer of showers. And when Laguna, a neighboring pueblo, borrowed and refused to return it, the American courts were called in to compel its restoration. The possessor of such magic was obviously a favored protégé of the deity and would naturally not want for converts. In a similar connection it may be recalled that it was a drouth in an arid country much like New Mexico that gave the Hebrew prophet, Elijah, opportunity to demonstrate his influence with Jehovah, and at the same time triumphantly to turn Israel from the heathenism of Baal to the true God.

While the Indians, like the Romans of Domitian's time, made no objection to the introduction of one god more, trouble began when they fully understood the claim to uniqueness which His worshippers made for Him, i.e., His existence as the one only God. The Padres' impious interruptions of the solemn rites of conception, growth, and maturation in the kiva and of the ordered cycle of observances which the tribe depended upon for success in the harvest and the hunt — these were the really important grievances which led to the great Pueblo uprising of 1680. It was everywhere believed by the Spaniards of the time that if there had been no priests and no missions, there would have been no Rebellion.

The tenability of the view rests upon the events which followed the outbreak. After the massacre of the twenty-one Franciscans there followed the burning of the churches and *conventos,* the desecration of the sacred vessels and utensils, and the destruction of ecclesiastical vestments. The apostates then bathed themselves with *amole* to wash away their hated baptism and renounced their Christian names and their marriages. While making an attempt to exterminate the conqueror, they vented particularly their rage upon the badges of his religion. Among all the pueblos the same was true, and this hatred, deeply felt, gave a powerful unity to the tribes which, except for the Spanish, possessed not even a common language. And after the expulsion of the friars they returned promptly to the gods of their fathers.

If all motives were transparently clear, the Pueblo Rebellion would probably be distinguished as the only Indian war actuated by religion. Seemingly, it was for their faith that both sides contended. Words, of course, cannot be taken at their face value, and a perfect simplicity of motive is rare, but the plain outcome of deeds seems to prove that Spanish dealings with the Pueblos — meaning largely, the dealings of the Roman Catholic Church — were uniquely inspired and directed by it.

To be sure, a similar note was sounded by colonizers elsewhere, notably among the devotees who settled New England. The Massachusetts colony, for instance, avowed in its charter that its end was "to win the natives of the country to the knowledge of the only one God and Saviour of mankind." And yet, in spite of that pious profession, they promptly adopted a policy of out-and-out extermination towards the Pequots. But the Pueblos are different. At the end of two and a half centuries of Spanish (and Mexican) rule they remained in the identical valleys — and are there today.

In short, the religion of the sky penetrated inevitably into pueblo hearts as far as it is possible for human beliefs to reach; and when an irresistible Catholicism overwhelmed it, there was first an ominous lull and then a terrific recoil. After the catastrophe, unquestionably nothing but the flame of an unparalleled missionary devotion would have returned to the attack.

Since 1692 there has been no more war. But through

the long generations, while one side has endeavored to abolish, the other has determined to maintain. As a consequence the Church has for three centuries been unequally yoked with a heathenism which it is still compelled to tolerate. The like exists nowhere else. It is as if our Saxon forefathers had gone out from High Mass at Canterbury into the forest to do sacrifice to Thor, the Thunderer.

CHAPTER EIGHT

PUEBLEÑOS

As organization of material unearthed by the spade progresses, one may see with increasing clearness how sky determined of old the puebleños' mode of life, gave its tincture to their religion and, indeed, to their whole culture, and nowadays permits their survival among an alien population. It explains, furthermore, their reaction to the Spanish contact which comprises their *written* history.

Of some relation to the Forgotten Ones not yet certain, the pueblo devised for himself a mode of life closely similar to theirs. While skeletal differences here and there make clear that there is not a complete continuity between the two, both were equally products of an identical environment, and for practical purposes the only distinction is one of time.

Like his progenitor, the puebleño is a house dweller, living in a settled community among his valley corn lands because the Sky Powers made him so. On the vast spread of unwatered and inhospitable land that makes up New Mexico, even an Indian community could not subsist, and, just as everywhere in the arid Southwest, they gravitated to the friendly watercourses. There in the flood plains lay the only fertile soil which the region afforded; there grew abundance of firewood, and thither came the larger game animals to drink; and, finally, there alone ran the water on which life depended.

Such a society would be compact rather than diffused. With small plots irrigated and under intensive cultivation, a very few acres would suffice for the community. But it was not until the advent of the white man's herds that the full significance of the fact appeared. Civilized man and savages cannot occupy the same range simultaneously, and the result elsewhere has been the extermination of the savage. Such was the uniform procedure on the westward march across the continent. But here the aborigines, satisfied with their own resources, did not molest the newcomers' property, and, concentrated by their own needs into small islands of population, did not occupy great tracts coveted by the invaders. Thus surrounded but not obliterated by the onrushing tide, they still hold their place. The mode of life enforced upon them ages ago by their native climate turned out to be their salvation, and thus today they are survivals of pre-history.

On account of the rarity of tillable oases in the vastness of waste land, they became unbelievably precious, so that the possessors had to defend them at any cost against the attack which would naturally be incessant. The ever-present threat of marauding enemies alone explains the adoption of a communal castle and citadel as the ordinary pueblo type of habitation. And to this day the removable ladders are a relic of grim days when there were no doors, and only a massive blank wall was exposed to the besiegers.

And exactly like his progenitor, the puebleño employed his resultant leisure and security to advance in well-being. Culture never flourishes among nomads, because uncertainty offers no incentive to painful progress. But with time for meditation on his problems, for dreaming and planning, and for the laborious construction of equipment and tools, the puebleño indulged his creative impulses not alone in irrigated agriculture, but in basketry, jewelry, pictographs, and above all, in pottery.

Closely connected, perhaps, with pottery, which afforded it a medium of expression, a primitive religion developed apace. Naturally its preoccupation would be with the means of life in an arid land — therefore, with the rain. The favor of the Sky Powers was indispensable, and their propitiation would be the chief content of religion. On this one problem the tribal devotions would consistently concentrate, and here would be soil for the evolution of a passionately sincere ritual. Here man would inevitably become more humble in petition, more zealous in placation.

Continuing from out a timeless past, precisely such a development has taken place. A priesthood of the rain would arise from the exigencies of the case; a ritual of dance and chant and pantomime would crystallize from the rich but nebulous mythology; and the suffusion of the tribal cult would go on until each member shared in it. The influence of a priest or two with the Sky Powers did not avail sufficiently; it was needful for the community to participate in unison. A rain dance is not an exhibition of a few virtuosos; the village dances. The Sun Priest does not intercede as an individual; he is supported by the Sun People. Like a son of ancient Israel, the pueblo feels himself a member of a priestly people, a royal seed; and each bears upon his shoulders the inherited tribal duty to the Powers.

When the first Spanish explorers came, the pueblo culture of the San Juan, the Gila, and the Mimbres Valleys was extinct. While the material remains are abundant, the reason of the wholesale depopulation is still the subject of guess. Some of the destruction can be attributed directly to plague — as at Cicuyé which was visited by "the great sickness" within historic times; and some of it to long-continued raids of the predatory tribes. But neither cause — in fact, none of the causes as yet alleged — seems to satisfy the archaeological requirements. On account of the presence of arid-country vegetal remains, with the absence of all other, and the detailed testimony of the Mimbres pottery designs — which included horned toads, plumed quail, antelope, and other dry-country animals — as to the fauna, a hypothetical change in climate seems about the least plausible explanation of all.

Yet from long observation one comes to lay almost every arresting mystery in the Southwest at the door of the Sky Powers. Their hand is in everything; and so, if not a permanent change in climate, a drastic, long-protracted drouth might have been the destroyer. A crop failure of more than two or three years' duration would probably be fatal to an isolated people with no commerce in foodstuffs. Furthermore, it is stated on the evidence of pine tree rings deciphered by Dr. A. E. Douglass that a great drouth actually lasted through the last quarter of the thirteenth century.

The memory of such a visitation would endure in folk traditions through a long period, and their tragic recurrence would furnish the spur of fear to a caste of ambitious priestly zealots. In this connection it is well to recall once more like a refrain the significant words of Castañeda, already quoted:

Those who have most authority among them [i. e., in the Rio Grande pueblos] are the old men; we regarded them as witches because they say they go up into the sky. . . . They worship the sun and water.

Sky, sun, water — the everlasting three! The ripening of their cult through uncounted generations makes clear what happened at the impact of a new cult brought by men of another race. The preceding speculations belong largely to the realm of archaeology; what follows, to that of written history.

Into this long-venerated system of nature worship, inelastic as an intense ancestral conservatism could make it, burst the emissaries of the most Catholic nation in Europe, superheated by the religious wars of the Protestant Reformation. Never since, and seldom before, has there been in any nation such irrepressible fervor for religion. Resisting like the rocks of their own mountains at the intrusions of molten granite, the puebleños were compelled to give ground. Into the fissures and joints of the strata was forced by volcanic pressure an irresistible, searing flood, yet the metamorphic results are confined to the immediate zone of contact. So with the new faith. Its results — to carry the geologic metaphor a bit further — have been confined to the zone of contact. Back from it a little way the primitive stuff remains unaltered.

The written history of the puebleños begins with the coming of the Spanish Padres. Who were the Padres? They were, in truth, the descendants of the famed Greyfriars of the Middle Ages, Franciscans, or begging friars, who, unlike the members of the older monastic orders, possessed no landed endowments, but were supported by the alms of the faithful. Like their founder, St. Francis of Assisi, they were vowed to the strictest poverty in order to pass their days in this present world as strangers and pilgrims. Naturally, they were zealous missionaries. Franciscans, besides being found in all parts of the pagan Orient from Abyssinia to Tartary, accompanied Columbus on his second voyage to America, and from that time onwards were a very spear point among adventurers in the New World.

So far as human motives and emotions are ever unmixed, their zeal was rooted and nourished in love, and if the civil authorities on occasion employed their services on non-religious errands, these were exceptions. With utter simplicity of purpose and true apostolic power they labored for the honor and glory of God, the propagation of the Faith, and the welfare of souls. Coupled with their extraordinary gentleness and fervor was another strain, however, which today few can comprehend or admire and yet without which there could have been no stark achievement — the inspired, dynamic strain of what would be named today fanaticism, the vivid yearning for self-immolation and the palm of martyrdom. It is necessary to remember that inside the velvet glove was the grasp of steel, lacking which the glove would have been only velvet.

And what aim had they in coming? True, they came to deliver souls from the powers of darkness, but the answer would be incomplete without reference to the unwavering Catholic insistence that the Church has a divine mission to teach and is the custodian of that completely rounded education which concerns the whole man as a Christian, as a member of a family, and of a commonwealth. While men may be condemned for what they do, they can be understood only in the light of what they attempt to do. They came not only to hold religious services; they came as civilizers. But the Padres were in the company of man and of the same blood as men who were merely adventurers and metal-hunters, and who saw in the Indians only animate objects for their lust and avarice. Hence, their best-intentioned plans were often embarrassed and often miscarried.

The Padres, then, not only converted and baptised the Indians, inculcated into their minds Christian morality and Christian conceptions of marriage and the home, but they taught them the Spanish language, the manual arts, the care of domestic animals, and improved methods of agriculture. While the mission church with its cross and mellow bells was the religious symbol, the *convento* was the broader symbol of enlightenment, both spiritual and material, and the Padre was not only priest to the pueblo, but teacher and guide as well.

At the missions the Indians learned from the Spaniards the arts of building. They acquired the use of metal tools and the rudiments — but only the rudiments, if one may judge from the free-and-easy dimensions of the structures — of measurement. Under the supervision of the friars they constructed chapels, cloisters, and massive churches whose adobe walls, having stood for ten generations, seem likely to last as many more. They built living quarters for the priest, with room for the entertainment of guests, and accompanying kitchens, granaries, and wine cellars.

Under Spanish tutelage they learned to speak, in addition to their mutually unintelligible dialects, one common language of civilized men; they learned also to sing the ancient chants of the Church, and the young boys were trained to serve at the altar. If irrigation was practiced among the pueblos, the Padres appear to have developed it still further, and they introduced fruit trees and the vine. Indeed, the place where the grape was first introduced into New Mexico is known to have been Senecu, where there was a church and a *convento* dedicated to St. Antony of Padua, and among the other appurtenances of civilized life, a fish stream and a vineyard. The reverend founder was Friar Arteaga, and a chronicler says that he had a garden "where he gathered grapes from his own vines, and made wine which he distributed to the other *conventos*."

But more important to the Indian's eye than any other innovation was the introduction of the horse. For him the horse was to become what the railroad and the automobile have become to civilized man, and he soon learned "to ride on horseback and to salute the Spaniards with an Ave Maria." Then before a long time elapsed some of the animals ran wild on the wide ranges and propagated their kind, so that in later generations there was at hand an unlimited supply of wiry horseflesh for the mere taking. Cattle and burros were also brought into the country by the earliest colonists, and sheep presently became, with the crops, a main support among the puebleños. It is a matter of record that De Vargas, who reconquered the country after the Rebellion of 1680, captured at Cochiti seventy horses and nine hundred sheep, and that later he gave to the Friar Alpuente one hundred and six head of animals for his proposed mission at Zia.

From the foregoing it will be apparent that the effect of the Padres was profound. And for three centuries it has been percolating into the deep places of the Indian mind. A new language, a new religion, the introduction of domestic animals, and the use of the metals which enter everywhere into the sphere of common tasks — these are among the most basic things of human culture, and even when imperfectly assimilated they were the means by which the priests were able to lead their charges a long way towards civilization. As among the California missions founded a century and a half later by the Franciscans under Fr. Junípero Serra, the plan was beneficently conceived and ably and humanely executed.

But there enters a new complication. The Padres were forever attempting in subtle ways to abolish the ancestral worship of the rain gods. In the end, as the brooding Indian mind looked at it, their benefactions brought more ill than good, and it became necessary to exterminate them.

In the main the contacts of the pueblenos with the Spaniards will be seen to have been contacts with the Cross rather than with the Crown. Before 1680 there were white settlements at Santa Fe, Taos, Santa Cruz, and perhaps a few other places, and there were Spanish families living at the scattered haciendas, but the pueblos probably saw nothing of the soldiery except when they came on punitive expeditions, and still less of the civil power. While they were required to pay a commensurate tribute of corn in return for protection against the Navaho and other enemy tribes, there were as yet no mines in the province to be worked with gruelling toil, and the only compulsory labor was at the missions.

When the Rebellion of 1680 came to pass, the essential basis of that tragic outbreak lay not primarily in industrial oppression and injustice, but in obscure religious emotions. There has been much loose and confused talk — possibly exacerbated by the Spanish-American War — about the cruel enslavement of the Indians by the Spanish colonists, but when documentary proof is requested, it is not readily forthcoming. And, on the other hand, there is record of a lengthy series of enactments designed to protect the Indians who were wards of the Crown itself.

The Indians themselves, seeing nothing wrong about slavery, bought and sold captives. But the Spaniards imposed slavery, in theory at any rate, only as a punishment — sometimes as a penalty for witchcraft, but ordinarily for war against the Crown. And such was the regard for the humanitarian fervor of the Franciscans that one edict after another was promulgated against enslavement. The *repartimiento* system, by which Pueblo Indians were distributed and placed out at a servant's wage in Spanish families, was not slavery. Seen from another angle, it was a humane attempt to civilize them by intimate contact with Catholic family life. And whatever abuses may have crept into the practice, did so in spite of the viceroy's vigilance. In a letter of February 5, 1621, he lays down various restrictions, directing that not more than eight out of each one hundred inhabitants in any given pueblo are to be allotted for service; that a native is to be paid one-half *real* a day with board, or one *real* without board. The practice of giving Indian women in *repartimiento* for personal service is to be forbidden, since it is contrary to law, and the natives are not to be required to carry heavy loads, since this has been forbidden by royal order. Furthermore, the governor is not to levy new tributes without the viceroy's express consent; he is instructed to heed all complaints made by the friars in the name of the Indians, and in his dealings with them is to be guided by consultations with the friars, the *cabildo* (citizens' committee) and the military.

To be sure the Pueblo, in return for protection from the Navaho and his other enemies, was required to pay a tribute to his protectors and to take part in public work, but not to serve a private master. No less a personage than Governor de la Peñuela himself, after information had been laid against him at the court of New Spain, was told by the viceroy that he must at once discontinue drafting the services of Indians for his own personal benefit, and that further transgression of the royal. edict would be punished with a fine of two thousand pesos and damages to the Indians. This instance, cited by Bandelier, is part of his well-documented discussion of the question, which shows that, "It was not easy to escape punishment for cruelty to Indians under Spanish regime."

The probable truth at the bottom of the matter is that while evasions of law then, as now, were common, the intent and the official dealings of the Spaniards with their wards were not less humane than those of our own government. Significantly, it was not the captive Navaho, regularly enslaved by the colonists, who tried to exterminate them in 1680; it was the puebleños who had never been enslaved. The volcanic upheaval shot out not from labor-deadened peons, but from the rain priests, for Indian fortitude and stolidity were tolerant longer than Indian superstition.

But the Friars, though themselves the patrons and chief protectors of the pueblos, ultimately gave to their spiritual sons grounds for rebellion. In the first place they had the right to conscript labor to erect their massive mission churches and *conventos*. The construction of walls of stone or adobe, not infrequently reaching a thickness of four or five feet and a height of fifty feet, represents an effort which must have occupied whole communities for years at a time. And the Franciscans, being themselves vowed to poverty, had nothing but spiritual rewards to bestow in return for labor; and consequently the extensive service which they required for dotting the region with their buildings must have grown irksome in the extreme.

In addition, the Friars kept up from the beginning a firm and incessant effort to eradicate witchcraft and the heathen ceremonies of the *estufa*. But these venerated and timeless observances having to do with rain-making and the germination of life in both plants and animals were the most tenacious imaginable, and the manifold attempts to embarrass and suppress them were naturally interpreted as persecution. The superstition of the primitive human mind nowhere yields readily to missionary endeavor.

And there is reason for believing that by means of a great climatic pulsation the Sky Powers themselves took a definite part in fomenting trouble for the Spaniards. As happens today in equatorial Africa, a happy fortuity may send a succession of good seasons that greatly advances the evangelization of a savage tribe, yet an unfavorable one is quickly seized upon by their native witch doctors as evidence of deific displeasure at the tribe's apostasy, and thus the missionary effort of years may be largely undone.

Such would seem to have been the case among the pueblos. Professor Huntington is authority for the statement that while there is tree-ring evidence of particularly propitious seasons in the earlier years of the Spanish occupation, a marked falling-off in the rainfall begins to be apparent about 1665, which rises to a climax in a series of drouth years about 1680. He says:

If we interpret the curve in this way [i. e., of the tree rings], it appears that perhaps one reason why the Spaniards were able to establish themselves in New Mexico almost without a blow was that from 1600 to 1650 the amount of rain and the general conditions of the growth of vegetation were not only more favorable than now, but were becoming better from year to year. . . . Under such circumstances the ignorant Pueblo Indians would naturally look upon the coming of the Spaniards as a blessing. A decrease in rainfall begins to be apparent between 1650 and 1660, but it is unimportant at first, as we infer from the fact that the growth of the trees (and impliedly of the crops) continues to be well above normal until about 1665. Thereafter a rapid deterioration takes place, which culminates about 1680 or soon after. During that period a widespread uprising took place against the Spaniards, the Pueblo Rebellion which ousted the Europeans for some years. . . . Want and famine must have prevailed, and if the Indians were like the rest of mankind, they doubtless ascribed their misfortunes to their conquerors. . . . After 1680 conditions appear to have improved. (*The Climatic Factor*, pp. 137-138.)

Such causes for resentment, aided by sorcery and the work of devils, as writers of the day declared, culminated on the tenth of August, 1680, in a general massacre of the Spaniards. The Padres naturally were the first victims, and in a single day twenty-one of them achieved the palm of martyrdom. The first to die was a priest at Tesuque. Of him it was said:

On this day the venerable Padre Juan Batista Pio, a native of the city of Victoria in the Province of Alaba, having gone to celebrate the holy sacrifice of the Mass at the pueblo of Tesuque, which is a mission of the City of Santa Fe, the Capital of the Kingdom, was killed by the Indians of that very pueblo. Passing from sacrilege to robbery, they carried away the scanty supplies which the *convento* had for its own subsistence, and like the wicked in the proverb, without knowing who pursued them, fled away to the mountains. (*The Franciscan Martyrs* quoted by Twitchell in *Leading Facts*, p. 361.)

There was slain at the *convento* of Portiuncula, Pecos, the Reverend Father Fernando de Velasco, who had served thirty years as priest at the beautiful six-towered church there, and at that of San Gerónimo de Taos, the reverend Padre Fray Antonio de Mora and a lay brother. At Santo Domingo three priests were martyred. All these, with isolated missionaries living at Jemez, San Ildefonso, Acoma, Oraibi, and the other pueblos, lost their lives on the same summer morning.

In addition to the Franciscans about four hundred other Spaniards were slaughtered. Governor Otermín and his soldiers were compelled to abandon the villa of Santa Fe and retreat down the Rio Grande. With the town in their power the Indians embarked upon an orgy of revenge. Besides taking the captured white maidens for squaws, they looted and burned the buildings on the plaza; they desecrated the Church of San Miguel and set fire to it; they arrayed themselves in ecclesiastical vestments and rode about the town crying that they had killed God and the Blessed Virgin Mary and, in all the pueblos except Zuñi, they buried the church bells, crucifixes, and sacred vessels or else desecrated them in other ways. Finally, they abjured the use of their Christian names, washed themselves with soap made from the *amole* in order to cleanse themselves from the last vestige of the hated faith of their conquerors, and returned to the ancient cultus of the rain and the practices of the ancestral kiva.

The record makes several facts quite clear. The pueblos were not ground under the iron heel of the military. The missionary had not even a guard to defend him in the hour of his death. And when the massacre was complete, the jealously vigilant Franciscans did not accuse the cruelty of the civil and military powers. They alleged Indian sorcery and the work of the devil. With that conviction their future course was plain. The issue was between Christ and anti-Christ. They had no choice about their return to the attack. For twelve years after the Rebellion Spanish power was unable to reassert itself, and the pueblos remained in complete paganism. But with the *entrada* of De Vargas in 1692, they were compelled to own the white man's sway once more, and to accept, at least outwardly, his religion.

In the history of the Reconquest, the religious note again comes out with extraordinary prominence. In the Captain-general's own account, it would seem to be uppermost in his purposes. And while the reader must be on his guard against being misled by fine sentiments, it is hard to disbelieve in the writer's sincerity. In the light of the general's subsequent dealings, one can hardly deny him an intention that was in the main beneficent.

As quoted by Twitchell in his *Leading Facts* (Vol. I, p. 289), he writes:

December 16, 1693.

On the sixteenth day of the month of December, date and year above, I the said governor and captain-general, about the eleventh hour of said day, made my entry into this town of Santa Fe, and coming in sight of the walled village where the Teguas and Tanos reside and seeing the approach on foot of the very reverend father custodian, Friar Salvador de San Antonio, and in his train the fifteen monks, priests and reverend father missionaries, and the lay brothers of our father Saint Francis, chanting on their march divers psalms, I got down from my horse, and my example was followed by the said corporation, . . . and then I made due obeisance as I was passing on my way to the entrance of said village and town, and the same thing was done by my followers, and in the middle of the square a cross had been raised, and when all present knelt down and sang psalms and prayers, including the Te Deum and in conclusion the Litany of Our Lady, and the said very reverend father custodian, atuning his voice, sang with such joy and fervor that almost everyone without exception was duly moved by the happiness of hearing in such a place the praises of Our Lord

God, and His Most Blessed Mother. And after he sang the hymn three times, I offered my congratulations to said very reverend father and the rest, telling them that notwithstanding the last year at the time of my happy contest, I had given possession to the very reverend father president, Friar Francisco Corvera, . . . I would do it again and would grant it to him anew with great pleasure, considering the great resignation with which all, together with their very reverend father, do so heartily and freely agree to employ themselves in the administration of the Holy Sacrament in this newly conquered kingdom.

To the said natives in the plaza of said village, I told and repeated what Our Lord, the King, had sent me on the news I gave His Royal Majesty of their surrender last year, with orders that this kingdom should be re-peopled; that with the information I had given of my having pardoned them, and of their obedience which was the cause of said pardon, all his displeasure had vanished, and he would again call them his children, for that reason he had sent many priests in order that they might be Christians as they were; and that likewise he sent with me the soldiers they saw for the purpose of defending them against their enemies; and that I came not to ask anything of them, but only for two things: that they should be Christians as they ought, hearing mass and saying their prayers, and their sons and women attending to the catechisms as the Spaniards did, and the second was that they might be safe from the Apaches and friendly with all, and that this was my sole object in coming, and not to ask or take away anything. . . .

To the matter-of-fact reader of today such language from a military man savors of an absorption in spiritual matters which appears either hypocritical or incomprehensible. Strange men, these Spaniards. Arrogant and fierce, not hesitating to enslave and kill and on occasion even to torture, they were animated, even when most ruthless, by an astonishing zeal for religion.

A search for the underlying motives of such zeal

would lead one far back to the religious wars which rocked Europe after the Reformation. In fact, from the first discoveries in the New World the thought of evangelizing the natives never ceased to fire the Spanish imagination; and as early as 1493, Pope Alexander VI bestowed forever upon the Most Catholic Sovereigns, Ferdinand and Isabella, and their successors, in consideration of the zeal for the conversion of the savages, the possession of all lands already discovered and still to be discovered. And the long line of Conquistadores in both North and South America was goaded by the twin spurs of patriotism and religion into herculean labors which looked toward the building up of a new empire which, being both Spanish and Catholic, would atone for the loss of northern Europe to Protestantism.

In thinking back upon the giants of the Reformation, the student of history is sometimes tempted to forget that the Counter-Reformation had also its giants. By the year 1680 or thereabouts, while the puritan minister, the Reverend Samuel Walker (or was that his name?) , as is narrated in Mather's *Magnalia,* was preaching the gospel to the Indians twenty miles from Boston; the French Jesuits, having sacrificed some martyrs to the Mohawks, had penetrated to the Mississippi Valley and the interior of the continent; while the Spanish Franciscans had already dotted the southwestern deserts with their missions.

In brief, the dynamic missionary zeal which spurred Spanish priest and layman alike in the seventeenth century, is, without its historical background, incomprehensible; yet when viewed sympathetically, it makes clear, as nothing else can do, the nature of the impact made upon the red culture by the white. Labor and hardship incredible, blood and martyrdom — these were poured out without stint like the offering of a sacrifice in order that the red men, the "gentiles," might be brought into the Catholic fold. History has no record of men more indomitable than the Conquistadores in North America. Coming to bestow religion, as they understood the same, there is no doubt that they bestowed it. Thereby they deflected the whole course of Pueblo life. Even so, their religion overlies, without abolishing, the ancient worship of the water from heaven. The interaction of the two has been the impact of an irresistible force upon an immovable object — and this always and everywhere has been the essence of the dramatic, furnishing as it does variety and richness of episode, agonizing effort, pomp of majestic tragedy.

But go to a pueblo. Go not during a ceremonial when the people are furnishing a spectacle for the tourists, but when they are leading their everyday life, placid and busy like other human beings. The first impression which the visitor gains is that here the two great genii of the white man, gasoline and electricity, have no place. In fact, the existence seems alien, almost uninfluenced by the contact with our modernity. . . .

It is a still morning in late December. In the plaza of Tesuque patches of snow lie unmelted in the band of shadow along the north-facing wall. From a chimney or two curls blue smoke suffused with the unforgettable incense of cedar. Anastasio welcomes us into his house. He is sometimes a woodcutter, who hauls his fuel to Santa Fe, where its thin essence, laden with the breath of dwarf conifers from the foothills, will later float above the rooftops. Two days ago he was a tribal dancer, intent upon the great Christmas ceremonial. This morning he is at home delicately threading minute blue beads upon a string. Sitting before the open white fireplace which rises, Spanish-fashion, in the corner of the room, he is not without unconscious pictorial quality. His hair, black as pine charcoal, is bound back from his face with a red band according to Indian custom. On his feet are native moccasins, and he sits upon a goatskin rug. A fine physical type of man — no mistake.

The room, too, is interesting. The floor is of trodden earth — smoothed adobe like the rest of the pueblo. On the wall in front of me hangs a bundle of grey eagle feathers, the glorious headdress which Anastasio wears when he steps out of the twentieth century into the immemorial past. Through a door I can see his wife bending over a *metate,* and as she grinds the corn the meal trickles away snow-clean, like everything else there. My eyes had rested a moment on a little religious picture beyond the door — the Adoration of the Magi. Just then his father enters with a three-year-old child, his grandson. The old man with a kind face salutes us as one saying in pantomime, "Señores, my house is yours." He does not speak English, and round his throat he wears a bead necklace. But the little one is wearing shoes which perhaps came from St. Louis. Outside the door lies a freshly cut young piñon, the discarded Christmas tree. Along with the Magi, it seems to belong here quite as naturally as the *metate* and the headdress of eagle feathers — or the small rain gods which tourists carry away as souvenirs. Baked in the beehive ovens, these sphinx-visaged images sit with feet extended, posed with the stiffness of a contemplative idol. Balanced between their hands, a deep *olla* holds the rain. Formal, archaic, painted on the breast with symbolic clouds of red and black, they preserve the calm of all religious statuary.

Or go to Isleta, whose name commemorates its ancient situation on an island whose feet were bathed by the waters of the venerated Rio Grande. Go on some autumn afternoon when the corn is ripe and the women sit on the flat housetops, tearing the husks apart with noisy laughter and fragments of folksong — Isleta, where all summer the white-walled church is full of a cool dimness in the midst of the sun's shimmering fire, and where back and forth on pink adobes move enchanting lacy shadows of the tamarisk tree.

Or go to San Ildefonso, where all day the brown children play in the plaza under the giant cottonwood, safe under the patronage of Ildefonso, Spanish abbot of the seventh century. Note well also the large circular kiva, which stands for a quite different order of things. But fail not to visit María Martínez, creator of exquisite black pottery. You take this two-toned bowl in your hands and raise it to the eye level. The lovely silhouette is a bit uneven, as in all handmade things; but set it on the floor where it belongs in an Indian home, and the irregularity is no longer perceptible. Encircling it in a wide belt, Avanyu, fabled water serpent of the heavens, sky god and rain-giver, undulates through the clouds. From his mouth goes forth the crooked lightning, and the plume of his head bends backward with the swiftness of flight. His only rival in popularity is the Thunder Bird. With flapping wings that reverberate among the mountains and eyes that gleam with lightning fire, it ranks as trusted rain-bringer, savior of crops, vanquisher of want, omen of good fortune. Amongst all the rich variety of Indian decorative motifs, the favorites are everywhere serpent and bird.

In the land where the Sky Powers determine all things, their cult of wings and serpents and clouds is perhaps the one which the Indian takes most seriously. But here the white observer looks only at the shell of things. To the Indian everything means more than it seems, and while a symbol may be only a conventional decoration on his *olla* or his jewelry, it may be in some indeterminate measure his prayer. The circle with its four sets of rays represents the sun, but can anyone say that it does nothing more? This butterfly is the emblem of happiness, and this squash blossom of fertility — but what signifies the sign?

At San Ildefonso, as at other Tewa pueblos, the age-old ritual of the Sun People is still performed to bring the summer rains. Studied by Mrs. Matilda Coxe Stevenson, it was described in *Smithsonian Explorations,* 1914 (p. 73):

Almost every breath [i. e., of the Tewas] is a prayer, in one form or another, for food. "May we be blessed with food, more food!"— this great thought is paramount among these people who have lived in an arid country from time immemorial. Having no outside resources, everything, life itself, depends upon their own exertions and their influence with the gods.

Dealing thus with the essentials of life, the Pueblo rain religion thus possesses a tenacity that is not surprising — it is inevitable.

And here annually on the night of February 17, the Sun God is presented with a heap of offerings and devoutly invoked by the members of his clan, who sing: "We give these offerings to you; you the great, the ancient one, you who have lived always — that you will be happy and contented; that you will see that all the world receives much water, that all crops may develop for good. We pray that you will talk to the rain-makers, urge them to play their games and go out and be happy, and to send rains to every quarter of the world, such rains as will uproot trees, wash out canyons, and cover the Earth Mother in water. Let her heart be great in water. And we pray that you will lift the Earth Mother from her sleep, impregnate her with your rays, and make her fruitful to look upon. Bless the whole world with her fruitfulness."

Through the entire night the supplications continue, and then at the first light of dawn, the offerings are carried to the Rio Grande and laid reverently on the water, which bears them to the gleaming Sun Father.

Or go to Taos, most famous and loveliest of all the pueblos — Taos of the painters. The best time will be in October. Then come brilliant days when the high peaks beyond are powdered with snow from their summits down to the ten-thousand-foot level, when cottonwoods and aspens turn golden, when apples hang ruddy on the trees, and when noons are drowsy but mornings sting with frost — days when through crystal air the white sunshine is shot like shining arrows from the Sky God's bow.

The pueblo is at its forenoon tasks. An Indian, white-clad, sits on the ground dressing a cowhide, clawing out thin tufts of brick-red hair. A woman wearing white moccasin boots is stooping beside a beehive oven of adobe, while across the clear little Rio de Taos another is hanging out a line of rich-colored clothes. With hair bound in red fillets and with a heavy silver necklace upon his shoulders, a statuesque boy astride a bay pony fords the stream — an equestrian group for any of the arts, including the cinema. No wonder the young girl stands on the footbridge looking after him as he rides away toward the mountains. Two youngsters, brother and sister one might guess, scurry up a ladder with the graceful rush of young squirrels or of naval recruits. Halterless and with creaking packsaddles, two benign and venerable burros enter with accustomed slowness, bearing logs of red cedarwood. While the driver tarries somewhere, a nondescript dog trots in from behind the picket corral and lies down to sleep in the shade of a farm wagon. On platforms made of long poles corn is drying in the harvest sunshine, and here and there along the wall hang strings of chile peppers ripening into crimson. High on the roof up against the sky a graceful *olla* limns its curves sharply like matrix in a turquoise gem.

The great terraced communal house rises quite five stories, each story having for its dooryard the roof of the one below it, in typical pueblo style. Thus the builders have in the remote past evolved a cube type of architecture that is native and distinct, harmonious in its lines and supremely adapted to its setting. The building material is adobe — the red earth of the valley tempered with pebbles and straw. While durable beyond expectation, its corners and edges weather rapidly, and what with the molding of the elements and with constant patching it soon comes to assume the rounded mellowness of age. It has none of the uncompromising obstinacy of stone, which requires generations to lose its look of newness and blend into its surroundings with an air of permanence.

Long ago the Indian builders came to understand the genius of their material and to perceive its limitations. They understood well that it is scarcely strong enough for towers which have to support heavy bells, and that it is not adapted to outdoor arches — in fact, in all of the mission churches there is said to be but a single arch, which is in the Pecos ruin. Roofs are supported by pine log beams called *vigas,* whose projecting ends stripe the walls through days and days on end with bands of geometrical shadow, and which may justly be called the most characteristic note of pueblo architecture. But everywhere the square little windows with their wooden bars emphasize the blind, fortress-like appearance of the structure, and recall the onslaughts of aboriginal time.

Finally, visit Santo Domingo to witness the noble ceremonial known as the Green Corn Dance. As everyone knows, it is not what its name implies, but a dramatic performance with theurgical intention, combining the qualities of a religious procession and a mystery play of the Middle Ages with those of the choral dances of the ancients in Greece and the Orient. Among the most primitive steps in the ritual of worship, it remains one of the most truly impressive; and as a kind of universal litany which gathers up all the prayers to the Sky Powers, it occurs in one form or another in each of the pueblos. Its amazing and sensuous beauty, which is the delight of artists and travellers, is non-essential, the action being impersonally aloof from public praise or censure, a concern only of the deities and the participants. It is somewhat as if grand opera were performed without an audience, its music a lovely possession for only the orchestra, the singers, and the spirits of song; and in truth, like a priest robed in chasuble and stole, the Indian would seem to be equally absorbed in the importance of the solemnity which he is presenting before his holy deity.

Whatever esoteric significances may be discovered by experts in ethnology, the plain meaning of the spectacle lies open to any beholder who approaches it in the right attitude of reverence. By beautiful gesture of the whole living body instead of by word alone, as with us, it dramatizes the eternal human application, "We beseech Thee, hear us!" The sum and substance is just that. And unless one's being chords sympathetically with this emotion "from the first drumbeat of the first dance he sees"—to borrow Witter Bynner's fine expression — further knowledge and study will not do much to unlock it.

Indeed, Pueblo religion has much in common with all others. The fatherhood of a Great Spirit, propitiation, purification, sacrifice, protection — these beliefs, as in ancient Israel, are among the things by which men live, and even the Padres strove not to root them out but to fill the primitive pagan forms with a Christian content. And the rain priest endeavors to effect by "sympathetic magic" exactly what our own heathen forefathers strove to do with the Christmas Tree — to convey to the Sky Powers by pantomime that which in the deities' own language they know not how to express. In the dark Germanic forests men tied summer fruits to the boughs of the evergreen fir tree that the beneficent gods might know what to do; in the pueblo, men with gourd shells imitate the sound of showers for the same reason, and with the same reasonableness.

When the fourth of August arrives, the pueblo, like any other Catholic village, is all *en fête* to celebrate the anniversary of its patron saint, Santo Domingo, or in English, St. Dominic. It is at the time of year when the young shoots of the corn, having been already fertilized grain by grain, are filled with milk and are swelling into heavy ears — the time of year when seasonal rains will put the crop out of danger until full maturity. Galisteo Creek carries a trickle of water on its sands, and the earth for a while is green with rough weeds and grasses. White clouds silently jostle one another across the turquoise firmament, and in mid-afternoon frequently bring heavy thunderstorms. It is the background which profiles of pinkish adobe require. Shadows lie black and geometrical beside the walls. Incongruous booths have been erected for the sale of ice cream and pop to the carnival crowd, while densely parked automobiles from many states, adding their sophisticated tints to the ensemble, heighten the chromatic confusion.

A great medley of sound rising from the plaza where the dance is in progress strikes the ear as one approaches. A barbaric drum executes a monotonous obbligato above the chanting voices, while a multitude of little rhythmic bells tell of hundreds of feet keeping time on the earthen floor. The sound of gourd rattles shaken in the dancers' hands imitates the sound of rain.

The first glimpse of the dance itself remains an unforgettable memory. Seen in the pulsating white sunlight of the far Southwest, it is an impression first of color, then of movement, then of sound, gorgeous, indescribable. It gives one the sensation of participating in a primeval epic wherein the actors are gods and ancestral spirits as well as mortals, and the setting a fantastic world of imagination all compact. Among the dancers personal identity has disappeared, as from assistants at a religious solemnity garbed in uniform vestments. Each female head is alike with straight black hair and green *tablita*, a wooden board painted with symbols of cloud and rain. The feet are bare, like the left arm and shoulder, and a red sash encircles the waist. The rest of the costume is black. But the men are resplendent. Each wears a ceremonial rain apron of white, embroidered along its margin with mystic symbols in red, green, and black — which the sky gods all comprehend. A russet fox skin depends from the girdle, sweeping the wearer's heels, while his feet are hidden under cuffs of black-and-white skunk skin. Around the knees are, half hidden, the little bells which sound at every step. The upper part of the body, according to barbarian fancy, is gaudy with symbolic turquoise necklaces, and on the arms are bands into which are thrust sprigs of piñon. Tied into the hair are a few feathers — to make the dancers light, and to put them in mind of beings that inhabit the sky.

But there is a third class, the Koshares, and in them the inviolable heathenism of the rite becomes most keenly felt. With faces and bodies grotesquely smeared and spotted, divided half and half between black and white, with dried corn husks tied into hair which has been matted with clay, they personify the invisible spirits of the ancestors — of those perchance sleeping in churchyard soil, encircled by an adobe wall, overshadowed by a Cross, yet whose souls after leaving the earth by way of the heathen *sipapu,* have ascended into the sky to become dispensers of the rain. Blood brothers to the shaman and the witch-doctor in the first low twilight of evolution, these capering creatures convey sharply to the more civilized mind reminiscences of the abysmal superstition from which the race has emerged. Between the two minds there is a chasm which seems immeasurable, and from one side to the other none can cross.

At the end of the plaza an image of Santo Domingo, himself, contemplates his children with the reproach of three hundred years. After the festal mass in the mission church, he had been carried in solemn procession to the leaf-covered booth erected in his honor, and there the little red-robed *santo* waits during the afternoon, insensible to their tribute of many flaming candles. Throughout the wide world, wherever his memory is venerated, the great intelligence so filled with the concept of the unity of God, could hardly envision a stranger commemoration than this.

But the dance proceeds in devout supplication to the Sky Gods who cannot resist. In the crowd of watchers stand tourists from distant cities, Mexican señoritas, artists, and newspaper reporters. From the housetops Indian spectators watch with inscrutable faces. On a terraced roof where someone has built a canopy of poles and thatched it with cottonwood boughs, some seek the grateful shade. The sun has become very hot. There is lightning from the direction of the Sandia Mountains. While the drum throbs like a tireless heart, the Thunder Bird approaches.

The dance is now well along. It is hours since the Koshares came rushing forth from an opening in the kiva roof to encircle the pueblo with patriarchal blessing; hours since the enacting of the symbolic pantomime which portrayed the departure of the runners and the preparation for battle with the enemies of the corn. More thunder! Some of the spectators are leaving. The rain priest seems about to prevail. Under his potent, feather-tipped standard, the files of dancers continue in their untiring rhythm. Rain is flooding the western scarp of the Sandias.

Leaving the strange scene at length, we pause for a meditative look into the church. Not one of the oldest Spanish edifices, it preserves their finest characteristic in the terraced wall which sustains the bell, and with its façade traversed by an outdoor balcony, its white walls, and its viga-supported roof, it is typically Franciscan. The interior is simple. There are no seats, for the worshippers kneel upon the floor. At one side there is the group of statuettes representing St. Joseph and the Virgin beside the Christ Child's crib in the stable of Bethlehem, which tells the Christmas story to the humble who cannot read. There is a picture of Santo Domingo in his conventional habit of black and white, not in barbaric red like the *santo* of the plaza. Except the altar, nothing of interest; and we depart, thoughtful, in a storm of rain.

In the arroyo which lies between us and the highway already swirls a turbulent, clay-colored flood which we dare not try to cross — the Sky Powers' answer to the folk incantation.

High Mass and the Rain Dance! The two can never blend, and in three hundred years neither one has been able to supplant the other. Almost since the end of the sixteenth century the puebleño has lived his life within sight of the cross, within sound of the mellow-toned mission bells — those bells "which praise the true God, which call the people, which lament the dead"— and his cultural history since that time has been largely the story of the conflict between his richly colored Spanish Catholicism and his native cult of the Sky Powers.

The puebleño is thus no more than his white brother the untutored child of nature, and his atmosphere has been suffused with Christianity until, like our own, it appears to be nearing the saturation point. Into the Christian Faith he is baptised in early infancy, is instructed in its mysteries and attends mass like the men of the other four races. He spends his years in the nurture of the Church and leaves his body at death to rest in consecrated earth.

And yet . . . and yet. . . .

CHAPTER NINE

MEXICANOS

IN LOOKING BACK UPON THE
four hundred years that have passed since the advent
of the white man in New Mexico, one needs no great
acumen to see that here Sky has consistently determined
the course of his history. Logic, starting from the given
premises, followed pretty much inevitably one train of
reasoning, for the record was destined to be the story of
an arid, barren land resisting the labors of a poverty-
stricken and isolated people. An acre of clayey, stony
soil requires as much cultivation as a black acre; yet its
return for the husbandman's effort will be a niggardly
harvest or none. And in other pursuits the same principle holds. Where the bounty of nature is scant, human
effort does not much avail.

The diversity comes out in comparisons. A glance
at the history of Illinois makes clear the basic differences
between a typical mid-western commonwealth and New
Mexico. Though a settlement was made by La Salle and

Tonti on the Illinois River in 1680 — earlier than **Penn's** venture at Philadelphia — the actual development of the state scarcely antedates the opening decades of the nineteenth century. At that time Santa Fe was a village of several hundred inhabitants. One hundred years later, owing to natural causes not at all intricate or obscure, it was still a village.

In the same century Illinois was filling up, not alone by the increase of her own population, but by the influx of multitudes from the eastern United States and from every country in Europe. Chicago grew from a village to a million-peopled city and then doubled in size. Once it became clear that a metropolis must stand at the foot of the lake, the labor and capital of the New World were eagerly placed at its disposal. The energetic and adventurous from everywhere swarmed to the scene to contribute their measure of achievement. And they built Chicago — the corporate result of incalculable effort of men and women who spent themselves for it, and in so doing won for themselves whatever of profit was possible.

But the world's work was not to be done at Santa Fe. On its arid hills there was neither the need nor the possibility of creating a metropolis, for there no titanic task called for the employment of myriads of hands and brains. In Chicago there had to be created facilities to care for the bulky output of America's most productive section — vast plants for the handling of grain and livestock; transportation accessories, such as railway terminals and stations, warehouses, docks, etc., in addition to the streetcar lines; great factories for the treatment of raw materials; huge stores and office buildings for the general purposes of trade. Labor created wealth and, in turn, wealth created labor. But while Chicago was the trade center of that fertile portion of the country whose natural task was to provide food for the nation, no task of such magnitude existed at Santa Fe. There, for the work at hand, a few hundred pairs of hands unaided by machinery were ample.

The land's aridity was not merely an inert obstruction. It gave an active opposition. The isolation of Santa Fe, of course, did its share in creating backwardness and poverty, but it worked also in another way. For conquest, being a man's task, was not an enterprise to lure Spanish women away from the south where life was safe and pleasant. Even after the colony was well established, the unbearable hardships deterred them from coming up to the remote outpost. Consequently, there were not enough of them to mother the sons of the Conquistadores, who, therefore, mated where fancy led them. Amalgamation, naturally, was here unavoidable for men whose views on the subject were not strict. So almost from the start there grew up a generation of half-breeds, sired by Spaniards but born of Indian squaws; and this middle group, which shortly came to comprise a large percentage of the total population, was the beginning of a new people.

The progressive amalgamation of the white and red races thus began, never ceased; and while the first generation of those who came up from Mexico was Caucasian, the majority of their descendants were Caucasians *plus*. Indeed, it is possible to point to one tribe of Indians — the Navaho —and say that from them came the predominant red strain in the mixed race. Almost constantly at war with the Spaniards, they were enemies of the Crown, and as such, fit subjects, when captured, for enslavement. The Padres laboring among the Pueblos were always militant defenders of their wards both against slavery and debauchery; but the Navaho had not any such champion. His women when taken captive were sold without a qualm, the price being from one hundred to three hundred dollars. Unlimited concubinage was the result. New generations of a slave population grew up closely related by blood to the owner, and the line between half-breed and pure-blood tended to become blurred or ceased to exist. Some of the fine unmixed strain remained and still remains. But it is futile to contend that the bulk of the Mexican population is of the same strain as the brave men who marched behind Coronado.

The consequent grading down of the human stock from the Conquistadores in shining armor to the modern Mexicans — speaking only of those north of the Border — is fairly amazing. Measured by any standards, the sixteenth-century soldiers completely filled the human mold, and the world will not soon look upon their like. But from their loins sprang no race of lion's cubs.

The vicious circle of causes, once set in motion, was never arrested. Where slavery existed to any appreciable extent, the status of free laborers would tend to grow more and more precarious. Like the unfortunate "poor whites" before the Civil War, they were ground between the upper and the nether millstones. Because of insufficient employment they were unable to make a living and keep out of debt, and so in consequence, they bound themselves "voluntarily" to the creditor. The resulting peonage brought upon the people a double curse — the rich became richer and the poor became poorer. In time the point was reached where a man might spend his life toiling for a master without ever once getting out of debt. His state was in a sense worse than a slave's, since no master was charged with the care of his old age. And the bondage might be, and often was, entailed upon his son.

The grinding and degrading poverty had its effect upon both minds and bodies. In a society too poor to educate its members, there could be no intellectual advance; in one too poor to feed its members, physical energy and virility itself would at length succumb. The point is brought out in a paper read recently by Dr. Helen Burton of the University of Oklahoma before the twenty-first session of the Oklahoma Academy of Science. As quoted in the press, Dr. Burton states that Mexicans are below normal height and weight because they eat too many beans. "Mexican children," she says, "are fed beans usually twice a day and their growth is stunted in their early years. Absence of Vitamin A in this food hampers normal development." Certain it is that, in general, the Mexican as a physical type is unimpressive, and even under American conditions his children in a great number of cases come to school pathetically undernourished. Natural selection working through a long period on meat-fed Americans has produced a very different animal in, say, Texas, from the slighter native breed across the line.

The higher authorities in Mexico, while rendering such aid as they were able to their northern colony in the performance of its two-fold function as military post and missionary center, left it for its economic support dependent on local resources. And these, after the Eldorado myth exploded, were just two: farming and stock-raising. But the Spaniards were not farmers.

This fact became obvious in the very beginning, when the colonists proceeded northward and left the Lower Sonoran Zone behind them. It is only in this zone that extensive farming could take place in New Mexico. Here they could have raised grains, cotton, hay, and fruits. The valley was wide and the soil fertile. But they marched straight through the inviting bottomlands of the lower river (Rio Abajo) and built their village on the stony soil of the Rio Arriba, or upper river. By its inception the venture was thus destined to depend for its well-being rather upon ranching than upon farming. Tiny fields would afford necessary cereals, in case Indian tribute or Indian barter did not, but hope of economic advancement and prosperity was based upon livestock.

It is significant that every one of their earliest settlements was in the life and crop zone known as the Upper Sonoran. There the summer heat was not enervating, and the rainfall was much heavier than in the Lower Sonoran. There the *rancheros* had far more abundant forage for the browsing herds, and there they had pines for building and junipers for firewood — a matter of great importance where coal was not available and the only fuel, worthless cottonwood. There, if the frosts came earlier and the growing season was shorter, water was more abundant for the *acequias* (irrigation ditches), for the Rio Grande in its northern reaches maintains some of its character as a perennial mountain stream, whereas farther south it frequently dwindled to a shallow ribbon and often disappeared for long periods beneath its flat sandy bed. (This, of course, was long before the practice of impounding flood waters in huge reservoirs changed the flow of so many western rivers.) The standard crops were corn and wheat. No attempt was made to cultivate the rich variety of grains and fruits which the valley now produces in profusion. The necessary farming they were willing to do; but no more.

But in fairness it must be said that agriculture also, along with the other practical arts and crafts, was always retarded by lack of equipment. The poverty was thoroughgoing. There is an illuminating letter of the date of February 5, 1621, cited by the late Professor Coan in his *Shorter History of New Mexico* (vol. 1, p. 68), in which the viceroy in Mexico City promises the governor that he will furnish to the colony, with ammunition and other supplies, the following: 160 pounds of iron, 200 pickaxes, 100 hatchets, 30 adzes, 20 shovels, 80 plow-shares, and 500 sickles. The enumeration is worth notice. The crying need undoubtedly was hardware, yet so costly was iron that only one mule-load of it, apparently, could be forwarded. The pickaxes probably point to the construction of irrigation ditches and the digging of wells; the hatchets (more likely axes) indicate that a considerable share of the colony's energy was absorbed in wood-cutting; and the large collection of sickles suggests, in view of the small number of Spaniards at that time, the practice of slavery. The total weight of the goods could scarcely have exceeded two or three tons, and yet the labor involved in their transportation would have made them extremely costly in Santa Fe. (As a matter of record they were never delivered.) The point might well be elaborated, since the creation of all wealth depends upon the possession and use of tools.

The twenty shovels, it may be remarked in passing, help to dispose of the myth of great mining activity in the colony. Twenty shovels, if they were to be used in mining — which is doubtful — would indicate the employment of twenty men. Twitchell (who quotes Gregg's romantic assertion that after the Rebellion the Indians filled up and concealed the pits whose secret location they alone could tell) summarizes the treasure stories and declares that "all of the traditions concerning lost Spanish mines, buried treasures of the Franciscan friars and kindred tales are only myths." His prosaic conclusion is that mining of any consequence did not begin before the first years of the nineteenth century, and this view is that of the best-informed contemporary opinion. There were two occupations, and only two, by which the struggling colony could support itself — agriculture and stock-raising.

The most appealing aspect of Spanish culture in the New World is that which is symbolized by saddle and spur. At his best the Spaniard was a centaur — whether in New Mexico, the Argentine, or in the eighteenth-century mission-bell days of California. Astride a horse whose lineage kept some obscure strain of old Arabian sires, with his lariat swishing through the air above a pair of curved and fleeting horns, the *vaquero* has persisted as a figure for song and romance.

On the immense free ranges of New Mexico and Texas he found ultimate fulfillment in a setting completely congenial. Fancying himself too spirited for the uninspiring tasks of farm life, he cast his lot with the Upper Sonoran country and elected to be a man on horseback and an aristocrat. In other words, when New Mexico society settled into final form, it was not democratic and agricultural, but aristocratic and feudal, depending upon the possession or use of vast untilled tracts of land. Accordingly, the development for two whole centuries was predetermined along a direct course.

The grazing industry was encouraged by the Spanish Crown's practice of bestowing upon soldiers and deserving nobility great grants of land in the colony. While areas were given to each of the pueblos, private grants were far more numerous, and of these some three dozen are still shown on the map of the U. S. General Land Office. And when recently the validity of similar two-century-old grants was questioned in California, the courts upheld the titles. Naturally, the rich *ranchero* in due time came to dispute the preëminence of both priest and soldier. No longer a mere colonist, he assumed the status of a feudal grandee.

His cattle on a thousand hills were of a hardy breed. They had to be. The ranges were not then, as now, dotted with windpumps, and water was available only in widely scattered locations. So toughness was the first requirement — toughness to the summer's thirst and blistering sunshine, to the spring dust storms, to the winter's snowstorms and freezing nights. The product of such an environment was a scrubby, thin-flanked animal that ran to horns and legs instead of beef, but which was a competent forager on tough bunch grasses and yucca, where anything but a jackrabbit would succumb to starvation. While mules and burros were plentiful, horses on account of Indian thievery were always much less so. But in sheep the province led all of New Spain, and in them for many generations its chief wealth consisted; although for lack of an adequate outlet the price fell as the number of range animals increased, and both wool

and hides sold for a pittance because there were no manufacturing facilities for turning them into cloth and leather goods.

Each year, however, there were two temporary markets which made up in turbulence whatever they lacked in commercial efficiency. The Taos Fair was held in early autumn. Primarily, it was a trading venture with the northern Indians, but it always had a tendency to take on the aspect of a fête. It came about in this way. Somewhere in the vast territory known as Louisiana, some New Mexicans had made contact with French traders and purchased from them $12,000 worth of goods. Then as speedily as word could travel to Mexico and thence across the ocean and return, there came a royal edict, in 1723, forbidding such commerce. In the reasoning of the authorities there was much cogency, for at that time the French were the Yankee traders of the frontier, and, as rivals, quite as dangerous. So Spain insisted on a monopoly, and in addition to the handicaps of nature placed this further restraint on the free movement of commodities through the natural channels — a restraint later to be laid on the Missourians who came in wagon caravans across the Great Plains. In effect, imperial Spain had formed unholy alliance with the Sky Gods for the more effective promotion of poverty in her northernmost colony.

The edict allowed trade with the Indians who came to Taos and Pecos, the aim being a master stroke, both in business and diplomacy, as it was hoped to win thereby both Indian friendship and custom from the French. As a direct consequence, Taos grew in population from 160 in 1760 to 1,351 in 1799 — a convincing exhibition of the power of trade, which to the rest of New Mexico was firmly denied.

In the time of the fair the streets of San Fernando de Taos (which is quite distinct from the pueblo and three miles distant from it) must have been filled with pageantry wilder and more esoteric than any which its artist colony finds there today. Colorado Utes wearing grim necklaces of grizzly bear claws brought down their peltries; Navahos came displaying bright, barbaric blankets handwoven from the wool of their own sheep; scalp-hunting Comanches from the east brought captives and buffalo hides; and all came to trade, to enjoy, and to drink, since very early the whisky of Taos acquired a name for effectiveness. Among them was an ever-increasing sprinkling of mountain men — long-haired, bearded, none-too-clean trappers of French or American name, who were taking beaver along the streams of the southern Rockies. For them all the little Spanish town made carnival, with song and wine and women combining in the full etymologic meaning of that interesting word to "solace the flesh." When the traders had all of the Indians' blankets, deerskins, and corn, and the pelts of the trappers, they packed up and started south, leaving behind them customers feasting their eyes upon precious new knives, axes, bridles, cooking pots, and other light hardware. The gamblers and wine sellers found it worth while to remain.

Then in the great mid-winter fair of Chihuahua came the other opportunity for trafficking in the articles which civilized men require. The traders leaving Taos would take the trail to Santa Fe and thence follow the Camino Real down the Rio Grande and pause for a rest at El Paso del Norte, where a growing settlement made their goods welcome. At length, lading their pack mules and ox-carts once more with corn, wool, hides, blankets, and peltries, and driving with them their great herds of livestock, they continued on their way. At the Chihuahua market the standard price for a sheep was one dollar, for a beef five dollars, for a horse eleven dollars, and for a mule thirty dollars. But payment was not made in coin — there was no coin. Here the raw products of the colony met the manufactured articles from Europe and were exchanged for guns, ammunition, groceries, medicines, and above all else, cloth and hardware. But so expensive were the imports that the balance of trade was always unfavorable to New Mexico. While the peon could not make a living and keep out of debt, the colony as a whole seemed able to do no better. Striking evidence of the general poverty is contained in a military order of the late eighteenth century, in which the governor commands all citizens who do not possess firearms to provide themselves with bows and arrows! About the mystery of slow growth there really is very little mystery after all.

Only in the house of the *rico* were there opulence and charm. The hacienda was a fragment of Old Spain in exile, and as such preserved something of continental grace and tradition. From many sources comes testimony to the effect that there, with women for amours and *bailes* for display, with fine horses resplendent under silver-mounted saddles, with walled gardens and wine and tobacco, life even in banishment had its possibilities. The great *casa* stood in a bower of cottonwoods, whose unresting leaves tempered the caress of that sun which none endures recklessly; and with the protection of two feet of earthen adobes, its interior was cool, and, in contrast to the outside glare, agreeably dim to the eye. The fireplace of oven-like shape rose in the corner of the room, and beside it lay one of the treasured Spanish chests, covered with ornamental carving and fitted with cumbrous iron lock and hinges. The chest and the floor furnished seats, for there were few chairs. In a niche beside the chimney stood a severe-faced *santo*, very crudely executed and ugly if one may judge by the specimens that have survived, but expressive of a pious intention. As the makers were generally members of the Franciscan Third Order, the statue was oftener than not a representation of St. Francis; and as mark of peculiar devotion, it was commonly dressed in the best style of the time.

In the kitchen serving women bustled about on inconsequential errands, turning the spits and tending the adobe oven beside the door; peons lolled in the shade, rolling cornhusk cigarettes; horses waited, ready saddled; servants went with idle laughter about the corral; and in the enclosed court, gracefully busy with her roses, the *señora* gossiped among her maids.

At Santa Fe it was no different. Men in sombreros smoked, gamed, wagered on cock fights and horse races, or made love elegantly, in Spanish fashion. Black-eyed beauties, making the most of their charms with the aid of fan and *rebozo*, counted their conquests by the score, and afterwards succumbed to matrimony and grew old at thirty. Meanwhile through half a dozen generations, the country stood still, while the motto of its people became *mañana, mañana* (tomorrow, tomorrow). Roads were not built, schools not established, mines not developed, and the predatory Indians not conquered.

The roll of Spanish governors in Santa Fe during the seventeenth and eighteenth centuries is long and, no doubt, illustrious; but one by one they held office in the Palace that overlooks the shady plaza, and then went ingloriously away, or were recalled, or died. Their names, and but little else, are preserved on yellowed documents in the archives. One built a church, and so his name survives in the carving on a roof beam; another pacified the Zuñis, and in journeying westward past the famous Inscription Rock, left some chiselled lines to say that he "passed by here" (*pasó por aquí*). Another sent out men to look for mines, and in so doing unlocked to knowledge a section of the Colorado Rockies; many another made explorations, for always the Spanish blood leaped to the call of the long trails; another, Don Juan Ignacio Flores Mogollon, will be remembered by all posterity — though perhaps for no virtue of his own, since he was tried for malfeasance in office — from the lovely Mogollon Mountains, a buttress of the main Continental Divide, which perpetuate his mellifluous name.

But what chance had the best of them against the odds which eventually wore down both energy and ability alike? Beyond a mere livelihood incentive stopped, bowing to the stone wall of inevitability. And so dry rot set in. Moreover, in the new world both feudalism and villeinage were out of date, and a society of brutalized peons supporting an ineffectual aristocracy was doomed. Poverty continued invincible and aided everywhere enormously in the social and physical disintegration. While individual courage in the upper classes remained, industry went, and with it, the virile discipline of their forebears. So when an American army marched through the land, the once proud sons of the Conquistadores were able to offer no armed resistance.

The other fact no less amazing about the society of the *ricos* is its perfect disappearance. It collapsed like a house of cards, and except for the Franciscan missions, left scarce a wrack behind — no art, no literature, no music except a few folk songs, no great highways, and no adequate governmental system. The collector must search deep in the remote Mexican villages for a few carved chests, old candlesticks, and such like. Occasionally a spade or a plowshare will unearth rusted coins, a spur, or a knife.

One article of this kind the writer recalls with peculiar pleasure — a steel lance blade, very narrow and sharply pointed, once used in buffalo chasing. Inlaid with silver by some craftsman down in Old Mexico, it is ornamented with the figures of two diamond rattlesnakes, two vinageroons (a southwestern scorpion), and two herons. But, at most, the relics which antiquaries prize are hardly monuments of a culture.

So for admirer and critic alike the history of Spanish civilization in New Mexico concludes invariably in a minor key. Founded by an imperial race with sword and Cross, suckled upon the heroic milk of patriotism and religion, it was overcome at length by poverty, isolation, and ignorance without having produced any principalities or shining metropolitan cities and works of genius; so the ancestral fire and inspiration which in more favorable environment might have left a lasting impress upon the affairs of men, here lapsed at length into a decadence whose highest quality was only picturesqueness. If sometimes the laurel-crowned ghosts of Coronado, of Oñate, of De Vargas, or of De Anza must expiate the sins of their mortality by revisiting the scenes of their desert travail, their eyes surely fill with "the tears of things," and their hero hearts swell with a Vergilian sadness in contemplating the ill-fortuned posterity that issued from their loins.

The society of aristocrats lost the virility to do what alone justifies an aristocracy — to produce commanders and leaders. Into this stagnation came aggressive American traders from across the plains, lured to the adventure as naturally as bees to honey by the extraordinary level of commodity prices in Santa Fe. When American commerce came, American domination was not far behind.

When one attempts to write of contemporary Mexicans — meaning always those north of the Border — the best descriptive word is "disinherited." (The following was first written during the Great Depression. Its intention was compassionate. In the intervening years the status of the native people has risen greatly.) A stronger race came and took away their inheritance — New Mexico, Texas, Arizona, and California. And the Mexicans have been denied the privilege commonly accorded to conquered peoples of mixing their blood with that of the conquerors. Accordingly one finds today in New Mexico three perfectly distinct peoples, Indian, Mexican, and American, lying side by side with the sharp contrast of strands in a Navaho blanket. The weaver lays, for instance, pure red alongside of pure white, but the two nowhere blend into pink. The fat of the land — and in the thousand-mile strip of territory preëmpted by the force of arms, there is a great deal of it — goes to the "Anglo." And the Indian, in spite of much propaganda to the contrary, is not badly treated by the Great White Father at Washington, and has a far more secure living and probably more happiness than when his forefathers were possessors of all that they surveyed. But the Mexican, sharing neither in the paternalism of the government nor in the natural resources of field, forest, or mine, is in his own country an outcast, a poor relation. Lacking capital, he is shut out from all participation in their development, except as a laborer. Though happily there are exceptions, he and his family are still enchained in the poverty that enervated his ancestors a hundred years ago. The masters still rob the cream and take the cake — only the masters are different now. So his share is always the rockiest field and the shabbiest section of the town.

Notwithstanding a mixed origin the culture of the American Mexicans is distinctly Spanish. Their speech, their customs, their religion are all Spanish, and such modifications as exist are the evolution of their long-protracted isolation and poverty — two curses sent by the malice of the Sky Gods.

Particularly in religion the Mexican is a Spaniard — that is, a Catholic with the ascetic, self-torturing instinct. Among his favorite saints are San Lorenzo, who gave up his life tortured by a slow fire under a gridiron; Santa Barbara, virgin and martyr of the East; and Santa Rita, upon whose brow came the miraculous imprint of the Crown of Thorns. Even St. Francis of Assisi, apostle of sweetness and light to the rest of the world, became for his somber soul the patron of flagellation with yucca whips. And this austerity goes a long way toward rendering intelligible the elemental stoicism that underlay the iron dauntlessness of the Padres.

Indeed, from the Americans' point of view, there remained a curiously invariable strain of cruelty in these Indianized men of Spain. Of this, no one who examines some of the flamboyant bridle bits and spurs can have a doubt. Occasionally a curio seeker runs across one of these old bits, with its abnormally high port and its metal ring which fitted round the horse's lower jaw — a real instrument of torture. The spurs were no less severe, and from some extravagant notion about ornament were fitted sometimes with rowels of enormous size. A friend of mine once owned a pair that had been picked up by a sheep-herder near Magdalena. The rowels were unequal in size, one being eight inches in diameter and the other eleven, both being set with spikes sharply pointed and shaped like nails. It was noted that the larger one was for the left foot, and at once the reason for the inequality became apparent. A man with an eleven-inch wheel on his foot could not throw his right leg over the saddle! One suspects that the *caballero* looked slightly ridiculous.

The instinct for religious cruelty manifests itself, not in witch-burning, but in the rites of the Penitentes, a secret, debased, and unorthodox offshoot from the Third Order of St. Francis. As an instance of their perverted and savage emotion, the practice of flagellation (self-scourging), which in Europe fell into general disuse at the end of medieval times, is customary among them to this day. While misinformation is abundant on a subject so obscure, it is commonly reputed that in Holy Week the devotees lash themselves with yucca scourges, and that on Good Friday there is a "Crucifixion" which consists in tying the victim to a heavy cross, where he is permitted to hang until all but dead. In *The Land of Poco Tiempo* the ceremonies are described vividly (if unreliably, as Catholic writers say) by Lummis, who obtained a photograph of them at great personal danger. The rites are commonly explained as being due to the isolation of the province. When the missions were secularized and the priests left the country, it is said, lay devotees undertook to keep the Faith alive. But popular ignorance, left without the guidance of the Church, relapsed naturally into fanaticism, and the Mexican zealot inheriting from the Spaniard a tragic interpretation of Christianity, and from his Indian forebears a recent and thinly covered savagery, evolved presently a cruel and schismatic cult of the scourge.

But even with the restraining guidance of the clergy, the *Mexicano* tends towards a bizarre note in his religion, of which his American Catholic neighbor has neither understanding nor approval. In Silver City, for instance, whose colorless name, bestowed in the early seventies by prosaic miners, overlies the older sonorous name of San Vicente, the patronal festival is celebrated annually with mighty detonations of blasting powder, which begin as the bell rings for first vespers on the preceding eve. And at the remote settlement of San Lorenzo they hold a fiesta in their unique Mexican way. High Mass first. Commemorations of the fiery torments of their saint and requests for his intercessions, who is particularly a protector of the needy. And heaven knows that among his children there is need enough! Then the athletic contests — boxing matches in the roped square, foot races for both girls and boys, horse races in which the fleetest ponies of the Mimbres Valley compete — with betting of course; and then a bronco riding contest, in which the *vaqueros* vie in their traditional sport. In the evening a *gran baile* with jazz orchestra, where rustic *señoritas* display ancestral Spanish charms before a rustic chivalry.

And riding through the byways of New Mexico, one notes here and there crowning a hilltop the silhouette of a cross, an unaccustomed sight from American roadsides. Many years ago one stood on the cliff above the famous Kneeling Nun of Santa Rita, the giant lava monolith one hundred feet high, statuesque, bending exactly like a Sister of Perpetual Adoration. And still one rises starkly white upon the azure at Cross Mountain, a few miles distant. From far plains below one notes on a holy eve in May a bonfire twinkling red in the sky — nothing more.

And the wayside Mexican cemeteries, too, make the traveller wonder at times if he has not unwittingly crossed the Border. The *campo santo* is weed-grown and unkempt, but it blossoms with Christian crosses on every grave — pine boards with a transverse arm for the name and years. Most of them are laboriously notched and scalloped with some pathetic intention at ornament, and they are often hung with rain-faded paper wreaths. Seldom will one find poverty with attributes so touching.

And there is a disproportion of little graves. Mortality is high among tots reared on beans and peppers — which recalls how sparely life goes among these humble folk. I can hardly remember having seen a Mexican man who was fat. Uniformly the men are spare. Lined faces are the rule. The commonplaces of sewage and water supply, the danger of flies and mosquitoes as disease carriers are unfamiliar to them, and out of those whom inadequate diet and insufficient clothing spare, unsanitary living conditions take their toll. Their thick adobe houses, frequently chilly in summer and, in winter but half warmed by a handful of wood coals, are lurking places for pneumonia.

Naturally, poverty has compelled them to explore pretty thoroughly the native beneficence which their land concedes in the matter of food, drink, and fuel. So in the desert sections they gather the sweet pods of mesquite and boil them or grind them into a meal. They dig into the sandy dunes for the roots and haul them home as the best substitute for coal. They collect and eat the purple egg-shaped tunas or fruits from the prickly pear. In a country barren of mast they go into the foothills and gather cones from the piñon trees and dry them in the oven until the brown nuts drop free. In the higher country they go out in mid-summer and cut the heavy, succulent flower stalks of the mescal and concoct therefrom an effective liquor.

But most they depend for a living upon pinto beans, corn, and chile peppers, which not even the most optimistic could call a rich or varied diet. Cornmeal ground from fresh hominy is baked into little cakes called *tortillas*, and a red, fiery pepper sauce is poured over them and the tear-evoking result is an *enchilada*. Or else the cornmeal is cooked with little chunks of meat, peppered, and rolled in a corn husk and called a *tamale*. But the real mainstay of life is beans (*frijoles*) and a pot of them, seasoned generously with ground chile, is kept always simmering over the fire — that is, when there has been no drouth and when there is enough employment to go round. In lean winters when depression overclouds everything, such comparative affluence shrinks to a vanishing point. For these disinherited people, life is hard!

Living among them, one grows at length to comprehend with compassion their backward indolence, their credulity and gaiety. Even the thriftiest alacrity finally slackens into improvidence where "The struggle nought availeth." Of what use to wear out body and soul where only a bare livelihood at most can be coaxed from rock and clay? What sense in saving and scraping together for a motor truck when a living can be made more simply with a burro? So runs their thought. Naturally, the music sinks to a minor key with many a retard. And naturally they have been surpassed by fleeter ones in the race, and while their advancement continues haltingly, they have been outdistanced by a half-dozen generations. *Mañana, mañana,* it will be time enough.

This world, after all, cannot last always; so better take it as it is, and grow reconciled to its futilities and frustrations. Thus out of an unprogressive indolence flowers the quality that endears Mexicans to travellers, artists, and writers — their quaintness. Placidly they drift through an existence that is unashamedly poor and grim, yet interpenetrated with a certain adorable beauty. Neither is their credulity beyond explanation. When society and government can help so very little, there is a natural turning among the troubles of the present to the invisible, yet forever hovering world of angels and saints. Somewhere in a divinely guided scheme, say they, there must be help for the helpless. Hence their excessive faith which runs so readily into error. A childlike superstition — would they not affirm?— is better than no faith at all. If their sick rush to venerate a relic in some apocryphal shrine and there drop a coin or burn a candle to the eternal Misericordia, is this not finer than despair?

And by some profound paradox, gaiety like credulity springs up naturally in this beaten people. They sing, perhaps, lest they fall to weeping. Apparently it is — and if I knew a more humane phrase, I would use it — a "defense mechanism." When one must choose between tears and laughter, one is wiser not to weep. The early "Anglos" who came out from Missouri to Santa Fe were appalled and disgusted at the light-hearted way in which the native people appeared to treat the death of a child. In ignorance they imputed heartlessness where the real reason was a pretended rejoicing that the little one had escaped the sufferings of life.

But excepting the sociologist or the hardened reformer, no one would have the Mexicans otherwise than as they are. Product of a desert culture eclipsed by isolation and stunted by poverty, they add to standardized American life a well-aged mellowness which one would not willingly lose. Nor do they themselves appear to hanker after the travail of progress. And until some time remote in the future, New Mexico will probably continue to drowse through slowly changing years, while brown, unfashionable women tend cube-like adobe cottages, banded with their processional of hollyhocks, jewelled with blood-red strands of chile peppers shrivelling in the autumn sunshine, and painted at the door with the color of heaven — that blue which places the house and its dwellers safe in the protection of the Holy Virgin, Santa María. And brown children of a sweetly vowelled speech will imagine indefinitely battles between Conquistadores and Indians. Mouse-colored burros of a Spanish race brought long ago from Palestine by the Moors — each strangely marked along his back, like a Jerusalem ass, with the sign of the Holy Cross — here will long regard the world with meek-eyed reproach. Through the length of uncounted summers their masters will recline like a tattered frieze against the wall until golden October. But in the season when frost begins to nip the embrowning corn, and Capricornus, leader of the winter signs, swings southward through the nights, the chill of the rolling year will urge them forth to the forest once more as reluctant woodcutters. Then along highways which know the roar of high-powered automobiles and motor buses, they will return at evening, trailing their file of packsaddled burros against the autumn sunset; while the measured clinking of the leader's bell cuts through the sound pattern of unshod hoofs, and the burdens of copper-red firewood, fresh from the axe, exhale the incense of split cedar. Sharp-etched in strokes of grimness and splendor, such scenes persist in the land where *mañana* is like the yesterdays.

CHAPTER TEN

APACHES

In his own arid country the
Apache was on the side of the gods — the Rain Gods,
native spirits of sun and air and rain, who stood mili-
tantly with him. Together they made their astonishing
stand. Although the decision of the struggle was inevitable, as it always is where the Stone Age meets
civilization, the duration was meaningful, and here Sky
Determined. The writer's concern is not with the denouement which was, of necessity, certain, but with the
causes which operated to postpone it through more than
two and a half centuries.

History has persisted in misunderstanding the Apache.
He has been viewed exclusively and constitutionally as
an enemy, a sort of rattlesnake among men. Historians
have taken up the word *apachu,* "enemy," which the
timorous Zuñis applied to him, and the name has stuck.
To the unwarlike Pueblos, no doubt, these free-roving
falcons of the desert were indeed enemies, but it is unfair

to withhold a certain tribute of applause from the soaring hawk because he must get his living from buccaneering.

The fact is, that so far from being by constitution an enemy to the rest of his fellow creatures, the Apache was nature's supreme example of adaptation to arid environment. Yet, even here, it is only fair to say that the desert was not his first choice of a home. While never essentially farmers, the tribesmen in the relatively untroubled days of the eighteenth century maintained their *rancherias* in the well-watered valleys and there tended their fields of corn. Their permanent homes, so far as they had any, were in the places where men always make their homes — along the streams, by the margin of the forest, at the mountain's base, where water and game and fuel and fertile soil served their everyday needs. But when forced by the exigencies of self-preservation into the predatory existence of the desert, they fitted as admirably as birds of paradise in gentler climes.

Never a debased savage living, like the Diggers, or like the lower types of California aborigines, on a fare so degraded as to be unfit for human use, he possessed something in his make-up that transmuted a lean diet not into an ignoble, spiritless being, but into a man-o'-war, a more than Spartan foeman worthy of the American nation through forty years of bloodshed. Outnumbered ten to one, he kept up the fight against a great soldier like General Crook and dealt him blow for blow. Even with all the paraphernalia of civilized warfare the regular trooper was no match for the Indian on his own ground, and through nearly two generations the vast resources of man-power and treasure were expended by the government at Washington as vainly as sand is poured down a rat hole.

Through all that time the struggle was a running sore, which over and over healed at the surface, only to break forth again still more malignantly. The West grew sick and tired. In the East there were not wanting some who felt distressed at the futility of all the fighting, and more than a little ashamed at the spectacle of the armed forces of a great nation at war, year after year, with a handful of naked savages. During the administration of President Grant, Congress appointed an Indian Peace Commission, headed by no less a person than General W. T. Sherman, and consisting of five other high military officials and two U. S. senators. In their report they declared that the government had spent in the preceding fifty years the enormous sum of $500,000,000 and twenty thousand lives in Indian warfare, and that during the time, it had been uniformly unjust to the Indian. Somewhat later a United States commissioner, Vincent Collyer, declared that our inhuman treachery and cruelty had turned the Apaches into implacable foes, and that this policy had resulted in a war that "in ten years, from 1861 to 1870, cost forty million dollars and a thousand lives" (Twitchell's *Leading Facts,* Vol. II, p. 434). All of which suggests that if natural adaptation be the basis for such a resistance, it is worth study. Incidentally, it is clear from the record why the Apache was an "enemy."

When the end arrived the red man was not so much defeated as overwhelmed. His skill and speed were not surpassed; they were smothered under the white man's strength and awkwardness. The process of clearing the country of its native inhabitants for new occupants was thus analogous to the process of clearing the desert for agriculture. It can be done — for, in the end, the heavy tools of industry are bound to triumph, but the task is

unconscionably expensive, and it involves many wounds. Nature, with a mother love that is always tenacious, planted the Apache in the desert, and before any alien species not specifically adapted could supplant him there, it would be necessary to modify, in some real sense, the environment. Otherwise, it would be as rational for a cornfield to supplant a patch of cactus.

Essentially, the tragedy was unavoidable, and the record of the white man's advance is full of such stories. In the larger sense no one was to blame, for the life purposes of the Apache ran counter to those of the paleface. They could not occupy the same ground at the same time. Latterly, the same feud continues between the rancher and the mountain lion. The big splendid cat is not by nature an *apachu* — he merely follows the mode of living that was destined for him. But deer are encouraged and even bear are protected, while the order has gone forth that he must be exterminated. To much of nature's scheme civilization is an intransigent enemy.

Boundaries expand, frontiers advance. The westward-thrusting spearpoint reached New Mexico. There the green valleys became the apple of an eye to the homesteader; the grama ranges were an object of desire to the ranchman; more than all, the mountains of metal were coveted by the miner. And thus, when the Americans seized the country, they terminated abruptly the equilibrium which had persisted only because the military arm of Spain and Mexico was too feeble to change it. Naturally, such an advance could not be withheld.

But in the duration of the struggle, the Sky Powers, as always in the thirsty Southwest, hold the explanation of much that happened; for in all campaigns water and the lack of it played the trump cards. Without the aid of thirst, which everywhere and always fought for him, the Apache's courage and his metallic sinews could not have kept the enemy from his throat while millions of dollars were being expended to crush him. The troopers, too, were fighting men.

By pretending for a moment that all highways have been erased from the map, that automobiles capable of mile-a-minute travel do not exist, and, above all, that there are no wind pumps sucking up to the surface life-giving water from deep borings, we can, in imagination, attack the problem of ninety years ago. Mathematically the equation was simple — troopers versus the Apaches, plus great distances, plus waterless wastes and the whole compendium of desert craft. But the point of the matter consisted in the fact that the balance, which remained more or less complete during the Spanish-Mexican régime, had now changed, and that for the purposes of civilization the symbol "equal to" had to be superseded by "greater than."

The advantages of the red warrior were manifold. He knew the waterholes of the country, how good they were and how large, and whether or not they were permanent. It would be awkward to risk death to reach a guarded spring and then find it dry — for when the army blundered upon a spring they cunningly posted two men to lie in wait and shoot all who came to drink. He knew also the trails and distances, and could therefore move expeditiously through the mountains by the safest, least-fatiguing routes, while the foe found himself trapped in box canyons and at the edge of precipices. Above all, he could move unseen. The real reason why during the interminable struggle so few Indians were killed was that they were so seldom seen.

And the Apache knew how to fend for himself in situations where a trooper would quickly perish. In fact, only an examination reveals the surprising extent of his traditional lore which possessed military value. The lifelong study of self-preservation made him a natural soldier, and if in combat he was no match for the heavily armed cavalryman, he could forage infinitely better while actively campaigning.

In autumn the brave could sustain himself on mesquite beans if he chanced to be on the desert; if in the foothills, he lived well on piñon nuts, the fruit of a dwarf pine. These, in fact, were and are a staple article of Indian diet. (It was while gathering them towards the end of 1931 that several hundred Navaho were overtaken by a storm on the high mesas of New Mexico and snowed in. To relieve their sufferings, pack trains, sledges, and even airplanes were employed in carrying blankets and supplies to them.) By September or October the brown nuts are ripe in the cones, but later they drop to the ground and are carried away by the pack rats to their dens, whence they are removed by the Indians.

Walnuts since the days of the prehistoric Mimbreños have been stored and eaten. And chokecherries, wild gooseberries, grapes, prickly pear fruits, the inner bark of the yellow pine, and even roasted grasshoppers are edible on the march when a stomach filler is imperative. And the mescal — that is a story by itself. This lethal-appearing plant, called by some Spanish dagger or century plant, is an amaryllis, closely related to the lilies, which after sojourning long in the desert has gone native. Its terminal thorns are needles strong enough to pierce rawhide, its fibers tough enough to use for thread, and its thickened base succulent enough to eat. It was, in fact, as vital to the Indian as the potato to the Irishman, and the Mescalero Apaches did it the honor of assuming its name.

Thus when not even a jack rabbit, a pack rat, or a snake could be taken, it was still impossible to starve out the savage. Indeed, by chewing the watery fiber of the cactus, he could even make himself temporarily independent of streams and springs. In particular there grows on the Lower Sonoran deserts a bulky species called *bisnaga* or barrel cactus, whose melon-like pulp contains enough stored-up moisture to preserve the life of a man through an extremity. While to cultivated taste a poor substitute for drink, it satisfies for a while the crying tissues of the human body. So whereas the menace of thirst and hunger kept the soldier always within reach of his base, the Apache could rove, free as the wind, wherever inclination led him or peril drove him.

Furthermore, in addition to his expert ability to live off the country while campaigning, the Indian had developed a set of tactics that against white troops were effective in the extreme. It is wrong to think of the conflict as waged on the one side by regulars, and on the other side by amateurs. The Apache was, in the truest sense, a professional fighting man from the time he could ride a pony and shoot with a bow. But he fought for a livelihood instead of for pay. Essentially, his theory of offense was to strike the enemy in a surprise attack and race for the mountains without waiting for the return blow. Not having a base of supplies to defend, the Apache always elected to make a running fight, which afforded him the immense advantage of ambuscade, and in this art he was conceded by the military authorities to be as expert as any savage the American continent has produced. How many canyons over the length and breadth of the Southwest have resounded with the yells and shots of his ambushes, none will ever be able to say.

But it was not alone that the Apache was a peerless man-o'-war, not alone his prowess with horse and rifle, his ability to forage, his cunning invisibility up to the moment of his serpent strike, nor was it his stoic command of flesh and spirit. Rather was it his lifelong schooling in the genius of his country, the harmonious way in which he compelled its total resources and peculiarities to serve him. He always moved with its current, never athwart it nor against it, and it repaid him by remaining consistently his provider, protector, and ally. And this cooperation it steadfastly refused to the white man's organized warfare. The desert is not amenable to standard military rules.

In a warfare which consisted so inevitably of pursuit, the savage invariably succeeded in interposing a desert or two betwixt his tawny back parts and the avenging cavalry. In a plains country he would have become in a generation or two merely a memory, like the great Illini, Tribe of Men, or else a reservation prisoner. In a continuously mountainous land his people would sooner or later have been corralled in some enclosed valley and taken captive.

But his own open country is a vast high plateau or plain over which are scattered at random hundreds of discontinuous mountain masses. The interruptions are irrational, without plan. The only rule for them is the old rule of thumb. For recognized military purposes infantry was useless on the immense plains; cavalry equally so in the craggy mountains. Artillery was everywhere dead weight — like a heavy rifle on a quail hunt. On the plains the Apache was light cavalry, fleet as the wind, cruising on his mount, trailing with his horse herd, league after league from one remote waterhole to the next. Among the crags, he became, by the simple act of dismounting, heavy infantry ready for any enterprise from fighting to scaling an abrupt canyon wall. In Apachería if horses were indispensable, legs were even more so.

Consider the country which Cook's Peak overlooks. From the heart of Apache land it towers high enough to be visible for many leagues down in Old Mexico, from the Rio Grande, and almost from the environs of El Paso; while from the hills that ring Silver City, it appears through the forty miles of clear air as though it were just beyond the doorstep. The dominant impression is that the peak gazes down upon a vast plain interrupted by the discontinuity of many ragged mountains, rather than — as one might infer from perusing the map — a jumble of mountains in which some plains are embosomed. To the south, close in, soar the treeless pinnacles of one of the most abrupt and broken mountains in the Southwest, named by the early Spaniards—for its indescribably magnificent color in the sunset, I imagine — La Florida, the Beautiful. Farther away, down near the Chihuahua line, like three inverted strawberries all exactly equal in outline and altitude, rise the Tres Hermanas; but the intervening tract is mainly a waterless desert checkered with olive-green patches of creosote intersected by bands of mesquite along the arroyos. Beyond the sharply rising Victorio Peak, named for one of the Warm Springs chieftains, the plain rises by gentle degrees to the Continental Divide, beyond which lies the high, cold Chiricahua Range of Arizona. Sweeping still in a grand circle to the right, across the parched plain, the eye rests agreeably upon a triple pine-clad peak called The Burros. Then closing in the whole panorama along the northern horizon rise the loftiest peaks of the region, the Mogollons, and their lower prolongations to the eastward which lift again into the mighty buttresses of the Mimbres or Black Range. Across this arid, dangerous land, which the Sky Determined until the final triumph of the machine age, Mangas Coloradas (Red Sleeves), Cochise, Victorio, and finally Geronimo, followed by ever-dwindling bands, wrote the name Apache in letters of blood for a great nation to wonder at through all time to come.

Looking back from the safety of the present, old-timers are sometimes tempted to underestimate the valor of Indian resistance and to make accusations of laziness and inefficiency against the soldiers who protected them or were expected to do so. At Silver City they will tell you that the troopers at Fort Bayard — the colored ones, especially — were more effective at consuming liquor than at fighting, and that hearing of a raid, they would ride over from the post, camp in the arroyo, or scour the foothills for a while and then ride leisurely back to the post. In the 'eighties there was much talk about forming a militia or volunteer military companies from the citizenry who would go out and in short order exterminate the enemy. But it did not come to pass. The citizens went into action rather as a collection of individual riflemen than as a disciplined military force, and in a few days when their indignation had been worked off by the killing of a few hostiles, they were ready to go home and stay until the next raid goaded them again into rage. They maintained no relentless pressure, which kept steadily closing in on the enemy until he was crushed. The difference amounted in the main to this — the citizens avenged depredations, while the military authorities tried in a bungling way to solve the Indian problem.

There were advantages and disadvantages on the side of the soldiers, but the difficulties which they faced were truly enormous. Being not only unfamiliar with the country and its trails, they also had very limited means of transportation. Each trooper had a horse, and usually but one. The brave owning a string of ponies, and riding a fresh one every day, could swoop down like a hawk upon his prey, escape to the safety of his native fastnesses, and there laugh at the pursuer vainly trailing him. The cavalry animals, though strong while fed on grain and hay, jaded quickly on ordinary range picking. And, being shod with iron, they were ready for rough going, but having occasionally the ill luck to cast a shoe, quickly became footsore on the rocky trails. Furthermore, the

Indian after riding down a pony cut its jugular vein with his lance, hacked off a few steaks, and roasted them. Refreshed, he took another mount and rode on. Or if hotly pursued, the band would dismount, kill their horses, scatter in the brush like quail, only to assemble later at some appointed rendezvous. And the Apache on foot was not quite helpless. He could travel — on the authority of army scouts — fifty or sixty miles a day over the roughest of ground.

Yet in the last analysis he faced a foe who had advantages which could not ultimately fail to turn the scale in their favor. Their superiority was as great in numbers as it was in equipment. They were organized and disciplined, and from Civil War days down to the end of hostilities in 1886, many of them were veterans. They filled their stomachs regularly three times a day; they slept inside forts away from the cold and rain in the midst of their stored-up reserves of meat and flour and whiskey; and when they were tired out or sick or wounded, they had a place to rest and doctors to take care of them. When the snows came, they kept warm with heavy boots and overcoats. They had far-seeing field glasses stronger even than the Apache's hawk-eye, and in a few minutes with their magic mirrors they could send a code message clearer than his smoke signal and farther than an Indian on a pony could carry it in a day's journey. Finally, they had accurate carbines and an abundance of ammunition that could be trusted. The Indian, when measured by the army standard, was a notoriously poor shot — he couldn't afford to practice — and often in earlier days he had nothing more death-dealing than arrows. But the army's mounted riflemen, armed until about 1873 with terrible 50-caliber Springfields and after that time with 45's that carried a load still more deadly, were capable of a most tragic execution upon their red-skinned foes.

The wicked 500-grain bullet of that weapon, propelled by 70 grains of black powder and directed by a keen sight, is conceded to have been the greatest man-killer our army ever used. On kicking up one of them from the sand, flattened at the point and now corroded by the elements, one muses upon what life must have been for an Apache in those days. Chased from plain to mountain and over and up and down; haunted by fear of confinement on a military reservation or of death, which was not much worse; dodging constantly the flight of those maiming, bone-crushing chunks of lead that fell in wasp-like hail; denied the ministrations of antiseptic surgery and with no hospital or walled fort to rest in during convalescence; scorned by a heavy-bellied, slow-footed enemy who wallowed in guns and powder; hopeless of finally delivering his race and his homeland from the oppressor, and with no death ahead but a dog's death. . . . God!

There is no great difficulty in picturing the feelings which the white man aroused in the Apache at first contact. Over the broad expanse of desert and mountain the Indian was unchallenged master. The puny cavalcade of Spaniards, sweating under metal armor and tortured by heat and thirst, offered to his superior numbers, his military prowess, and, above all, his knowledge of desert-craft, no conceivable threat. But gradually the scene changed. More and more of the enemy came to take up squatter's claim to his valleys and to trespass in his forests. And they thrust their roots down pertinaciously among the rocks. At length numbers became equal. But the enemy's strength was formidable because it was concentrated. It differed thus from the Indian's, which was vulnerable because scattered.

Friction would not be long in arising. To the red man's untutored moral sense, the distinction between *meum* and *tuum* was nowhere very important, and between himself and an alien it did not exist. So he became a predator. But among civilized men thievery cannot long go unnoticed, and so horse-stealing and raiding soon became a cause for war. The war thus started never came to an end.

In its large outlines the Spanish policy was to string a thin line of presidios along the two-thousand-mile front that began at the Gulf of Mexico and ended on the Gulf of California — indeed, the line was ultimately extended up the coast to San Francisco — and from them to send out local punitive expeditions as the provocation demanded. Figueroa's map of 1784 shows that there were then only five in the entire Gila country as far west as Tucson, though perhaps others were built later.

A private stronghold designed to protect the famous mine at Santa Rita, which still survives in part, may possibly be taken as a representative of the type. Erected in 1803 by a wealthy Chihuahua merchant, Don Francisco Manuel Elguea, and his partner, General Don José Manuel Carrasco, who with the aid of a friendly Indian had previously discovered the mountain of copper deposits, it consisted of three round, squat towers connected by a triangular wall. The remaining tower, constructed of a four-foot thickness of adobes, was impervious to arrows, to fire, and — as it appears today — to the elements. But while the outposts of Spain held their own, it is doubtful whether they ever affected the Apaches with deep fear.

Technically, the American did not inherit the ancient quarrel. Yet the same grounds of offense were bound to result as before. Always the white man came as a usurper into the Indian's country. Unwanted and unwelcome from the start, he habitually mistreated his high-spirited hosts. Hatreds presently developed, and then mutual retaliations naturally.

Among the natives it soon grew to be an act of merit to steal from a white man or to take his life in ambush. Compared with their indigence, the settler possessed tempting riches in the shape of horses, firearms, utensils, and ornaments. Plundering soon grew habitual, and then came the inevitable retribution. But the Indian, being a savage, did not feel bound to conduct his warfare by his opponent's rules. He followed his own, and these included torture of captives and death to non-combatants. More salt in the wounds!

The civilized Spaniards had shown themselves apt pupils at savagery, and matters went from bad to worse until hatred between Apache and New Mexican rose to a ferocity beyond which it is not possible to go. And, in their turn, our own countrymen were not so far behind. Less than sixty years ago the Christian citizens of Grant County, New Mexico, were officially offered by their commissioners the sum of $250 for each dead Apache, the death certificate being in each case the scalp! After 1886 decency required the Americans to say comparatively little about the inhuman cruelty of Spaniard and Mexican. In fact, the scales tipped slightly in favor of the Conquistadores, for in 1785 Captain Martinez, scouring the region under orders from Governor De Anza at Santa Fe, was content with a somewhat more humane trophy — the ears!

The amount of punishment that the Apache nations could not merely endure but actually thrive upon in their protecting deserts and mountains becomes apparent only upon a historical examination that surveys the long accumulation of bloodshed. Fortunately, a late book by Professor Thomas of the University of Oklahoma gives a detailed and scholarly account of the Spanish campaigns against them.

When France yielded to Spain in 1763 the vast tract of territory called Louisiana, a Spanish officer named De Rubi was sent to inspect the border country which separated Mexico from the northern provinces. As a result of his recommendations the Viceroy sent an Irishman, who has come down in history as Don Ugo O'Conor, to reorganize the entire line of presidios along the border and to beat off Indian attacks upon a line nearly two thousand miles long, which ran from the Gulf of Mexico to the Gulf of California. A superhuman assignment! For the task, O'Conor had four hundred men, poorly armed. He reported that since 1748, four thousand persons had been killed, and that the property loss had reached a grand total of twelve million pesos.

By the spring of 1775 O'Conor had rebuilt the frontier defenses and was ready to undertake aggressive warfare. The attack which he planned was grandly conceived. He issued his orders to the provincial governors and to the captains of presidios in Coahuila, New Viscaya, New Mexico, and Sonora. Governor Mendinueta at Santa Fe was to furnish six hundred mounted men and combine his forces with those from El Paso near the Sierra Blanca. O'Conor himself was to come up from Mexico past the Florida Mountain, and the Sonoran army was to advance northeastward past the Chiricahua Range to the Gila and to follow that stream up to the mountain rendezvous of the Apaches, which was then loosely called the Sierra del Gila. Essentially, the Irish don was attempting to drive the tribesmen away from the Rio Grande into the Mogollon-Mimbres country, where they could be crushed between the jaws of the two armies advancing from the north and the south. The campaign began at the end of August, 1775. When it was complete the Indians had suffered fifteen defeats "of devastating proportions." The Spaniards had killed 138 warriors, taken 104 prisoners, and recovered nearly 2,000 stolen animals. It was no comic opera warfare which the doughty Irishman waged, but it did not settle the Apaches long.

The next soldier to receive command of the Interior Provinces was a chivalrous Frenchman named Don Teodoro de Croix. His attempt to conciliate the savages, while it accomplished nothing, adds luster to his name, and shows also the humane concessions which Spain was willing to make.

De Croix, as he says, "following the King's command to win the Indian by gentle rather than by warlike means," proposed to the Apaches that they should live in organized pueblos and receive priests to teach them. He proposed that they learn to sow and reap and give up vagabondage, and offered to furnish them tools for agriculture. And while the children would be required to embrace the Catholic religion, the adults would be under no compulsion. The chief to whom the bargain was offered wheeled his horse and rode away, bellowing defiance. A little later war was on again.

In 1786 the Frenchman had Governor De Anza marching down from Santa Fe to join Captain Martinez, who was marching up from Carrizal. They were to come together by the Rio Mimbres, near the sharp cone which they called Picacho and which is now known as Cook's Peak. Again the Sonoran troops, led this time by a captain with the melodious name of Vildosola, scoured the Chiricahuas. In spite of an offer of twenty pesos for the body of each Indian dead or alive, only thirty-one Apaches were killed and twenty-five captured. Four Spaniards held in captivity were freed and three hundred head of stock were regained.

As a reward for this and his other brilliant achievements the Frenchman was made Viceroy of Peru, and a former governor of California with the genuinely Spanish name of Felipe de Neva was promoted to his place.

Again a complicated campaign was to be executed with the aid of five divisions. This time the main push was to come from the south and southwest, and the strong fifth army was to proceed up from the Hatchet Range to the Mimbres, where it was to ambush the Indians fleeing eastward. To one who knows the country the enterprise, like the others, was a search for a needle in a haystack. The surprising thing was that they ever chanced upon a foe. Yet in April and May of the year 1784 they killed sixty-nine of the enemy and captured eleven. It is interesting to note that among the spoils taken were some buffalo hides, which must have come from somewhere over in the Pecos country.

When the Spaniard died, Commander-Inspector Rengel, who if not a German at least had a German name, stepped forward to continue the *"strafing"* of the red men. Rengel, with more craftiness than his predecessors, attempted to seduce the Navahos from their Apache alliance. He sent Captain Martinez north again from Old Mexico, up past La Florida and Cook's Peak, to scour the headwaters of the Rio Mimbres, while his second and third divisions under Captain Don Antonio Cordero came up through the Animas Mountains and the Playa of Santo Domingo to beat up through the Burro Mountains. Captain Don Antonio, less romantic and chivalrous than his name might indicate, succeeded only in killing five women and a boy. The warriors somehow eluded him, and he related seeing only some smoke signals exchanged between them and their allies on Cook's Peak, forty miles away. Proceeding downstream on the Gila, he hunted through the San Simon country, but was forced by a great snowfall on the desert at the beginning of December to return southwards. Sixteen of his men were ill, and he lost fifty horses from starvation in the snow. His total kill was nine — six squaws, two children, and one warrior. Captain Martinez fought several engagements near the Picacho, but reported no fatalities among the enemy, who retreated northward into the Mimbres Range. But he had worn out all of his horses and could not pursue them — which became almost a refrain in later accounts of cavalry operations. So he returned southward to his base at Carrizal in Chihuahua.

The totals seem to indicate that the Apache, hunted for ten years up and down the length and breadth of his native land by the combined abilities of an Irishman, a Frenchman, a Spaniard, and a German, endured, according to enemy communiqués, a total loss of just two hundred and seventy-six lives.

It was in the year 1785 when Captain Cordero withdrew his troopers from the pursuit. It was an even hundred years later when General Miles finally settled the Apaches. . . . What other savages have ever fought civilized man a hundred years — two hundred years?

We have seen now how Spain made war. The Apache made war differently. His tactics included massacres, raids, thefts, manifold depredations. The chronicle of them is a long, bitter one.

On the southern slope of Cook's Peak, not far from the great Spring, occurred in 1861 an episode of a kind that was to become tragically common before the end. The Civil War was going on. Seven young men, Union sympathizers, were salvaging property of the Butterfield Overland Stage Company. Taking away one of the heavy stagecoaches, they stole north along the Rio Grande to Old Mesilla, where they struck westward across the desert, hoping to make connection with the oncoming California Column. The Trail led past Cook's Spring, and thence through a dry, winding canyon over the divide. At the Spring, Mangas Coloradas laid his ambush. After their horses fell the defenders had not a chance of escape; so turning the coach on its side and piling a barricade of stones around themselves, they made their stand. When five of them had been slain, the other two pencilled a message and laid it under a stone. They planned, it stated, to attempt to slip through the enemy in the darkness. . . . Three days later a freighter, pausing to water his horses, found what remained of seven bodies and the blood-stained sheet of paper. And Mangas Coloradas with his warriors was already in Old Mexico with the stagecoach, where he sold it with other booty.

Years later, in the fall of 1879, a little beyond the Spring in the same canyon, Victorio, often called the greatest chieftain of them all, surprised a wagon train in characteristic Apache fashion. A party of sixteen Mexicans from Mesilla was on its way up to the mining camps of Pinos Altos and Silver City. Their cargo contained whiskey, calico, shoes, and general merchandise for the miners. As they were making camp in the October dusk, tan bodies stripped for war lay all around them in the shadows. At a signal the massacre began. The killing kept on until none was left alive, man or woman. Next day when the stage driver passed by with the mail the carnage met his eyes. He carried word to the soldiers at

Fort Cummings, who came out to inter what remained. While at their task, one of them spied a far-off moving speck out on the desert. Reconnoitering, they found it to be a yoke of oxen; and in the cart sat the driver — dead. An old army teamster, who was there, told me that he afterwards scoured the hills for the loot, which Victorio concealed somewhere in the vicinity. He found nothing — only he heard the Apaches signalling to one another with their well-known owl's cry. But, after being cached forty years, some of the bolts of calico were recently found in a cave. An old-timer showed me the labels. They were "Gordon prints."

In 1871 the Hulbert family, the first to settle on the site of Silver City, became Apache victims. While the father was away in Pinos Altos, the savages surprised the mother as she was hoeing the garden, killing her and the children. Only a year later John Bullard, from the same settlement, was shot through the heart by an Indian as he was leading a party of volunteers. A company of troops rode over from Fort Bayard and accorded him military honors, while a meeting of citizens sent a resolution to Congress, requesting $30,000 to raise volunteers for the purpose of gathering the Indians on reservations "where they will stay forever."

Another massacre which made southwestern history was the one in which Victorio's band ambushed James Cooney and a band of miners in the Mogollon Mountains in the spring of 1880. The body of Cooney, beside that of his friend Chick, was found lying in a creek near the famous old silver camp to which he gave his name. His brother afterwards hollowed a tomb for him in the solid rock, and over it the miners placed a hewn porphyry cross. And then there was the murder of Judge McComas and his wife, with the abduction of his son, Charlie, which still haunts the memories of old-timers. Where the Lordsburg road rises out of a green valley to start up a grade in the Burro Mountains, Chato and his warriors fell upon them. An old man who went out with a party to bring in the bodies tells me that both were stripped naked and mutilated. The boy's fate remains to this day a mystery. The wild riders, of course, escaped. The concluding tragedies occurred after Victorio was dead, when Geronimo was wielding the scourge of despair.

But for these lords of carnage there was no ultimate escape; nor could the state of affairs continue indefinitely within the borders of a civilized country. After a period of more or less tranquility, the ravages had broken forth again in the 'sixties, when the troops were withdrawn for campaigns against the Confederates. Mangas Coloradas and the other chiefs had been quick to seize their chance. But energetic military action presently brought about the surrender of some hundreds of the Mescalero Apaches, who were placed on a reservation near Fort Stanton, at the foot of the Sierra Blanca. However, with the fragments of other tribes there, they proved sullen and restive. Transferred later to Ojo Caliente, they were no better; and so at length the government, moved by protests of the settlers, ordered the agent, John P. Clum, to remove them thence to join the other Apache tribes on the San Carlos Reservation in Arizona.

But through the guarded lines of the reservations, there were always leaking stealthy war parties which rode forth to slay, rob, and burn. Naturally, there had to be punishment. And by the same token there had to be a final act, or in stricter dramatic language, a catastrophe, to the tragedy. And as that approached, the narrative becomes a merciless, mad, pathetic mess of slaughter on both sides. The troops had orders to slay the men and bring in the women and children as prisoners. The alternative for the warrior was unconditional surrender as a prisoner. And there was, let it be remembered, a cash bounty for each man's body. When a more or less humane nation acted thus, it is small wonder that savages remained merely savages.

Seen from one side, the close was sheer magnificence and heartbreak; seen from the other, it was economic necessity acting. Old men and women who lived through those days in the Southwest shed no compassionate tears in recalling them. But, again, the present writer's concern, let it be recalled, is with neither the ferocity nor the justice of the struggle, but with its duration and the reasons therefor.

With the American occupation new walls rose all over the southwestern part of the state for the accommodation of the ever-increasing soldiery. Besides the strongholds, little sub-posts were scattered widely over the region wherever villages, trails, or mines required military protection. At Santa Rita the old Spanish blockhouse was relieved of its long guard duty by the new Fort Webster. Near the gold and silver mines at Pinos Altos, ten miles distant, Fort West was erected later. In between them stood Fort Bayard, which became in the 'seventies and 'eighties the general guardian of the vastly rich mining district around it. Forty miles more or less to the southeast, Fort Cummings, designed in Civil War days by General McClellan himself, guarded the great Cook Spring. So important was this spring, incidentally, that it caused not only the erection of a fort, but it put a long bend into the Butterfield Trail, sending it away from the flat country and across a mountain range. Then along the middle reaches of the Rio Grande stood Fort Fillmore, Fort Craig, Fort Thorne, Fort McRae, and another at Mt. Robledo. Beyond the white summit of Sierra Blanca rose another — Fort Stanton, erected as a sentinel over the Mescalero Reservation. Forts, soldiery, horses, equipment — such reckoned in magnitudes that challenge belief — are the factors of the sorry, too-prolonged saga. The stream of men and treasure that the Apache tribe diverted from useful channels of advancement through a dozen generations explains in large measure why the beginning of the region's economic progress was delayed until yesterday.

After the removal of the tribesmen to Arizona the denouement of the two-and-a-half century tale comes swiftly. The curtain rises upon the last act. The stage is set. But now the stage is an immensely spacious one, a veritable amphitheater of war. It begins in the western end of Texas along the Pecos River, and extends in a deep band across southern New Mexico and Arizona far down into the Yaqui country of Old Mexico. Measured off into conventional squares on a map, no inconsiderable part of the Southwest, it will be seen, was involved. While numerous units of the U. S. Army participated, the Indian actors were astonishingly few. Victorio had, at times, it is estimated, three hundred braves in his command, but no other band approached that strength. In general, women and children far outnumbered the fighting men. And quite naturally! The Apache fought, as the great wars of the future will be fought, not with an army but with a nation. Yet still the statement is inaccurate, for the closing campaigns of Crook and Miles were executed against only insignificant fragments of the nation. Out of the thousands of Apaches only a few dozens, literally, went on the warpath in 1885, the others remaining quietly on the reservation or else accepting service with the army against their fellows. Those who put up the final agonized struggle against the white man were called "renegades"— but it was the white man who bestowed the epithet.

But while the tawny killers were few, they had horses — stolen horses in unbelievable profusion. And now they had firearms — repeating rifles. Gone were the Civil War days of Mangas Coloradas when, up in the Gila wilderness, twenty-eight warriors armed with bows were picked from a canyon wall by well-armed troopers, who were able to stay beyond arrow shot and so lost but a single man. Retaliations would now be more equal.

•

It is the spring of the year 1870. Victorio, after having twice fled the San Carlos Reservation and having twice been driven back, has left it again, never to return. In hiding among the Mescaleros for a time, he assembles a company of thirty bitter spirits, and they set forth. Going to Ojo Caliente, he kills six of Captain Hooker's men and captures for his raiders forty-five head of horses belonging to the Ninth Cavalry. One hundred and fifty patriots from the reservation join him. The Southwest in its long familiarity with carnage has never known such bloody days as are to follow now. Twitchell, the historian, writes:

Victorio was an intrepid warrior. He attacked, even while pursued by the government troops, wagon trains, ranches, mining camps, and American and Mexican troops. Entirely reckless of the outcome, he terrorized large mining camps and successfully eluding his soldier pursuers, he would suddenly appear in some unexpected quarter. He outwitted two generals of the American army and one in command of the Mexican forces. He captured from the governor of Chihuahua, in one campaign, over five hundred horses. He and his warriors killed over two hundred New Mexicans, more than one hundred soldiers and two hundred citizens of the Mexican Republic. At one time the armies of both countries combined to destroy him, but he made his escape. On another occasion, Colonel Buel, with one thousand cavalry and three hundred Indian scouts, pressing him on the north, Colonel Carr with six hundred cavalry on the west, and General Grierson with the 10th Cavalry on the east, were only able by the most severe fighting to drive him into Mexico at a time when he proposed to again invade the territory. In 1883, the American forces which had been coöperating with the Mexican, separated, and while the troops of our sister republic were returning through Chihuahua they discovered the Apaches under Victorio encamped near a lake, located in the vicinity of the Tres Castillos. Victorio had with him about a hundred warriors, four hundred women and children, and many horses and other animals and much booty. The Mexicans soon surrounded the Indians, who sought shelter in the rocks of the canyons. The battle began in the evening and continued during the entire night. At early dawn Victorio was seen on the summit of one of the crags of the Tres Castillos, basaltic hills which rose directly from the plain. For an hour after daybreak the firing continued, when suddenly the Indians ceased. Their ammunition was exhausted. The Mexicans now charged them with great bravery, the Indians falling beneath a pitiless fire. Victorio, several times wounded, finally fell, shot through the heart.

In a recent article written for the El Paso *Times*, Colonel M. L. Crimmins states that in protecting the western counties of Texas and the surrounding country from the Mescalero Apaches, the army sent out no less than 120 expeditions during 1879, and that they covered a total distance of 40,100 miles. The following year the army was still more active, covering, according to the same authority, nearly 50,000 miles. What the officer says is corroborated by an estimate of an old-time trooper, Anton Mazzanovich, who served in the campaign and writes in a Deming newspaper (1931): "The American troops during the duration of this campaign marched a total of 44,000 miles, all of it through rough and difficult country. At times they suffered from lack of water. . . ." Unconsciously the water refrain is interwoven through every war story of the Southwest.

After the fight at Tres Castillos came a lull. Then, presently, more gory business. Seven hundred Chiricahuas — men, women, and children — broke away, heading towards Sonora and Chihuahua. Making good their escape, they threatened from the inaccessible Sierra Madre Mountains much of southern New Mexico and Arizona. Though the border was patrolled by American troops aided by a large body of Apache scouts, Chief Chato and twenty-five bucks evaded them and swept north almost to Silver City. This was the band which murdered Judge McComas. After a few days, in which they took twenty-five lives, the riders galloped south again to the mountains of Mexico.

But this time their security was brief. General Crook took up their trail and followed them across the border, where he surprised their camp. By the end of May, 1885, he was on his way back to the States with nearly four hundred prisoners of the Apache nation, among whom were Geronimo, Chihuahua, Mangas, and other chiefs.

Just two years after this a desperate remnant, numbering only forty-two men, ninety-six women and children, broke loose again. Led by Geronimo, Chihuahua, and Mangas, this raid was the most spectacular of all and the last — the mad, spasmodic throe before quiet fell.

Pursued relentlessly by the cavalry, they rode for the ancestral fastnesses of their Mogollon Mountains, the Sierra del Gila, which had been so named by dead-and-forgotten Spanish fighters when the Apache war was young. Issuing thence after the custom of their fathers on tumultuous Valkyr raids "to choose the slain," they carried terror to communities which were enjoying the privileges of railroad, telegraph, and printing press.

The Silver City *Enterprise* of the time carried accounts of the massacre of a Mexican family three miles from town. This was included among news items of ore shipments and other matters of everyday civilized existence. And an issue some months later carried the proclamation of a reward offered by the Grant County commissioners for Apache scalps. In the same columns was recorded the killing of prospectors and ranchers on Blue Creek, of a young Englishman named Lyons of the S U Ranch, of some hunters in the Mogollon Mountains, of silver miners near Lake Valley, of a freighter on Cactus Flat, and of other men and women.

In the military cemetery at Fort Bayard the bodies of some of the massacred were buried by the soldiers. Now, even after eighty years, a vivid picture of savage mutilations is still suggested by the word on the grave markers — "Unknown," "Unknown Child," "Unknown."

Presently Geronimo was driven once more into Mexico, and an expedition organized to follow him. Though nothing of importance happened at the time, finally at the end of March, 1886, General Crook captured him. Four days the wily old fighter was a prisoner, and then he and twenty-five companions once more escaped. Again a pursuit into Mexico! But this time it was not directed by General Crook, for he asked on April 1 to be relieved. His position was filled by General Miles, to whom the President of the United States assigned the task of killing or capturing every hostile Apache within American borders. General Miles was opposed, says former Indian Agent John P. Clum, in the El Paso *Times* in July, 1931, "by thirty-four hostiles — only twenty of whom were men." After a five months' campaign of body-breaking hardship, Geronimo and his few followers surrendered to General Miles in Skeleton Canyon, Arizona, on September 3, 1886. The Apaches were conquered.

Geronimo, kept a prisoner of war until his death, never relinquished the hope of being returned to his native deserts. One day at Fort Sill, pointing to the west, he solemnly declared: "The sun rises and shines for a time, and then it goes down, sinks, and is lost. So it will be with the Indian. When I was a boy, my father told me that the Indians were as many as the leaves on the trees, and that in the north they had many horses and furs. I never saw them, but I know that if they were once there they have gone. The white man has taken all they had. It will be only a few years when the Indians will be heard of only in the books which the white man writes."

And thus ended the Indian Wars. The destroying sickle of empire had been sweeping westward from the Atlantic shores since 1620. Through more than 250 years the bravest and ablest of the aborigines had withstood it with brief might — the Delaware, the Mohawk, the Sioux, the Pawnee, and the Comanche — and then, one by one, had "fallen on sleep" or surrendered. Only the Apache, most irreconcilable of them all, survived and fought on. Meeting the Conquistador's steel in the sixteenth century, he was three generations a veteran in the days of Massasoit and his New England braves.

As he was the first to feel the white man's science, so also, he was last to succumb — he and his Desert Gods.

CHAPTER ELEVEN

RANCHMEN

OVER THE GREATER PART OF New Mexico it is possible in one only way to collect the land's scanty annuity — by grazing. Ages ago the Sky Powers determined that the domain should be a possession of ranchmen, and so denied formally most of it to agriculture, manufacturing, and the other pursuits of civilized men.

But grazing has unique problems and complications, and it has accordingly introduced a peculiar sequence of its own into the history, and has influenced the general direction of native culture. Leaving to one side the purely industrial developments of the last half century, one may say that the history of the country consists of the combat of man and his beasts with nature — and the magnitude of the adventure explains directly the caliber of the men who ventured. In certain limited localities human agency has materially altered conditions, ameliorating somewhat the harsh environment for the human species. But over the seventy-eight million acres which comprise the commonwealth such areas are few and far between, and the traveller may journey today for leagues on end, beholding landscape that has remained virtually unaltered since the Forgotten Peoples, and which for lack of all economic incentive promises to remain so.

It all settles down to what unaided nature will produce for man's needs, and the high, arid tableland approximately four hundred miles square must be taken exactly as it stands or not at all. By and large, the one possibility of utilizing it lies in harvesting the native plant life. And the harvesters must be grazing cattle, sheep, and goats.

Now, a plant grows not where it would, but where it must. Where it cannot maintain life, it simply dies and leaves the room empty. Consequently, this age-long battle with death on the desert and along its fringes has resulted in a striking amount of vacancy, where no entrant has appeared with sufficient adaptations to cope with the handicaps. Yet a great number of plant forms somehow manages to stay in the race, and the survival problem for humankind resolves itself into a quest among them for features which can be utilized by man and his domestic animals. Out of the three thousand varieties of plants known to occur within the state, some are poisonous — like the various loco weeds — to range stock; many are spiny — perhaps a majority of them, if one excepts the hundreds of grasses and the minor annuals which mature early and die, thus having no need for the protective devices of the hardy perennials — and only a few of them possess any economic significance. Yet if these are sufficiently abundant and are distributed advantageously so that some of them are available through all seasons of the year, grazing animals can manage to subsist. Successful ranching, therefore, is seen to be first of all a matter of food supply.

Back of the food supply is the rain — for there is no irrigating a ranch ten miles square. The necessary moisture must be free, and it must therefore come out of the sky. So it is not strange that in New Mexico when it rains, they say, "What fine weather!" Only the rancher can fully comprehend such benediction, for the farmer with his irrigation ditches is independent.

Towards the end of May, when the drouth has endured three long months, a come-by-chance shower fills the wells of his soul with rejoicing. Occurring outside the ordered scheme of the seasons, it is a pure gratuity. Violet-soft and violet-colored from the Sky God's *olla*, it comes across the horizon, descending like a curtain from the melting cloud base, washing down invisible dust from the atmosphere, tempering the strident, windy heat, bedimming the sun's aggressive stare. Subtly the very air enfolds the skin with the velvet of humidity, dissipating the harsh dryness from face and arms. Nostrils sniff joyously at the smell of raindrops sinking into desiccated pine boards; ears listen joyously to their wet lisping among the cottonwood leaves; eyes released from squinting, watch happily their minor ripples on the cattle tank's surface. Even the hand feels delight in their cool dripping at the eaves. And the Earth Mother, responding to the Sky Father's caress — as the Pueblo myth-makers discovered long ago — brings forth in her gratefulness a token of blossoms, grass, and crops.

But be the annual rain much or little, the range plants know well how to make the most of it. Nature is ever keen in cutting the garment to fit the cloth. The wild sunflower — to take a roadside example — will blossom and bear seed on a dwarfed stalk not two feet high;

yet the same plant along a moist arroyo grows into a giant herb ten or twelve feet tall.

But back of the food supply is also the soil, and back of that, the rock whence it came. Boulders are fractured from the parent ledge, roll down the talus slope, where freezing and thawing get in their work with increased effectiveness. Roots thrusting their fibers into crevices pry them continually wider, and finally rotting, form acids which assist in the decomposition. Descending waters carrying down to the valley floor the ever-decreasing fragments, leach from them excess potash, soda, and lime, and deposit them over the soil in a white crust — the alkali which is the bane of field crops. Feature number one is thus chemical.

Without remission the rock continues to disintegrate, finally losing its identity entirely in the surrounding earth. But the process is exhibited in all stages and acting upon all sorts of rocks. Hence the soil cover is nowhere uniform, and plant life must everywhere adapt itself to a crazy-quilt pattern. The rough stony slopes that connect mountain and plain are porous and well-drained, but contain too little nourishment for any vegetation but the utterly useless creosote bush. Likewise, the gravels of all degrees of fineness strewn by the summer torrents, furnish only the scantiest food for plants and absorb heat enough to sear all but the hardiest species. There occur, also, barren "desert pavements" — concentrations of innumerable pebbles which remain after wind erosion has carried away the embedding dust and gravel. Playas spread their surface of impervious clay where rain water collects in shallow sheets and remains until evaporation removes it. On these nothing at all grows. Another clay-like substance called *caliche,* or lime hardpan, occurs a foot or two below the surface in many localities and effectually closes progress to moisture and roots alike. Then the loams themselves — the good soils — combine silt, sand, and organic matter in ever-varying proportions, as color and texture indicate. Obviously conditions of plant life are infinitely varied.

Typical of the desert soils would be the Mohave series, which shows the characteristic dull red color so common in the New Mexico landscape. Developed from material washed out from neighboring mountains, and stained by minute quanities of the iron oxide, hematite, they lay originally in broad, sloping fans, but now are nearly level. In them much sharp, dark-colored gravel — the chippings of original igneous rocks — is intermixed, and through their deeper strata the flecks and spots of *caliche* become more and more numerous, until they form a sharply defined white layer. On account of the high water requirement and heavy texture, little or none of it can be brought under cultivation, although in spots it supports enough tobosa grass and mesquite to make fair grazing.

It is one of nature's ironies that the best soil of all is found on the forest floor, high among the spruces and aspens of the Canadian Zone, where it benefits neither agriculture nor grazing. The remainder must be taken as it comes, patches of good land lying among others that are poor or worthless. Naturally, the vegetation shows the effect of such diversity, and frequently it offers a direct clue to the kind of ground. For instance, on the western flank of the Floridas a limestone slope affords sustenance to abundant sotol, ocotillo, and considerable bunch grass, while a granite slope against which it is faulted down and separated only by a little wash, nourishes practically none of them, though it is markedly hospitable to barrel cacti. Viewing the country from a mountain top, even a careless observer is impressed by the tendency of native growths to form great colonies in a patchwork pattern over the whole panorama. From an outlier in the Burro Mountains, which stands on the exact border of the Upper and Lower Sonoran Zones, one may note, with the aid of good binoculars, a dark band of creosote many miles wide, which rises up against the desert slopes of the distant Tres Hermanas, and at the left of the prospect a band of red-earth dunes designated as Mohave soil, where only the mesquite grows. Nearer in lies a vast prairie on which is spread a buff carpet of tobosa grass in the sunshine, while at the border of the outwash slope sets in a giant tufted growth called beargrass (*Nolina*), which yields its right presently to the foothill species, piñon and juniper. Then a few miles in the rear, on the higher hills, begins the yellow pine belt. The margins of all the various plots are singularly sharp, which testifies to otherwise indistinguishable variations in the surface and in the rainfall.

On a still larger scale than the prospect which the eye can take in, the surface of the state itself is divided in the same way among plant societies. On a map prepared by agricultural experts at N.M. State there are shown great provinces into which the entire area is divided by the five grass "societies." The upper three-fourths of the state belongs to the famous blue grama society, the exceptions being only the highest mountain tops, a threadlike strip along the Rio Grande and the lower reaches of the Pecos. The southeastern section is occupied by the hairy grama society, and the southwestern, comprising a more or less desert region lying in the Lower Sonoran Zone between the Arizona line and the Rio Grande, is the habitat of the black grama society, which includes the well-known tobosa grass. Such, in brief, are the grass crops which the land yields for the benefit of man and his animals. There is no turf anywhere except along the Texas border.

There is, however, beside the grasses, another important source of provender described by the ranchman as *browse,* which includes the leaves and tender shoots of woody shrubs, vines, and trees, which with weeds and grasses comprise range vegetation. Where large trees, on account of too great aridity or coolness or alkalinity, cannot subsist, myriads of shrubs are able to thrive. On the western forest reservations more than one thousand varieties are found, and botanists list the desert plains, the bolson-basins, the lava-beds, the sand dunes, and the piñon formations of the Arizona-New Mexico region as favorite shrub habitats. A few species are poisonous and some are so unpalatable as to be grazed only under the pressure of starvation, but many of them are both palatable and nutritious. So the lowly shrub is to be regarded.

Considering that the difference between success and failure in ranching may consist in the utilization of a few varieties of humble bushes, it will not be amiss to take a cursory look at some of them. Nowhere else, indeed, shows up so sharply the importance of adapting an industry to its external limitations. When the country turns brown in a six months' drouth, they afford the slender fare by which man is able to turn the balance in his favor.

What are the essentials of a good browse? Ranchers agree that it must be first of all palatable and nutritious, and that it should be widely distributed and abundant on the range. It must have sufficient vigor and aggressiveness in its root system to withstand overgrazing and to reproduce itself. In addition, it becomes the more desirable if it is of a height within easy reach of livestock and free from burs and spines, which annoy grazing animals or impair their wool.

The species on which the range's carrying capacity depends must be in the fullest sense adapted to survive at all. They must be exceptionally drouth-resistant, and many of them are required to be tolerant of alkali. They are subjected to extreme variations of temperature, both annual and diurnal. Objects in the direct rays of the sun quickly heat up to high temperature, and then at evening cool suddenly and severely. The total quantity of heat is very great in the run of a year, which, while promoting rapid growth, makes for short life. Plants, moreover, must endure an intensity of light which is trying in the extreme, and with it, an excessively thin, dry air which causes evaporation to proceed at a rate which is elsewhere unparalleled. Unless fortified by some protective device, plants exposed to such conditions quickly sun-scald and lose their leaves on one side. Finally, the spring winds come to tussle with root and branch and to abrade the stem with blasts of cutting sand. And as a last touch of malice from an unsympathetic nature, there are the late frost bites. Thus, the more one reflects and observes, the more clearly he sees how narrow are the limits within which ranching is profitable, or, in fact, possible.

One of the conspicuous examples of a shrub that meets all the requirements of an effective friend of man is the mesquite *(Prosopis glandulosa)*. Common on many kinds of soil, it ranges in size from a tree twenty feet tall down to a spreading, aggressive shrub less than two feet in height. It is a typical Lower Sonoran plant, but within its temperature limits seems equally at home on flat gravel plains, on dry canyon slopes, or on rippled sand hills. Its adaptions consist of an armory of tapered thorns which are capable of piercing an automobile tire, a thin, lace-like foliage which slants its edges at the thirsty sun, and an underground development which exceeds that of any other known plant. Thirty feet below the surface the roots have been known to extend, and they furnish to the Mexicans the best fuel in the region, making a clear, intense flame and a clean bed of coals. Naturally, such a plant can defy drouth and overgrazing. In September and October it bears a sweet, pulpy bean pod from six to eight inches long, which is eagerly eaten by livestock of all kinds. It "greens out" early in the spring, and in drouth years when the grasses fail, offers its leaves and twigs for forage. As an afterthought it supplies the bees with the richest of nectar.

Another such shrub is the common sagebrush *(Artemisia tridentata)*, which is important because of its spread in abundant stand over immense stretches of accessible range land. Its twigs and persistent leaves are often a mainstay for sheep in the fall and winter, when other feed is not obtainable, and they sometimes acquire what the stockmen call a "sage hunger," when they will eat nothing else. In addition to being an open, scattered growth, it also possesses the advantage of an immense root system, which enables it to defy overgrazing and to bring up valuable mineral solutes from far beneath.

Then up among the junipers near the border line of the yellow pines, sets in the mountain mahogany *(Cercocarpus spp.),* favorite forage of deer. In parts of the Black Range, where they are numerous, its palatability is so great that they graze it to death, and it is a favorite browse also for sheep and goats. Though its twigs are cropped throughout the year, they seem for some reason more pleasant to the taste in winter than in summer, and to sheep more than to cattle. Yet the carrying capacity of a mountain mahogany range is figured at twenty or more head of cattle per section throughout the year, which makes an unusually high average.

While not everything is grist that comes to the mill of grazing herds of cattle and sheep, the variety of their forage is amazing, ranging as it does from the various grasses through herbage and weeds of many kinds to leaves and shoots of live oak, aspen, willow, hawthorn, grapevine, saltbush, and cactus. It is safe to assume that sooner or later every possibility of diet is explored to the extreme limit.

But when forage is assured the rancher's problem is still only at its beginning. Water supply here, as everywhere else in the arid country, is paramount. Only in the higher mountains can he be certain of ever-flowing streams, and so elsewhere he must depend upon damming up the flow of wet-weather streams, or upon excavated "tanks" and on expensive driven wells. Deep, cold springs are not a common form of nature's gratuity in the dry Southwest. Where such occur one may look for beads, obsidian arrowheads, and votive axes — symbols of man's immemorial gratitude. In every respect the relation between man and earth here is immediate, continuous, crucial.

While cattle must eat and drink, they must also have salt, and the salt hunger is linked with both food and water. Since this chemical is present in nearly all of the organs and fluids of an animal's body, it naturally forms an essential part of the food supply, and when withheld, it causes loss of appetite, restlessness, and a general falling off in condition. And because the proper distribution of it on the range goes a long way towards controlling the grazing and maintenance of the forage, the rancher devotes no little thought to the placing of his salt grounds. Their location is determined by a consideration of the watering places, the topography, the habits of stock, and the type of vegetation. Cattle when left to their own will naturally tend to congregate where forage is most accessible and most palatable, to the neglect of other areas. This results first in a spot on which vegetation has been trodden to death. Next, in the bare, friable soil cattle trails quickly form natural ditches, and by the end of the first rainy season, erosion and its attending denudation have got a start. So, to even up the matter — to draw them away from the waterholes and the bottomlands, and to increase the use of the lightly grazed slopes and benches — the stockman has recourse to the lure of salt. He is careful not to place it too near the drinking places, or much of the outlying browse will be wasted; and thus in the rainy season, or in the winter, when there is sufficient snow to satisfy the herd's normal water requirement, he cunningly removes the salt grounds to more remote portions of the range and encourages grazing beyond the usual walking-distance limit. Then there are areas which support for short periods of the year a growth such as the filaree (*Erodium*), which when green is very rich and succulent, but which matures early and shrivels. On them salt is put down and the animals are herded round it by the range riders. Instinct does the rest. And then, since springtime vegetation in the mountains develops progressively from valleys to summits, the lag being about a fortnight for each added thousand feet of elevation, salt is employed to lure the herds upwards into the zone of their summer range. And so, in short, the uniform utilization of feed over the entire range by the simple process of salting, is like the simple process of catching a trout — a matter of considerably more technique than at first appears. Sky and the seasons provide the annual pasturage, and man with his humble bait of salt teaches his beasts to make the most of it.

But there is also another device which has aided powerfully in the same business — the barbed wire. Indeed, within the last generation it has been more valuable to the rancher than his side-arms in the prevention of cattle rustling, and more helpful than salt in conserving the pasturage in any given section of his range. By stretching three tenuous strands along infrequent posts and staying them with yucca poles, he can close off at will by a thin partition any pasturage which he desires to protect. For such reasons the wire-cutting pliers have superseded the six-gun in the cowpuncher's standard equipment.

Then, in addition to grazing requirements, herds must breed so that there may be increase, and the "cow-drop" must be heavy or there will be no profit. And each animal must carry its owner's brand, or it is only a maverick, the property of the first who gets his iron upon it. Cattle must be protected from disease, from predatory animals — such as bears and mountain lions — and from thieves. When the great round-up comes, stock must be graded and separated as to age, weight, and quality.

Herding, breeding, salting, protecting — such are the homely occupations of the most popular figure in all fiction. The cowboy, shaded by a ten-gallon hat, his bowed legs hidden behind leather "chaps," his feet shod with sharp-heeled, quilted boots, is the premier American figure of romance. The motion pictures did not create a tradition — they merely decorated it. And yet, the shooting, drinking, and carousing of the "western" film and story are but incidentals to the men who by punching cows in the Southwest have earned an honored place in its sober economic history.

Looking back upon the storied past and looking round upon the prosaic present, one recognizes that the cowboy's primary concern has been, and still remains, animal husbandry, yet at divers times and in various places the essential outline has been blurred somewhat beneath crude intrusive details, and the peaceful herdsman's art has been spiced with such interesting side play as range wars, bronco-busting, and Indian fighting.

The truth is, very likely, that young men concerned strictly with the production of bigger and better beef cattle remained in the East, while those hungry for epic adventure came to the Southwest. The magnitude of the task here awaiting them explained the quality of the men who came, for the winning of the great arid spaces gave no invitation to weaklings. Before there was any aviation to call the adventurous, men with mettle of that sort regularly came out West to fight, to punch cows, and to seek their thrills on the free range. And it is no play on words to say that the history of the West would have been different without the Westerners — without the particular type of Westerners.

The "punchers" were men who lived dangerously, and prizes were only to those who dared. Among them aggressive courage counted more than all else. It counted more than truthfulness or honesty — though, in passing,

it must be said that honesty counted in the old West. Hence, the universal detestation of the cattle rustler and horse-thief. Professional gamblers, especially, cultivated a reputation for honesty, and in Silver City, when faro was legal, a gambler has been known to borrow at the bank a thousand dollars on his bare word. This, by the way, is not romantic fiction. I have it from the old gentleman who lent the money and made a business of doing so.

But if there had not been among those who came for adventure a fair sprinkling of those who were ruined by an excess of qualities in themselves virile and admirable, it would have been passing strange, and so, naturally, there were some in whom freedom degenerated into license, aggressiveness into aggression, and bravery into bravado. There were others whose skill with a six-gun beguiled them into a career of killing, and, inevitably, when there was "no law west of the Pecos," badly "wanted" men from all over the East gravitated to New Mexico and Arizona.

And when ranchmen's capital was invested in large amounts, and where it was well to be able to speak in the name of right in cases where the law was silent, such talents were sure of congenial employment; for the larger outfits had on call a retinue of "lawless resolutes," armed with Winchesters which, it was expected, they would not be timid in using. Accordingly, cow-punching was not seldom used as a false front for fighting and robbery.

For certain types of mind, when ordinary range pastimes began to pall and the routine excitement of poker and roulette could no longer stir a jaded imagination, it afforded some passing moments of happiness to shoot up a town or rob a train. Although such episodes were never so tiresomely frequent as the writers of wood-pulp fiction would lead one to believe, they nevertheless occurred.

Take, for instance, a story without blood-and-thunder embellishments which is still common property among the old-timers of Silver City.

In December of the year 1883 there was a train robbery on the Southern Pacific at a wayside station named Gage. The engineer was killed and the express car looted by masked robbers. The Wells-Fargo people vowed revenge. At that time there was a famous Sheriff Whitehill at Silver City. Nine years he had held office and then retired. Though no longer in office he was engaged by the company to get the criminals. The train crew could furnish just one clue. Back of the mask, one of the faces, they noted, was that of a Negro. And Negroes were few in the Southwest. A search of the ground revealed a newspaper caught from the wind by the thorns of a mesquite bush. It bore the name of a Silver City merchant. On being questioned, the merchant was able to recall wrapping it round a parcel for a cowboy cook from the L-C Ranch. Then among the hands on the great Lyons-Campbell domain, it was remembered that there had been such a one, George Washington, a Negro. Step number one! But Washington had left the country.

At Socorro he was found. Coming to the well to draw water, he was taken in swift surprise as the sheriff's persuader was pressed against his ribs. "You are the man who killed the engineer." The ruse worked. *"No! No! No!* Mr. Whitehill, it wasn't me. Mitch Lee killed the engineer."

Duped into believing that his partners were all in jail, the Negro made a full confession. The robbery was planned by Mitch Lee and was carried out by him with the aid of Frank Taggart, Kit Joy, and the cook. All belonged to the L-C outfit. Taggart was trailed over into Arizona and captured. Lee and Joy had also gone across the line and were found hiding out at a lonely ranch house along the Frisco River. When the man hunt ended, Mr. Whitehill's four desperadoes were locked safely inside the old adobe jail in Silver City.

While awaiting trial they were allowed to exercise in the jail yard. Dick Ware was guard. For some unholy reason his prisoners were obsessed with a desire to play under the gallows. There, where Dick Remine and "Parson" Young had recently come to the end of the rope, they would climb upon the scaffold and hold broad-jump contests. One morning Lee and Taggart got into an argument over the tracks and appealed to Ware to settle the matter. As the guard bent over, Lee leaped upon his neck and overpowered him, while Taggart took his gun and keys. Marching Ware ahead of them, they captured the night watchman, who was then asleep, and locked both men in a cell. Taking all guns from the jail office, they unlocked the other prisoners. One Mexican boy and one white boy went with them, while the others stayed behind.

At the Elephant Corral, a livery stable, they took horses — all the horses — and paraded down Main Street, shooting up the town as they rode with wild yells for the Pinos Altos Mountains. Only a short ride distant lay Cherry Canyon and the roughest kind of country, where pursuit would be difficult and capture more than improbable. One man watched them. He was driving a wagon, and quickly unhitching his horse, he followed them at a safe distance until sure of their intention. Then riding back to town, he informed the citizen's posse, which was already forming. But the robbers did not reach the mountains. It was on the rolling slopes near the location of the present cemetery that they made their stand.

The first to fall was George Washington, cleanly drilled between the eyes. Next a bullet took off the top of the Mexican's head. Lee and Taggart, seeing that flight was impossible, abandoned their horses and hid among the scrubby junipers. Joy was already lying in a shallow wash behind some bushes. Through a winter's day the shooting continued. Lee, shot through the abdomen, lay mortally wounded, and Taggart, with all his ammunition gone, at length surrendered. Joy, after killing a citizen named Joe Le Fur, escaped. The white boy surrendered. When the dead and wounded were loaded on a wagon to be brought to town, someone suggested a hanging. The suggestion was taken up with much alacrity. Instantly ropes appeared, and soon necks were inside nooses. The wagon was driven under a bough; it paused while the rope was thrown over. The wagon went on. Booted legs struggled a while in mid-air and then hung still. What Bret Harte called the "weak and foolish deed" was done. The outlaws had died with their boots on, and not ingloriously. It was a fine day's work. And it helped to establish a tradition.

The white boy, when captured, made no resistance. Innocently tendering his gun to the officers, he showed them that he had not fired a shot with it. Thus he beat the noose. It was not until later that they discovered that the mechanism had jammed on the first attempt!

But gun-fighting enough there was of kinds fairly considered legitimate, and no range rider who hankered for it needed to quit until he had his bellyful. There was, for example, the never-ending struggle between cattlemen and sheepmen, which was historically the oldest contention for such thin bounty as the land conceded. The cattle were comparative newcomers, for in Spanish times the preference had been by long odds in favor of their rivals. But sheep brought a lower return, and besides they ruined the pastures. A sheep's hoofs are sharp enough to cut the soil, and, moreover, a sheep's nose is pointed, and this makes it possible for a herd to crop the herbage not merely to the ground, but down into the ground and so kill the roots. It is no exaggeration to say that of two fields on a mountain side, one can tell at a distance of several miles the field in which sheep have been kept, for the denudation is so thoroughgoing as to change the color of the slope. Naturally, when sheepmen and cattlemen met there was war. And in a modified form it has lasted.

And when the herds of one brand were found using the waterholes that belonged to another, there also was war. Water was life, and life it still is. The most recent waterhole killing took place but a short time ago. Then there were the rustlers, whom to kill was an act of merit.

And perennially there was war between the large and small ranchers. Such in its origin and main outline was the Lincoln County War. But, unlike an ordinary range feud, it reached a magnitude sufficient to cause the intervention of the armed forces of the United States, and the President sent no less a person than General Lew Wallace to settle the trouble. And that brings us at once to Billy the Kid, New Mexico's best-known (God save the mark!) character.

About this personage a wealth of legend has grown up. Known in his brief lifetime of twenty-one years as the killer of twenty-one men, "not counting Mexicans and Indians," he has of late been whitewashed in a bestseller and erected into the hero of a motion picture. There has even been talk of raising a monument to him by public subscription, though for what reason is somewhat obscure, since Robin Hood traits seem to have been rare in his character. An old-time peace officer who knew him tells me with anger flaming in his clear blue eyes after fifty years, "Billy the Kid didn't have one redeeming feature."

Until lately Silver City was invested with the honor of being the scene of his first killing. Now some literal-minded investigator finds that he was merely imprisoned here for the inglorious theft of two shirts from a Chinaman. And when one night he tunnelled his way out of the little adobe jail, everybody was relieved to be rid of him and no pursuit was made.

But within a few years the boy, hardened by sundry daredevil experiences with Mexicans, Apaches, and the gambling fraternity, had developed into a formidable killer. If his marksmanship with a pistol was not superior to that of other dead shots, he had, as all bear witness, an exasperating, insolent coolness all his own, which never failed him in any proof of his skill.

Naturally, in such a struggle as the Lincoln County War, his services would be valuable. Indeed, it was a "starring vehicle" ready made for him; for whatever his value as a herder, his skill with firearms was indisputable, and so he was promptly signed up as a valued retainer by the Murphy-Dolan faction — the small owners' side.

Throughout the summer and early fall of 1877 he continued with them. Then, for some now unknown reason, he attached himself to the Tunstall-McSween side. But Mr. Tunstall, an English gentleman who seems to have had a uniquely humane influence over him, was killed in February of the next year by a party of the enemy. Among them was one said to have had the authority of a deputy sheriff, but it looked like cold murder, and the Kid vowed revenge. Herein lies the explanation of much that followed, for the range feud took on the aspect of a vendetta. The Kid went to work picking off one by one the men who had taken part in the killing. Matters went on from bad to worse. Then in July a Sheriff Turner, bringing warrants and accompanied by a posse of about forty men, laid siege to the McSween house at Lincoln, where the Kid and his band of seventeen men had barricaded themselves.

For three days a desultory fire was maintained between them and the posse entrenched in the Murphy-Dolan store. In the meantime, Colonel Dudley from Fort Stanton came riding up with infantry and artillery. Planting his guns in a depression between the belligerents, he threatened to bombard the side which first fired over the ground where he had posted his men. But by both parties the war was regarded as private, and the firing continued as before. The cannon remained silent and were ignored.

Even in its own time the foray did not remain unsung. The New York *Sun* in its Homeric account said:

During the fight, Mrs. McSween encouraged her wild garrison by playing inspiring songs on her piano and singing rousing battle songs, until the besieging party, getting the range of the piano from the sound, shot it to pieces with heavy rifles.

But the adornment is a bit too heroic for literal-minded Pat Garrett, who gives the unvarnished account in his *Authentic Life of Billy the Kid*. As he explains the matter, Turner had concealed a number of his sharpshooters in the hills overlooking the plaza, and from time to time their fifty-caliber bullets chanced to bring a discordant growl from the instrument.

The stronghold was surrounded, and about noon, as Garrett states, fire broke out. An adobe building burns slowly, but the defenders were without water and so it was only a question of time. By retreating to the extreme end of one of the wings, they were able to hold on until darkness. At this stage the defense rings like a page from the pen of Sir Walter Scott, or a strophe from the lips of an antique border minstrel. The fortress-like building, in flames now for several hours, afforded to the garrison but a single tenable room. Surrender was debated. Billy the Kid, who was then seventeen years old but the acknowledged chieftain, begrimed and bloody, standing with his back to the door, vowed to brain the first man that tried to escape. "Hold on," he said, "until the fire eats through and then we'll break through this door and take to the undergrowth on the Rio Bonito and from there to the hills." Their case was desperate. The arroyo lay fifty yards distant.

At ten o'clock, by the wavering light of the flames, they came boiling out. Instantly McSween fell dead. Nine bullets had found him. The Kid made his escape through the hail into darkness. Five dead men failed to follow him. Here or nowhere is the stern stuff in which ballads and epics are rooted.

In addition to the war between owners of sheep and of cattle and between owners of large herds and small, there was continually an informal war between ranchmen and rustlers. The rustlers had all the romance on their side. They were an adventurous breed of parasites peculiar to the great open spaces of the West. It is everywhere easier to steal than to produce, and in the thinly populated Southwest, where hideouts were available in every range of hills, cattle stealing became naturally a profitable and agreeable, if highly hazardous, occupation. The racket attracted the talents of various kinds, but as the penalty for detection and capture was regularly death at the end of a rope, it remained an occupation for desperadoes, both American and Mexican, in which fleet ponies and aptness with a Colt's forty-five six-gun were primary qualifications.

A box canyon whose slopes were capped with vertical rimrock, where stolen stock could be corralled, with some evergreen oaks for concealment, a spring that gave a little water grudgingly into a stony pool, and a cave—these were the accepted properties of an outlaw stronghold; and if one may judge by the number of secluded Rustler Canyons on the map, they were regularly utilized. Such a cave, closed in at the front with a rude attempt at a wall, was discovered not long ago in the bare Santa Rita Mountains. Two broken stirrups and a rusted spur of Spanish pattern lying on the floor told no tales. A vastly more formidable robber hangout is the breath-taking gorge known as Black Jack's Canyon across the Arizona line not far from Clifton. From this wild rendezvous Black Jack and his famous band of outlaws rode forth to terrorize ranches and settlements in both states; between its walls some eighty years ago he was finally killed, and a spring in its recesses is still called by his name. In such haunts the gangs lived well, no doubt, like Robin Hood's merry men in Sherwood Forest, and rode as free and idle as the idle white clouds that drifted across the strip of sky above their heads.

In a free-and-easy time they had their day, for the loosely owned cattle wandered at will, the ranges were unfenced, and the only token of an animal's ownership was its brand—a token that could often by the mere application of a rustler's iron be disguised beyond identification. Thus when accurate property lines could nowhere be determined, and where no cross fences prevented stock from being driven entirely out of the locality, and when in reality as well as in metaphor "there was no law west of the Pecos," the rustlers had their brief heyday; and the gangs of armed, free-riding, hard-drinking marauders — along with the Apaches — made New Mexico, as Emerson Hough said, "as dangerous a country as ever lay out of doors." The rustler was very often a good cowboy gone wrong, whose preferences ran to shooting and depredation instead of the more regular and laborious occupations of roping and branding; and it was to this kind of life that Billy the Kid quite naturally gravitated after his escape from the three-day fight at the McSween house.

After that occasion he was too deeply immersed in blood for peaceful pursuits. Although invested among the lower classes with something of a hero's reputation, he was thenceforth recognized by the more responsible elements of the community as a desperado outside the protection of the law. His life, as he well knew, was nowhere safe, and when amnesty was offered him by General Wallace, he, like a modern gangster, dared not lay down his arms. Instead, he took to rustling, and all elements of chivalry disappeared from the brief remainder of his history, for he was no longer a figure of romance but a cattle thief. So the sheriff's steady harassment was merely the impersonal exertion of a frontier society in ridding itself of an annoyance that was already becoming outmoded. For a time the Kid and others of his kind terrorized the West and forced upon cattlemen the choice between the law of the six-shooter and law of the other kind, but the handwriting was already visible upon the wall, for an organized community could not indefinitely tolerate murder and rapine. Economics determined the issue, since in places where it requires the sternest effort to make a living, theft is not easily overlooked. Like the water supply and the presence of predatory animals, the rustler constituted for a time a serious problem in the security of the herds; but since there was no satisfactory adjustment possible with him alive and free, the hunt went relentlessly on until he was dead or behind prison bars.

But long after the disappearance of the old Wild West, the prosaic statistics on homicide prove the effect of early schooling in lawlessness. Although here no racketeers help to swell the totals, neighbor still shoots neighbor on small provocation at waterhole or in rowdy dance hall.

Now the

> . . . old, unhappy, far-off things
> And battles long ago

have passed into history, and a new era of barbed wire has consigned the rustler to posthumous fame in the motion-picture pantheon. Billy the Kid, most reckless and most feared of them all, came to his end in Pete Maxwell's bedroom on a night in July, 1881. In his right hand he held a revolver and in his left a butcher knife. Seeing Pat Garrett's crouching form in the semi-darkness, he demanded in Spanish, *"¿Quién es?"* (Who is it?) For once he did not shoot first and inquire afterwards. The sheriff fired—at a distance of six feet. A few seconds later the most dangerous man of his time was a corpse. "He never spoke," writes the man who had once been his friend. "A struggle or two and a little strangling sound as he gasped for breath, and the Kid was with his many victims." He was a few months past twenty-one. But the notches on his gun were many.

It is more than eighty years since that night. What poison and the steel trap did for the lobo wolf, the high-power rifle is now engaged in doing for the cattle-killing bear. In the roughest of the mountains the lion-hunter's hounds trail their quarry still, though now really formidable marauders, both beasts and humans, grow increasingly rare.

But the ancient warfare with the Sky Powers goes on. It has been but a few years since they once again demonstrated their dread sway over the rain. Month after month passed without appreciable precipitation. In a sky of brass a pitiless sun sucked out the life-preserving moisture from grass and herb alike, penetrating deep into the mantle of soil. Each afternoon the wind cruised over the ranges to gather any drop which the sun had overlooked. The thirsty cattle congregated down in the narrow draws until the last vestige of green was parched to a sere and deathly brown. Then they reeled away to die with desperate rolling eyes and outstretched tongue. On the thin, corrugated bodies, skin dried tight to ribs, and scarce enough picking remained to interest the buzzards. In this way passed not one season, but three, five, and — as they reckon it in different localities — even seven. And in 1922 and 1924 the deficiency was the more sorely felt because it occurred in August, which is the peak of the growing season. During the time many starving herds were shipped to pastures down in Old Mexico.

And when the rains came again, the pastures were ruined — overgrazed and trodden to death. Where vegetation had spread a protecting carpet over the loose, powdery soil, binding it fast with myriads of tiny roots, the brown, dusty surface lay bare to the ferocious sweep of the March wind and the August flood. In the deep cattle trails erosion quickly began its ruin and spread its devastation backward up the slopes. Such fertility as was native to the earth became impoverished with the failure of the annual crop of replenishing organic matter — decaying roots, stems, and leaves. And with the increase of denuded surface, by an inevitable progression, the water requirement rose, for the run-off increased with each new channel eroded. Inimical weeds came up in pastures where grasses had been killed. And the evidence of those bitter seasons can still be traced here and there in the shortened joints of the cholla cactus, which record not only the age but the amount of annual sustenance of the plant. . . . By the year 1925, or thereabouts, the ranches of New Mexico had been taken over by the banks, and the banks in turn had been taken over by the receivers. At one time all but one or two in the lower part of the state had closed their doors.

And everywhere in the corners of the wire fence and at the bottom of the draws lay bleaching a sinister and arresting number of dry bones — ribs, vertebrae, and heads of disintegrating steers. I know a mountain cabin ornamented with these souvenirs — thirty-two of them, bone-white, triangular, and horned — which for the sake of record I carefully photographed. A stranger coming up the trail as the young moon strikes them with spectral radiance feels the decoration, I confess, *macabre* and in poor taste.

Such seven-year drouths with their concomitant evils explain the fact that in localities where formerly there were thousands of cattle, there are today only hundreds. Very significantly, the same diminution holds for more than cattle. In riding through the country, one notes everywhere ruins which would seem to indicate that two or three generations ago land which is now almost uninhabited supported a considerable population. And observations of this kind when applied to prehistoric peoples have led some archaeologists to presume that a marked change has taken place in the climate. Occasionally the ruins of large villages are found in places where no adequate supply of water appears to exist today, and this circumstance — so they reason — is evidence that desiccation has occurred on a vast scale. Perhaps the chief of those who advance this theory is Professor Ellsworth Huntington of Yale.

Beginning at some undetermined time in antiquity, the encroachment of aridity is traceable, he thinks, down to the abandonment of Tabira (Gran Quivira). But running directly counter to the theory is the inescapable fact that the government weather records, which in many sections of New Mexico and Arizona reach back ninety years or more, furnish no evidence of such a process.

And Professor Huntington himself cites in his erudite study, *The Climatic Factor as Illustrated in Arid America* (p. 71), an interesting incident which appears to have more significance than he has realized. In 1904, he states, there was a destructive drouth in Animas Valley which caused the loss of about fifteen thousand cattle from the "Diamond A" herd of from forty thousand to fifty thousand. Now, an investigator at some time in the remote future, on discovering that the cattle dwindled within a generation or so from fifty thousand to a pathetic fraction of that number today, might be tempted to believe that he had here direct evidence of a striking diminution of rainfall. Yet actually, the decrease proves only that the range was badly overstocked, as in many other localities, and that the fact was unsuspected until it was tragically demonstrated by the occurrence of a severe drouth. Superficially, the decrease in the herds, the general denudation of the country with the resulting drying-up of springs and small watercourses, the supplanting of useful forage plants by worthless desert species, and other such matters, might seem to point toward a progressive desiccation. But the meteorological records kept at Lordsburg, Deming, and Douglas and adjacent stations set us right. It was perhaps overlooked by Professor Huntington that a land which has fared badly at the hand of man, whether red or white, loses in time much of its fertility, its vegetation, and its available water.

On the valley plain which lies to the south of Deming, further evidence seems to controvert the theory that numerous ruins and a decrease in population point clearly to a progressive desiccation. A recent soil survey published by the U. S. Department of Agriculture states that while almost all of the tract studied had formerly been homesteaded, a large part of it has been practically abandoned, and that at present only 3.5 per cent of it remains under cultivation. Yet, by 1910, as the records show, the climate at Deming was no more moist than now. And it must be added that the land did not then actually support the number of homesteaders indicated by the adobe ruins — it only tantalized them through some years and cruelly undeceived them. In ancient Egypt, the seven fat years aroused high hopes of prosperity, and encouraged, we may assume, much over-expansion in the more arid localities, but the seven lean years devoured the surplus and left the country about where it had been before, and the arid localities reverted — with their ruins — to their original barrenness. Such may well have been the case with many of the unfavorably situated villages in the pre-history of the Southwest. Probably many of them were occupied only through a series of favorable years, and then ruthlessly extinguished by the irregular desert rhythm of drouth and rain. Whatever the truth may at length be found to be, one can far more readily find parallels for long-drawn pulsations in the climate of the Southwest than for its relentless, progressive desiccation.

And there is a further analogy between the deci-
mated number of cattle and the number of detached and
scattered ruins — as distinguished from the fortress-like
pueblos — which suggests the easy probability of some
deceptive conclusions about population. To say that because the remains of a large civilized village indicate a
large civilized population on the spot the same must be
true of Indians, is to ignore the fact that agricultural
savages, unacquainted with adequate means of maintaining the soil's native fertility, could sojourn upon it for
only a limited time without exhausting its strength. And
the leaner the soil, the sooner removal would become
unavoidable. So migrant aborigines, like early ranchers,
tarried only long enough to skim the land's cream, and as
barrenness threatened, emigrated to some virgin locality.

And such removals must have been made readily, for
to savages with nothing but time on their hands, the
erection of a few crude rock shelters could have been no
formidable task. Wherever a parcel of moist ground and
a trickle of water were obtainable, a vagrant band might
settle for a few seasons and then shortly, because all the
land lay free before them with new promise, abandon
their domiciles, and again move on — like other squat-
ters. And perhaps many of the smaller, scattered ruins,
which so intrigue archaeologists, mark the site of only
mere hunting camps at most.

Furthermore, it has been ingeniously suggested by
Sauer and Brand that the aborigines may sometimes have
had *two* sets of habitations — one home on the forested
slopes for the sake of fuel and game, and another out
upon the treeless lowlands occupied only during the
crop season.

Yet when all is said a turn of the tide has set in. It
happens in this way. While in past centuries, clear from

the days of the prehistoric cliff dwellers, climate has counted more than man and has thwarted his puny strivings and stunted and impoverished him, latterly a resolute, marching breed, reinforced with the earth-conquering tools of civilization, weighs down the balance now on the human side. They have brought to the arid spaces steam power and the iron horse, giant powder and machinery, and still more recently, two other powerful slaves, gasoline and electricity. Perhaps more irresistible than all is the capital which they have set to work; and, finally, what none before them possessed, they own the unconquerable and saving grace of industry.

In general their work has consisted in undoing, wherever possible, the immemorial malice of the rain deities. The well-driller, far more than the Indian shaman, is a priest of the life-giving Element, and each churn drill that bites its way down through the gravels to the water-bearing rocks helps to loosen by a little the tyranny of aridity. Each windpump straddling a three-hundred-foot pipe filled with water adds to the amount available for the herds. As long as cattle were dependent upon surface resources alone, immense tracts were next to useless, for a steer will graze only a few miles from water; but when deep borings brought up an abundance of drink over the several sections of the range, forage in the most remote valley could be utilized.

Such a well costs one thousand dollars, but with its dark ring of verdure — where living water flows down an iron pipe to plash into an earthen "tank" or pool, in which fleets of stray willow leaves cruise idly among islands of floating moss; where wasps and butterflies come to settle transiently on the boundary mud, while high above, the great bladed wheel sings in the breeze with the rusty accents customary for windmills — it seems worth a million to one who comes out of the glare and heat of the desert with parched mouth to its consoling, green benediction. . . .

To such a well, with empty kegs rolling and dancing in the Ford truck, we went down from our miner's shack in the foothills. Seven miles down a burning, sandy arroyo, fringed with a growth of grey rabbit brush, we went, until it lost itself on the oven-like plain among shimmering, mocking mirages. Red dust-whirls sped like frightened jack rabbits in front of us, but nowhere else was there motion of leaf or wing. Drawing up at length after the long descent, we stopped before a brown adobe standing on what the botanist Wooton described, graphically, as "a sun-blistered flat, where bulls paw up pungent clouds of dust while they bellow challenges at each other. . . . Miles away through the quivering air danced the distorted outlines of cool, timbered mountains." Piling off the truck, we drank until stomachs were filled and mouths were moist once more, and then splashed cooling water turbulently over heads, hands, and arms. . . . Poignant thirstiness has a way of making itself remembered.

From a clump of apple trees near, a coolness ran out to meet us from the dark shade — which is not a poetic fancy, but a fact. And there among the boughs was such a congregation of birds as allowed us to see why there had been none on the flats behind us. Within a few minutes I had caught sight of a rare and beautiful Louisiana tanager, besides an Arizona hooded oriole and a pair of Rocky Mountain grosbeaks. Nowhere is life so abundant and so jubilant as at the water's edge in the desert.

This one munificent well was the direct means of reclaiming for man's use some thousands of acres. Though set in the midst of what could in no sense be called good grazing land, there was sufficient forage for a considerable herd, since it is astonishing what thin browse can be utilized by animals if only there be water within walking distance.

And the same munificence multiplied a thousandfold over the state has transformed the worthless uplands into grazing land. Elsewhere, wells of a different size and purpose are also forwarding the rancher's advantage by irrigating land for alfalfa, sorghum, and cotton to provide emergency rations in drouth periods, and winter feed for cows when the ranges are picked bare of every leaf but the yucca's. Cows thus fed, always do better and produce a larger calf crop in the spring; and moreover, as the massive bulls have to be kept in condition by the regular use of cottonseed meal and other supplementary rations, the general widening of irrigation counts at every turn towards the rancher's prosperity.

Though in moments of generous folly, one may pause to salute the two-gun badmen of the wild Old West, it was not they who guarded the herds and conquered the desert. Then, as now and always, the world's work in the main has been done by men of a different intention; and so to the traditional desperado and cattle rustler, mustachioed, redolent of whiskey, and disguised under a fictitious name, a newer generation has said "Adios!" The more literal saga recites the drilling of deep wells, the laying of steel trails, and the development of mines, with gun-play as only an occasional interlude. By such labors has been created the economic security by which alone modern civilized life becomes possible.

CHAPTER TWELVE

WELLS AND TRAILS

THE PRESENT ERA OF LIFE IN
the Southwest may be summed up in succinct words:
Sky determines the underground water supply, and deep
wells have made it available.

For untold centuries the high tablelands of New
Mexico continued unsuited to man's needs. As long as
the tyranny of the Sky Powers persisted, only a certain
type of specially adapted plants and animals could survive; the aborigines, avoiding the waterless wastes, concentrated in the valley confines; and the civilized men of
Spain and Mexico, while enabled to reap at the edges
of the land's scanty harvest by means of their herds, were
narrowly circumscribed both in their farming and ranching by the radius to a water supply. Sky determined.

But the same influences circumscribed also their
larger plans for expansion and development, since the
advancement of culture was conditioned by their ability
to procure the necessary commodities of civilization —

above all else, machinery. Yet the possession of tools was restricted by their cost when delivered beyond the desert, and by the desert-caused lack of purchasing power. Cost naturally rose with the tariff added by difficult transportation, and this on many articles equalled or exceeded the expense of manufacture — all of which indicates some of the inherently connected points of the vicious circle. Isolation, as we have constantly observed, and poverty go naturally together. Likewise long, roundabout trails, infrequent watering places, and retarded culture. For centuries communication waited upon the availability of water, and it may be rightly said that the later era did not begin until that dependence was broken, and water was taught to rise in dry places at the bidding of geology. The importance of this power to discover and command water was — the only adequate word is *phenomenal*.

When water supplies could be planted where needed, and connected by fast, safe trails, the essential desert factor was sufficiently modified to permit the complete utilization — in one sense, at least — of the land. While the humanizing element was water, the devices which made it available were wells.

But wells were inextricably associated with trails, and the two must be treated together. Without wells and springs at intervals, trails were impossible; and without trails, population would have continued to be anchored, as in prehistoric time, pretty closely to one spot.

The first of the great trails into New Mexico sums up all of the factors necessary for the promotion of both intellectual and commercial stagnation — length, difficulty, danger, and inefficiency. It was called El Camino Real — the Royal Highway — and on it the red and gold banners of Spain were a familiar sight long before Englishmen established themselves on the Massachusetts coast.

The way was blazed in 1581 by three friars with an escort on their mission to convert the northern "gentiles." Within a year or so a military party commanded by Espejo moved northward by the same route to rescue the valiant friars, but arrived too late. Another party marched up the Rio Grande not long afterwards to arrest an explorer, one De Sosa, but it was Oñate's expedition in 1598 which finally set the tides of traffic flowing in both directions. The cavalcade numbered 130 soldiers, but with their wives and children and the friars, the count was brought up to about 400 souls. The baggage train consisted of eighty-three carretas or ox-carts, and several thousand head of domestic animals were driven in the rear of the caravan. So after its dust had been churned by the passage of so many feet, the Trail could never again be lost.

Eighty years later came the refugees from Santa Fe streaming wearily southward after the Pueblo massacre and rebellion, and it was this mournful band which bestowed upon a waterless section of the road a name which has persisted — *Jornada del Muerto* (Dead Man's Journey). At the Pass of the North the exiles halted, and there Governor Otermín set up his headquarters; and thus El Paso became the capital of New Mexico a century and a half before the Lone Star State arose to claim possession of the famous crossing. A decade later De Vargas, by the same Trail, made his grand *entrada,* which fixed for all subsequent history the white man's yoke upon red shoulders.

After that the processional plying up and down between the southland and the northernmost frontier must have changed but little. A proud new governor coming up with his retinue on Spanish barb horses, all armed with swords from old Toledo, all clad in silks and velvets, all riding in heavy, high-backed saddles with silver trimmings — he could create a stir; yet the long succession of governors must have been rather uniform. And always there were soldiers — footmen, swaggering dragoons, booted and spurred, and high-bred *caballeros,* the aristocracy of their time, insolent with pride of race and the profession of arms. And among them moved the brown Franciscans, receiving always the veneration accorded to the Catholic priesthood. Thither passed also the daredevil *vaqueros* herding their Spanish longhorn cattle down to the southern markets; and rarely, at first, but more frequently as years lengthened into decades, the traders, whose crawling caravans became increasingly necessary with the growth of population.

The Camino entered the province at El Paso del Norte, where stood the Guadalupe Mission — for with sure prescience the Fathers had seen that there where the river flows through a gap in the mountain chains a city must some day stand, and had accordingly raised their cross and hung their bell. Ascending, it ran along the right bank of the Rio Grande past the savage, granite pinnacles of the Organ Range and the lesser Sierra de las Uvas (Mountain of the Grapes), opposite which sets in the Jornada, where tragedy and suffering lay wait. The misery which nature's ferocity could exact from flesh and blood in the thirst-tortured caravans plodding with weary steps along that ninety-mile desolation may best be painted by imagination.

Nowadays traffic rolls smoothly on the opposite bank of the river, and the traveller's gaze prefers to rest upon the blue Elephant Butte Lake instead of the Jornada, with its memories. The tawny expanse is but little altered, doubtless, since the old road was abandoned in the middle of the last century, but the course is marked in places today by a strip of mesquite. The seed pods were dropped from emigrant wagons long ago — reminders of scant desert fare.

Beyond the Jornada lay the ancient village of Socorro, where life-saving provisions had been furnished once to Oñate's colonists. On the right hand rose the Manzano ridges, which continued to Albuquerque. There where the valley is wide and agreeable and the cottonwoods offer grateful coolness, the travellers refreshed themselves. Continuing northward along the flank of the bare, though imposing, Sandias, they labored up the many-winding ascent of La Bajada to the basaltic capping of the mesa eight hundred feet in the air. After more weary miles across its wind-swept plain, they came at last within view of the majestic, cloud-haunted Sangre de Cristos, titans of the true Rockies, whose sides are not barren but green, and in whose cedared foothills nestled the Village of the Holy Faith. From Vera Cruz on the sea to Santa Fe beyond the desert — two thousand miles!

Yet it was not distance alone that retarded commerce. Other trade routes have been as long. But, in the first place, hides and wool were not commodities of the sort to make exchange profitable. In fact, nothing but the production of compact and costly articles like spices, silk, drugs, and precious stones, as in parts of the Orient, could have made so laborious a commerce profitable to both parties, and such commodities New Mexico did not produce. Then there was the peril of the journey. The desert never ceased to be a threat. Then there was the blistering heat of the wastes. There were dust storms. There were rattlesnakes. And for the caravans that trudged so slowly there were no supply stations to prevent the possibility of running out of food and water between stops. Indeed, along the modern motor highway there was a stretch of sixty miles which, until recently, boasted of one house — and only one. Furthermore, there were neither bridges over difficult arroyos nor cuts to relieve the steepness of mountain grades. Finally, from the Pass north almost to the end of the journey, the route lay in territory that was harried by Apache savages.

Imposed upon the other handicaps was the very uneconomical method of transportation. Goods were carried either in the *carreta* or on the backs of animals. The *carreta,* an enormously cumbersome ox-cart, was essentially a platform mounted on two thick, low wheels sawed from a tree trunk. A railing of saplings helped to retain the cargo in place, and the clumsy, unsprung vehicle was drawn at a snail's pace by one or more pairs of oxen bending under a heavy yoke. Until a comparatively late period, the only alternative was the packsaddle. Now, a sturdy, well-fed pack mule will carry a load of about 250 pounds over rough country, twelve or fifteen miles a day. An animal accustomed to grain is stronger than one fed on grass, but it jades quickly where grain is not available; and steel shoes are an advantage, but if they wear through and cannot be replaced, the hoof quickly becomes sore from use. Considering the various matters involved, it would probably be safe to infer that for the Spanish mules employed in freighting, two hundred pounds would be the maximum burden. But the smaller the load, the higher the cost. Commerce needed to roll smoothly upon wheels. Far to the northeast across the Great Plains the wheels were turning, but they were not of Spanish make.

About the end of the Spanish regime, there was coming into existence on the eastern side of North America the Iron Horse, servant of civilization, which was beginning to push westward, revolutionizing the old order as it came. The young giant whose name was known in southwestern rumor as the United States was beginning to create goods in a large way and to disseminate them to the four corners of the world. In the new age commodities were being produced and transported cheaply; so the possibilities of a market were therefore being explored in all lands. Hence it would have been surprising had the southwestern outlet been overlooked.

The fact not commonly emphasized by writers in their examination of the Santa Fe Trail is that, owing to its desert-caused isolation, New Mexico was — to borrow a metaphor from the weather map — an area of extremely low pressure commercially, and that goods from the outside tended naturally to flow thither with all the abandonment of a downhill sweep. "What a market!" sighed the St. Louis merchants, as they listened hungrily to Lieutenant Pike's recital and then turned to survey the prices which their wares commanded at home. Profits of several hundred per cent awaited them only a few hundred miles distant at the back of the plains. Such was the lure which underlay the effort, and such was the underlying reason for the amazing development of the Trail.

And the New Mexicans, having at length a favorable outlet for their goods, were able to buy what they needed. They were able to export the gold which they were panning in paying amounts at the placer deposits in the Ortiz Mountains and the silver which they were beginning to obtain from various small mines. And, although they themselves were not trappers, they obtained at Taos and other posts peltries from the "mountain men," who were trapping beaver in the region, and sold them in turn at a profit to the Missourians, since furs, not valuable in the tropics, were highly so at St. Louis. This was the heyday of the industry, when Mr. Astor's great corporation was gaining control of the fur market in New York and London — and before silk had displaced beaver in the manufacture of fine hats.

A two-thousand-mile haul could not compete with one eight hundred miles long, and New Mexico began to face no longer south, but east. The new Trail, which lay mostly upon green plains where the spring and autumn grass afforded forage for the mules, where water was almost always within safe reach, and where buffalo herds furnished food in abundance, effected the change within a few short years. Indian raids at Pawnee Rock and elsewhere were sharp and often tragic annoyances, but were no more able than shipwrecks at sea to disrupt commerce. The shortage of firewood along much of the way was a much more constant, if less dramatic, inconvenience. The early wagons used to carry bags for chips.

New developments in 1822 transformed the trickle of commerce into a flood. The year after the Mexicans gained their independence from Spain, William Becknell turned his back on the American frontier and set out for Santa Fe with an escort of twenty-one men to protect a pack train and *three wagons*. The Missouri mule had already made its debut in the Far West, but now for the first time it came in splendor, drawing wheels. Within a few years the sturdy Conestoga wagons were to be filing westward in great fleets, flaunting their white canvas tops over the green prairie like schooners at sea — prairie schooners, as they soon came to be called. In their capacious holds they were able to transport from one to three tons of goods; and powered by an eight-mule team, or by four or five yoke of oxen under the tender hand of a bull-whacker, they revolutionized — the word is not too strong — the frugalities of New Mexico living.

Becknell's three wagons and the pack train had ventured forth in 1822 with only five thousand dollars' worth of goods. But since the cargo of one of the wagons cost, it is reported, one hundred and fifty dollars and sold for seven hundred, the moral was plain. Consequently, in 1824 the spring caravan numbered twenty-five wagons and the value of the goods had increased 600 per cent. Even more gratifying was the value of the return cargo. The expedition carried back furs worth $10,000, and gold and silver to the value of $180,000. The effect of so favorable a balance of trade would be hard to overestimate.

It was the beginning of a vast expansion. New Mexico, so long deprived of creature comforts and the appliances of progress, responded to commerce as the desert responds to the summer rains. With the utmost graciousness the Mexican officials at once legalized the trade between the Missouri Valley and Santa Fe, doing all in their power to foster it. Their motive was two-fold: the modernization of the country and the filling of the exchequer. To them the trade was a godsend indeed, for the revenue of the province soon came to be derived almost exclusively from import duties. At first the tariff amounted to 15 or 20 per cent of the Missouri value of the goods, and rose presently to as high as 60 per cent. Still the goose continued to lay golden eggs. In 1839 Governor Armijo laid an arbitrary tax of $500 on each American wagon — which resulted naturally in the employment of the largest vehicles that could be brought over the mountains — and there were times, it is said, when the duty rose to a height equal to the value of the cargo. Still, buyer, seller, and officialdom all benefited.

Figures tell the story. An official report of 1804 showed that importations into New Mexico via Vera

Cruz amounted to $112,000, of which considerably more than half came from Europe. One-third came from the United States and the small remainder came from Asiatic ports. But the exports totalled only $60,000 — the old chronic cause of poverty. But in the era of overland commerce with the states, the amount of merchandise soared as follows:

Year	Amount	Wagons	Men
1824	$35,000	26	100
1825	65,000	37	130
1826	90,000	60	100
1828	150,000	100	200
1831	250,000	130	320
1843	450,000	230	350
and after the Mexican War			
1846	937,000	500	375

Of the total freight, American cotton goods made up approximately 50 per cent, and the remainder consisted of hardware, machinery, notions, and the myriad of articles which would be sold in a general store of that day.

The effect of the new Trail was shown in the sudden drop of prices in Santa Fe. When it was first opened, calico was selling at two or three dollars a *vara* (a measure three inches shorter than a yard). Soon the price dropped to about seventy cents, and on occasion considerably less. So naturally it was a red-letter day in Santa Fe when some villager raised the shout, "*Los carros! La entrada de los carros!*" which drew the population in a rush to the covered wagons assembled in the plaza before the Palace of the Governors. In holiday mood they all came out to surround the traders and inspect their wares — young, brown-faced boys in excited admiration; garrulous housewives, even under the somber black mantilla, inveterately coquettish; señoritas modest of demeanor but with roving eyes that missed no personable young man among the Americans; grave "Spanish" men with sideburns, wearing bright sashes and ornamented sombreros. And no wonder that all through the spring night the guitars were kept strumming the airs of the fandango! In the same caravan, commerce and carefree romance arrived hand in hand.

The freighter's charge on his cargo was ten or twelve cents a pound, and even so, the merchant's profit averaged from 20 to 40 per cent on a journey that required only two months for the westward haul and a month and a half for the return. So with a much lower initial cost on the Missouri River for goods that were themselves superior to those of the southern make, the American contest for the New Mexico market was no contest at all. From the day when Becknell's wagons halted before the old Palace on that day in 1822, the handwriting on the wall was visible. No supernatural gift of prophecy was necessary to foretell that the lot of New Mexico would henceforth lie not with the old decadent South, but with the young and virile East. The separation came, of course, by conquest. But it was in the cards, and probably would have come at some later time willingly and without the force of arms, brought on by the peaceful penetration of American citizens and American capital. Better to advance towards the national destiny in material comfort than to stagnate in desert-born privation.

The remaining thoroughfare was not, like the first two, a natural outgrowth from the exigencies of commerce, but a direct creation of the United States Post Office Department set up in order to provide an overland route for the California mails. The Butterfield Trail was the name it bore, and it ran from St. Louis to San Francisco.

For once the Sky Powers favored the desert. The route across the extreme southern section of the United States was chosen solely for the mild, dry winters of its mountain region, which would permit the regular all-year operation of the stagecoaches. The contract was awarded in 1857 to John Butterfield, William G. Fargo, later to become one of the founders of the famous Wells-Fargo Express Company, and some business associates.

Swift commercial development was foreseen. In his report for 1858 to the Postmaster General, the Superintendent of the western division of the Trail said: "Our line is already forming the basis of a new state, rich in minerals, half-way between Texas and California." The new state which he foresaw was then the Territory of New Mexico, which included the present Arizona with its immense copper mines, now the richest in the nation. The Texas *Almanac,* cited by L. R. Hafen in his *Overland Mail* (p. 107), spoke with the same enthusiasm:

We therefore assume that the establishment of this line must lead to the rapid and speedy development of the country throughout the entire distance, giving us within a very few years a continuous succession of farms, ranches, hotels and military posts, stage offices, etc., from one ocean to another. There can be no doubt that this is very soon destined to be the great overland, interoceanic thoroughfare of the nation. The immense amount of travel will soon make a railroad a measure of necessity.

A certain grandeur surrounded the Butterfield Trail as well in its epic difficulties as in its grandiose hopes. The scope of the project was such as to deter any but empire builders. The length of the Trail as given by the Post Office Department was 2,795 miles — practically the same as the width of the Atlantic in the latitude of the steamer lanes. And there were perils from Indians, perils from Mexicans, perils from white cutthroats and highwaymen, perils from sand storms, perils from hunger and thirst. The remarkable thing, as one looks back upon the enterprise, is not that the Company was able to make the runs reliably and on time, but that it was able to make them at all.

Entering New Mexico through the Pass of the North, where stood an adobe village, then called Franklin, the Trail ran northward along the east bank of the river to Mesilla, where it crossed the stream and struck out upon a red-earth desert of mesquite towards the great cool spring near Cook's Peak, where a few years later Fort Cummings was to be erected, and thence through the foothills in a westerly direction to the adobe station at Oldtown on the Rio Mimbres and towards Cow Springs beyond. Thence it took a course roughly followed today by the Southern Pacific railroad past the site on which Lordsburg now dozes in the sunshine, to Tucson, beyond which it reached the Gila River, which it followed to its junction with the Colorado at Fort Yuma. From the Rio Grande to Fort Yuma the route lay across the deserts of what was then Socorro County, N. M., which included an east-west trending band of territory some seven hundred miles long — a tidy administrative unit for the sheriff and his minions. Finally, winding through the California deserts, where wheels sank deep into the drifting sands, it reached Los Angeles, and ultimately San Francisco, its terminal.

The roadbed — at least through the long stretch from El Paso to Fort Yuma — being a Federal Aid Project, was constructed with the thoroughness of government highways. The engineer, Hutten, who had charge of the work, reported that he had improved the older road by smoothing out its surface and by reducing the grade; that camps had been spaced along the course so that the greatest distance between any two stops was but twenty-seven miles and, by his new survey, there was an increase of seventy miles within reach of running water. Furthermore, there was now no slope which could not be readily ascended by a six-mule team drawing a load of two tons. The proximity of Mexico may have suggested to Washington the need of a highway which could be utilized by army mules and wagons.

The Overland Trail was in effect the nearest thing of its time to a railroad. Its coaches carried passengers and mail, bringing to the country both population and communication. With roads on which goods could be freighted in huge three-ton Conestoga wagons, it was a far cry from the days of the primitive Mexican *carreta*. On fine stretches 165 miles could be traversed in twenty-four hours. Letter postage dropped to ten cents, and in a short time coaches were put on a daily schedule. Money was being sent into the country. Prospects for colonization and the development of the great mines seemed on the verge of fulfillment. A new era had arrived, so people thought.

More than 100 years have passed since the first Butterfield stage pulled into El Paso. It was late in the afternoon of September 30, 1858. Mr. R. P. Conkling, who recently explored the entire route, thus reconstructs the scene for the El Paso *Times:*

The watchers can now distinguish, through the sunset haze and golden dust cloud, the swaying stage wagon and the flashing yellow wheels with six great foam-flecked horses racing toward them over the desert road on a dead run. With crack of whip and blast of coach horn, it comes thundering on amidst shouts and waving of hats from the excited little populace. The driver stands on his brake, and with steady hands and strength of arm brings his team to a standstill. . . . Six of the station boys spring to the heads of the wheelers, swings and leaders, while six others begin loosing the traces to run them out. Not until now does the driver release the reins from his heavy-gloved hands, and climbs down from his high seat, retaining his whip with jealous care, while he shakes the dust from his broad-brimmed hat.

The mail coach stopped in front of the arches of a long, low adobe building on Overland Street. While passengers supped, the axles of the heavy coach were being greased and candles lighted in the side lamps.

Mr. Conkling continues:

Once more the bugle sounds. "Let 'em go, boys," comes the driver's crisp command. The boys leap back as the six fresh horses, with one great lunge spring away, the coach straining on its sturdy thorough-braces as it swings through the thick dust of what is now El Paso Street, at a wild pace past the rows of dimly lighted adobe houses. The populace of Franklin cheers and shouts and waves farewell as the swift-moving mail turns on San Francisco Street, heading for the Pass.

Overland Street. . . . San Francisco Street — romance still broods upon the names. But ominous rumors were in the air. Within three years the Civil War put an end to the vast economic possibilities of the Trail. The reverses suffered then retarded the opening up of New Mexico by a generation. Mail, for instance, which was destined for California had to be sent all the way back to St. Joseph, Missouri, and thence by stagecoach around by way of Salt Lake City. As things turned out, the great Trail was only a brilliant might-have-been, an immense frustration. It was not until full thirty years later when the steel rails of the Southern Pacific Railroad were laid along its route that the brave hopes of the Old Butterfield Trail achieved fruition. But by that time the parade had gone down the other street, and the tides of history had gone pouring westward across the continent far to the north.

Today only a few crumbling adobe walls remain on which a memorial tablet can be fixed — walls of the old stations where weary travellers refreshed themselves with food and potations of whisky, safe overnight from Indians and white renegades; walls of old-time corrals into which sweat-crusted animals were turned after the day's run for protection against nocturnal horse thieves.

One other link the Southwest had with the Missouri Valley before the steel rails bound them together permanently — the telegraph. A military line was strung westward from Fort Leavenworth across the plains and reached New Mexico in 1869. Although not commercial and intended only for the transmission of intelligence regarding troop movements, it played no minor part in making the country safe.

To the red men the talking wires were completely an enigma. There is a famous painting by Farny which depicts an incident that could not have been uncommon. In the snowy twilight a forlorn Indian scout is standing with his ear against a telegraph pole, listening to its singing vibration. Two gaunt ponies are seen in the distance, and a bleached buffalo skull lies at his side — symbol of the setting sun of his people.

Sometimes the savages made the strangest use of the telegraph poles. Once, according to an old friend of mine who recently died in his ninety-ninth year, a twenty-five-wagon train set out from Fort Leavenworth over the Santa Fe Trail for Fort Union, New Mexico.

He was one of the muleskinners, presiding over a big Conestoga drawn by six animals. A certain Henry Farmer was wagon master and a man named Carpenter was herder for the outfit.

One afternoon a war party of Sioux, ranging southward, surprised the caravan as it trailed westward along the banks of the Arkansas River. Instantly, in the approved plains tactics, the wagons were corralled — drawn into a close circle — the mules unhitched and tied down. Each man with a rifle was stationed at the end of his wagon to await the onslaught. The Indians, having only bows and arrows, dared not assault the wagon fort, but contented themselves with cutting off Carpenter and the extra mules. Him they tied to a telegraph pole just out of rifle range, but in plain sight of his companions. Then riding past on their ponies at full speed, they shot the unhappy man full of feathered arrows. At first he called frantically for help from his comrades, but the iron-nerved wagon-master forbade anyone under penalty of death to venture forth. Carpenter could not be rescued by a small band, and the loss of a large one would imperil the safety of all supplies and every life. So the torture went on.

Next morning on the empty Kansas plains there was nowhere the silhouette of a single pony nor the glint of a single war bonnet. Silently they loosed the stark body and laid it in a shallow grave. Pulling out a Sioux arrow, they sent it to Washington — taps, as it were, for an unsung freighter who gave his life in the line of duty.

The first great trails had Santa Fe as terminal; but on the later ones New Mexico was merely a wayside station — an important distinction. Transcontinental traffic had no time to waste in detouring for water, and where water did not exist already along the main line, imperious need required that it be brought up at whatever cost from underground. So geology, an extraordinarily important servant in New Mexico, at length enters the picture. With the aid of a few hundred wagons and stagecoaches, American enterprise had modified the standard of living in New Mexico; with the tools of industry, power-driven and directed by scientific knowledge, it was now ready to go ahead and modify the environment itself.

The railroads came at last. Since 1850 the shining dream had stirred imaginations. Surveyors had explored five feasible routes for the westward-pressing commerce and had been unanimous in saying that for all-year traffic, the southernmost along the Border was best. Then the famous Gadsden Purchase had been made in 1853 to acquire a right-of-way that would lie exclusively on American soil. But the Civil War had intervened.

When the project was again taken seriously in hand, the Union Pacific had already connected East and West and captured the commercial lead. Fortunately, there was more than one path to empire. The second was to run across New Mexico. And when at last it came, the throwing open of communications with the outside affected the country as no other event had ever done. After waiting two and a half centuries, development of the towns, mines, and ranches came to pass, and with this fruition the population increased within some thirty years by as much as 400 per cent. The advance had taken New Mexico at last beyond the control of the Sky Powers.

It has now been many years since Albuquerque commemorated the fiftieth anniversary of the coming of the Santa Fe. The great railway system's name suggests that in its humble origin it aimed at nothing more ambitious than the linking of two Kansas towns, Atchison and Topeka, but that later, becoming inspired with visions of a destiny, it sublimely added the two eloquent words, *Santa Fe*.

As years passed it kept on growing at both ends, consolidating, pushing its terminals wider and wider apart until it spanned the continent from the Great Lakes to the Pacific — from the second city in the New World to the immature giant which sprawls across southern California. But still the great system clings to its brief familiar name — the name it takes from a New Mexico village which it does not even enter. And is not this one more tribute to the unique place that still affects imagination beyond all reason?

Following closely the course of the great Trail along the Arkansas River, the railroad crossed the Kansas plains and came up against the Rocky Mountains. From their ponies the Indians watched the iron monster that was to put a period to the possession of their ancestral buffalo ranges. Day by day the construction crews — Irish and Mexicans predominating — swarmed over the westward-stretching grade, laying the ties, spiking down the rails, and stringing the telegraph wires. All day the work trains went puffing busily back and forth, and then when evening came, the laborers reclined against a pile of ties and puffed cigarettes to the music of a Spanish guitar or played the American game of stud poker in the light of a camp fire.

End-o'-track advanced at an astonishing rate. Where it paused there sprang up a succession of what Stevenson called in a memorable phrase, "roaring, impromptu cities full of gold and lust and death." In one of them was a famous Boot Hill where they interred the badmen who met their end without the formality of undressing, and there repose some thirty men who thus died in their footwear. For several brief months track-end became literally what it was euphoniously named — Hell-on-wheels. But commerce, nonetheless, relentlessly pressed on apace.

Reaching the ramparts of the Rockies, the rails bent southward to the Raton Pass, which they traversed partly by means of many altitude-gaining curves and partly by means of a half-mile tunnel. The one hundred miles of track between the summit and Las Vegas, which had been founded as a way station on the old Trail, were completed in the spring and summer of 1879.

For some years preceding it had been the custom of New Mexico ranchmen to drive their herds to Newton, Kansas, the end of the railroad, and a little later to Fort Dodge, which in its turn became the shipping point. But now the Chisum Trail, worn deep by the cutting of innumerable hoofs, would be trodden no deeper. Henceforth the steers would be shipped by rail direct from New Mexico.

In 1880 the main line reached Albuquerque, missing Santa Fe by many miles. The first train consisted of an engine and one coach, and there was no regular passenger service until two months later, for in those days the important contribution of the railroad was not tourists and health seekers, but heavy freight.

Though change was now at hand, Albuquerque was still the sleepy Mexican town that had been drowsing beside the River for two centuries. An old photograph of somewhat later date shows a scene in the plaza, where a yoke of oxen are enjoying their siesta, and a diminutive street car, from which the mules have been unhitched, waits vainly for a fare. But when shipments of machinery began arriving, the somnolent natives became conscious of a world elsewhere.

The rolling stock on which modern progress rode into

New Mexico seems, after the lapse of over sixty years, archaic and somewhat absurd. The locomotive was still but an iron horse, low of silhouette, fitted with a high, box-like cab, a tall, funnel-shaped smokestack that rose from behind a cumbrous headlight, and only two pairs of driving wheels. Yet it served. And as an agent of transportation it surpassed the prairie schooner even more than that famous vehicle surpassed the pack train. The renowned *Jupiter* and the old "119," reconditioned some years ago for use in a motion-picture spectacle, represent the general type of engine; and resting on a siding in El Paso, the Southern Pacific still keeps another as a relic where it may receive daily salutes from the contemporary monsters which are its grandsons. The coaches were, of course, built of wood and, in keeping with prevailing ideas of beauty, painted a barn-red color.

Descending along the Rio Grande, the line got to San Marcial in October of the year 1880. Just at this time an agreement of the utmost importance was reached by the Santa Fe with the Southern Pacific, which meantime had been approaching New Mexico from the west coast. The two systems were to meet at Deming, and the Santa Fe trains were to run over leased rails to tidewater. The state at last had an outlet in both directions, and thus came the fulfillment of plans that antedated Gadsden Purchase days.

But the raw, crude energy of the American nation was by no means wearied, nor its appetite for development satiated. The Santa Fe, with the aid of the Frisco Line, created an Atlantic-Pacific Company and went ahead opening still another avenue to the ocean. Speeding the task of placing tie and rail, the track layers on the northern route crossed the Arizona line in July, 1881, having already proceeded two hundred miles from Albuquerque. Prodigious headway was made in those hectic months at the beginning of the 'eighties.

During the same period, construction of branch lines went on apace, for a great era of mining development began, and boom camps springing up in every valley began with boundless optimism to roar for immediate rail service. The rail officials were singularly sympathetic to these appeals, and during the decade a number of branches were built to connect mines with the main system. In 1881 a short one was built in Colfax County out to Blossburg, to provide coal for the company's locomotives; a similar one was built to Madrid in Santa Fe County, another in San Miguel County. A branch was built from Socorro to the immensely rich zinc and lead mines at Magdalena and later extended to Kelly, making a total extension of thirty miles. The great silver deposits at Lake Valley were tapped by the railroad in 1885, the year after the much longer branch had been built to those at Silver City. This last, the most important by all odds, was built from Deming, a distance of forty-seven miles. Later it sent off a spur to the immense copper deposits at Santa Rita, and the smaller iron, lead, and zinc mines in the vicinity of Hanover and Fierro, and another to the copper mines at Tyrone. Over it was shipped the heavy machinery for the stamp mills, smelters, and concentrators that were employed at the famous camps at Mogollon, Pinos Altos, Georgetown, Tyrone.

The impressive production of some of these now worked-out mines enables one to comprehend the place of the railroads in the development of New Mexico. Chloride Flat, a narrow thread of valley back of Silver City, is officially credited by government geologists with an output of about five million dollars worth of silver. Lake Valley, before its marvellously rich ore was exhausted, produced a like amount. Pinos Altos, primarily a gold camp seated accurately on the Continental Divide, has a score of deep shafts which enriched the Hearst family and others to the extent of several millions. Mogollon, which owns above all others the perfect setting for the old western mining town of fiction, yielded both precious metals in munificent quantity, and a stage driver told me that he once hauled out a single load valued at $80,000.

This camp, which is strung along a thin trickle of water at the bottom of a profound notch in the mountains, lies at the end of an eighty-mile haul from the railhead at Silver City. At the stamp mill which once crushed the ores there still lie fragments of massive machinery rusting in melancholy ruin, and high on the side of a windswept mountain there remain still in use some giant engines, which suggest the equipment of a city power plant. One traverses the old road today, grinding in low gear over the bare stone of its slopes beyond Glenwood, crawling at a snail's pace round its hairpin turns, nosing his car up a grade that rises a vertical half mile in topping out a canyon. (Like many other bad roads in the Southwest, this one has since been improved. Only trucks need to use low gear now.) Up this road every ponderous piece was hauled by horseflesh. Old photographs show one of the boilers drawn by a string of teams containing thirty horses. If labor of that herculean magnitude remained after the railroads came, one wonders what it must have been before.

With the advent of railroad transportation, mining promptly entered a new phase, and tasks that had been achieved formerly by the toil of hands were now expedited by steam power. At Santa Rita of the Copper the Spaniards had previously used peon labor and divided their unproductive effort between mining and the manning of their three-towered fort. And they had freighted their ore far down to Chihuahua. Later miners had attempted to do their own smelting, but now the crude little adobe furnaces, hidden among the hills, found themselves suddenly obsolete. Teamsters were suddenly without a job, as wagons gave place to freight cars.

The commercial effect of the railroads is well shown by the rise of silver production in Grant County. In a real sense it was the making of the district. Figures given by the U. S. Geological Survey show that in 1875 there were produced 181,450 ounces of the white metal. Six years later (1881) the total had increased to 213,179 ounces, and in 1882 to 329,457. Then in the spring of 1883 came the rails. In the same year production leaped to nearly one million ounces (930,232).

Silver City now sprang into sudden leadership among the surrounding camps, and before long a smelter was built at the end of the track so that ores which had been hauled in six-horse wagons through the mesquite to Deming could now be treated locally. Looking back after half a century, one can well understand why on that eventful day in May, 1883, when "Silver City and Deming clasped hands in sisterly love through the medium of the great civilizer," they called out the Fort Bayard military band and a company of artillery to fire a six-round salute in honor of the occasion. The orators of the day were a Judge Ginn and a Doctor Kennon, and one may imagine for himself the speaker's flag-draped stand and the pitcher of ice water. . . . It is a picture from an America that now belongs to history.

Silver City enjoyed hilarious prosperity in its dual capacity of mining center and cow town. Saddled ponies with hanging reins dozed on three legs under the cottonwoods while their owners spent silver dollars lavishly across the bar. Gamblers — who were then licensed by law — grew opulent on lucky strikes where they had lifted neither pick nor shovel; while the crude western village took a blatant pride in homes where the grand piano and the Italian harp were not unknown, and in citizens whose dignity required the wearing of a frock coat with their rakish Stetsons.

The connection which had always existed between the trails and the waters developed at the coming of the railroads into a still closer interdependence. The railroads needed water in quantity for their locomotives, of course; but they were concerned also about the economic progress of the country which their lines served. Since water was the *sine qua non* for agriculture and the growth of towns along their right-of-way, they naturally conducted the search for it with all the technical resources at their command.

At Gallup, for instance, the surface wells yielded water of inferior quality and in small quantity. But the geologists, knowing the underground structure of the land, advised deeper drilling. Explorations which penetrated through the coal-bearing rocks to the underlying standstones proved successful. Similar inferences have been rewarded in measure beyond all dreams of earlier water witches, who took their observations with peach-tree wands. In the light of geological science, catchment areas have been studied, and level, waterless plains, for example, have been found to be underlain by gravel strata through which abundant subterranean moisture percolates. Even bare sandhills have been found valuable for catchment, since rainfall sinks into them and is not afterwards drawn out by field crops and dissipated.

In particular, where a sloping porous stratum, such

as sand — with one end open to the rains — lies between two impervious strata of clay or rock, the force of gravity makes practicable an artesian well. The water, being under pressure and having no escape either above or below, must obviously ascend into any shaft which pierces the upper impervious stratum. Known since the twelfth century from a boring in the French province of Artois, from which the name is derived, the principle has been widely employed in the Rocky Mountain region in connection with the famous water-bearing Dakota sandstone. Sloping gently eastward underneath the Great Plains, it supplies wells in Colorado, Nebraska, and Kansas, and on the western slope, it extends across New Mexico to Gallup, near the Arizona line. In the Pecos Valley geological explorations were rewarded by the discovery of great supplies of artesian water in 1888. There, with Mr. Eddy, Sheriff Pat Garrett started an irrigation project that was to earn for him a finer gratitude than the killing of Billy the Kid. The venture was destined to have more importance than the opening of a gold mine, for other important developments soon took place near them. Two years later Roswell made discoveries that were shortly to produce wealth; and the roll of towns, Carlsbad, Artesia, Hagerman, Roswell, with Clovis and Portales not far away, shows the agricultural activity that presently resulted. Almost simultaneously came the railroad. The Pecos Valley and Northwestern, coming northward, reached Carlsbad in '91 and Roswell in '94.

Presently the San Juan Basin sprang into sudden prosperity, for there the largest artesian water supply in the state was waiting to be employed in the irrigation of orchards and farm crops. Then, stretching down from Durango to Farmington, came the Denver and Rio Grande in 1905.

Possibilities of development — apart from the ore deposits — depended upon water. Where the wells were few in any given locality, ranching held its sway; where they were many, agriculture superseded it; and where water was still more plentiful, the townsman supplanted both ranchman and farmer. In the Southwest, the world beats a path to the best well and — then settles down beside it.

When for some minor consideration — such as silver or gold — a community takes root in a spot and begins to multiply, the Sky Powers are likely to show their displeasure plainly. At Silver City, whose location was determined by mines instead of by wells, there has been felt ever since the handicap of a constant water shortage. Only a few years ago the authorities there paid ten thousand dollars for a single spring. (In the drouth year of 1946, Silver City suffered even worse than other municipalities of New Mexico. One of the newspapers there referred appropriately to "the annual and always unexpected water shortage." Current developments, however, promise to cure the long-standing trouble.)

Deming's history is different, but there, too, sky water counted. A story in the *Railway Age* for April, 1881, mentioned the intention of officials to place the town ten miles east of its present location. But at the point decided upon for the terminus no adequate water supply could be obtained for the engines; so the drillers tried again, not in the fertile loam of the Mimbres Valley, but among the red-earth dunes of a desert plain to the westward. There they found an abundance of what has been called "the best water on the entire Santa Fe system," which is 99.99 per cent pure. Such is the reason that the junction of the Southern Pacific with the Santa Fe occurs not among the fields of cotton and sorghum, but in the midst of a mesquite waste. And today Deming's most impressive sight is the twenty-nine windpumps that stand up to be counted on the south side of town.

And what private enterprise had already projected, federal aid was ready to carry through later. Thus the United States Reclamation Service entered the field; and in coöperation with the Geological Survey, which explores and maps the water resources, and the Forest Service, which conserves them, it has made a green oasis of the Hondo Valley, another of the Mimbres, and has fostered a far-reaching development of the Pecos at Carlsbad. At present the Middle Rio Grande Conservancy Project is spending millions of dollars near Albuquerque in draining "waterlogged" valley lands.

The whole matter of water production is thus taken seriously in New Mexico. The United States government prepares beautifully executed and highly detailed maps showing the level of the water table — i.e., the distance below the surface at which it stands in the wells

of a given area — and the location of known borings and their depth. Both data are essential, since one affords a guide to further explorations and the other determines the cost of gasoline or electric current employed in the lift to the surface. If the lift is too great, the expense of the pumping will be prohibitive to both farmer and ranchman. In the Deming area, for instance, agriculture is limited to land having water at a depth of seventy feet or less.

On the almost level plain which now marks the pre-historic course of the Rio Mimbres as it bends down towards the Mexican Border, the survey contains hundreds of red symbols, which indicate the volume of the supply, the gentle slope of the water table to the south-east, and even the dry holes which failed to yield good water. The great springs of the region have, of course, been well known for centuries, and to each the desert dwellers have beaten a wide path. Though widely scattered, they usually occur among the hills, while the wells avoid the rock outcrops altogether and are concentrated on the plains.

But while throughout the past, water supply has been associated with wells and springs, it tends nowadays to become associated more and more with rivers and reservoirs. And it is on the Rio Grande at the great Elephant Butte Dam, that the thoughtful observer is most impressed by the epic exertions of civilized man in the age-long combat with the Sky Powers, who at length are compelled by the mechanical forces of engineering to recognize that their opponents are not pygmies, but titans. Elsewhere there may be masses of masonry yet more monumental, but it would be impossible to find a place where the victory of intelligence over brute matter and its strength smites the imagination with sincerer awe than at the foot of a giant dam. Built from the wealth of a rich nation acting from Washington, it symbolizes the best in the conquerors.

Through the sluice, under the pressure of millions of tons of the green, imprisoned element behind it, comes spurting, as through the bore of a rifle, a tumbling white mass which resolves itself into a madly tumultuous spume. Two hundred feet above one's head, high in the quiet sunshine above the deafening roar, is the crest of the dam; a quarter of a mile away, braced in a socket of the opposite cliff, rests the end of it. Nearly forty miles upstream lies the beginning of the reservoir of impounded water — the largest artificial lake which engineering has yet created! (It has since been dethroned by the still greater Lake Mead at Hoover Dam.)

Behind the barrier lies what alone can extort fecundity from a grudging nature and constrain it to bring forth food for man and his beasts.

The famous four-fold increase in population that took place between the coming of the railroads and the granting of statehood in 1912, brings us well up towards the New Mexico of today. Many of the exuberant dreams of twenty years ago have failed of fulfillment, but it is fair to say that the flowing of waters and the readiness of communication have in a measure banished the former curses like isolation, backwardness, chronic poverty. The despot sky no longer determines — except within limits. Bringing with them the machinery that drilled and heaved, that ploughed and sawed, the advancing hosts of the last half century have loosed its tyranny.

Over the physical aspect of the land the modifications of the last fifty years will, many of them, be permanent. Yet such changes appear to be nearing an end. There will certainly rise no metropolitan cities across New Mexico.

About that the experience of the last four centuries leaves no doubt. The number of homestead cottages will, perhaps, increase somewhat in future years, and along horizons now unbroken a windpump here and there may lift up its solitary Water Symbol, but the mountains that billow starkly against the sunset will not change. The high, thin purity of the air will not change, and the holy sunshine will not change. And when the last *Americano* in the fulness of time follows the last Spaniard and the last red man into the shadows, this will still be the same poignantly unforgettable land of beauty, its arid mesas, canyons, and deserts lying perpetually beneath an ocean of pure light, and its Sky Gods still pouring frugally from their *ollas* the violet-soft rain.

CHAPTER THIRTEEN

TO NATURE,
FORMIDABLE GODDESS
(A pardoned digression)

NATURE STEADILY OBSERVED AND correctly interpreted is a formidable goddess, the august Fate ceaselessly spinning the thread of life which ever and anon she cuts with her inexorable shears. To speak of Mother Nature on a quiet Sunday morning in the woods is to employ a fallacy feebly devised by sentimentalists for the sentimental.

The universal scheme is ambiguous, capable of diverse interpretations, but it can scarcely be proved to be directed solely at justice, beauty or any other perfect fruition. The observable sequence, instead of being a perfect line of causality, seems often so far as unaided human reason can penetrate, unjust, unintelligible, frequently malignant—only at intervals purposeful. Below the human plane where is any compassion? Lion and lamb seem to exist in a frightening cross of purposes, the eternal predator and its prey, until one day both lie down, solitary and yet together, to merge quietly into one unclassified mold.

Our whirling globe actually is one mausoleum, and all its hosts now alive are under one immutable sentence—for presently all will lie down to fatten the humus out of which they arose. "Dust thou art and unto dust shalt. thou return," says the ancient sage. Dying and living are two sides of one coin, for the drama is so rigged that each organism which lives is trailed by its horde of specific enemies whose function is to keep the species in balance with its competition. For each there is so much room, so much food, and no more. Each living creature is followed in unrelenting, deadly pursuit, like a stag by the hounds, by its own train of appropriate enemies—the worm by the minnow, the frog by the heron, the mouse by the snake, the bear by the man, the man by another man with club or guided missile; or with still greater malignity by bacilli whose only function in the economy is to reduce all living tissue to the status of carrion.

Yet it is not all tragedy. Like a cryptic vision of heaven in the midst of a nightmare, the lonely searcher discovers everywhere in this dance of death an equal and opposed design for life. Aging leaves like snowflakes keep drifting down to thicken the blanket out of which new sperm, new generation, new birth arises in a renewed quota of creatures to continue the action everlastingly. And when the argument for chaos begins to seem unanswerable, there usually appears from the obscurity a still stronger argument for cosmos.

And rising lightward through the mold there become visible the green shoots of resurrection that were there all the while and what had seemed the triumph of death becomes recognizable as a drawn battle where the odds are more than a little in favor of life.

Nature is, above all, birth. Upon all her creatures she lays one imperious urge and injunction: "Increase and multiply." The species must reproduce to continue. Desire, the hot sweetness of pursuit and the climax of fulfillment are her lures, but her serious aim is generation, growth, maturity. It is noteworthy that in all her scheme no such thing as lust appears. Male and female she created, but the female's function was nowhere for the male's barren pleasure. She was to be fertile, and her motto was everlastingly, *Fero,* I bring forth.

So death forever coming downward is forever meeting life stretching upward into light. Where the battle seems a tie, it is the stubborn, instinctual heart that makes up its own odds. It is the heart alone, though endlessly refuted, which still brooks no contradiction and declares prophetically that nature in spite of each monstrous disguise is yet on the side of angels.

Natura naturans, the Formidable Goddess forever bringing life, sending death, ceaselessly working out her planned evolution of things, is also for some men the source and chief giver of delight; for in her manifold splendors of light and color, her wonders of design, motion, repose, they find an emotional release which not literature nor the arts, nor philosophy, nor any of the civilized distractions is able to bestow. For those men nature is relevant because delight is relevant. To members of the Brotherhood, life without the free prospect of field, sea or sky is an existence that lacks wholeness or even sanity.

In this age of the jittery two-ulcer man, Nature is

peculiarly the Restorer. Where else in a tired civilization can be found renewal that equals the primitive, beneficent contact of earth? Here in this respect Nature, the Goddess, neither malignant nor indulgent, seems most clearly inclined toward beneficence. Man on his human side is one of her creatures, closely bound with the rest of creation by an iron chain; for like Antaeus, the giant in the meaningful Greek myth, man was born out of Gaea the earth, and he is part of her. Once when Antaeus battled the mighty wrestler Hercules, he was downed many times; but at each fall as he lay against the earth taking the count, new strength was infused into him from his mother's body, and he sprang up refreshed, stronger than before. It was only when the thick-skulled, slow-thinking Hercules at length comprehended and held him high in a Graeco-Roman spin away from the earth that Antaeus grew impotent and died.

Perhaps it never happened at all—or perhaps it is always happening. And we the sons of Gaea still need, as he did, the feel of earth underneath us, the free firmament overhead, the enduring landscape before our eyes. And some of us feel a penalty when we are absent too long.

Into the inner brotherhood of naturalists I was initiated, as it is clear now, by an unforgettable experience that occurred in Illinois one hot June forenoon along a sluggish prairie creek when I was ten years old. The slow water crawled along the bottom of a deep trench, impeded by sedges and confined between banks which rendered it invisible except on near approach.

When I was almost on the bridge by which a lonely road spanned its current, there flew up, so close

that it seemed almost beneath me, a great bluish-white
bird. It was unlike anything I had ever seen on the
wing, and far, far more imposing. As it took heavily
to the air in surprise, moving away downstream with
slow wingbeats, its great pinions appearing almost sil-
vered in the sunshine, there came over me a breath-
stopping excitement and delight which can never be
erased from my memory. I kept my eyes fastened to the
unknown habitant of the prairies until it had completely disappeared.

A long time afterward I learned I had seen a great
blue heron. The mystery at length was explained away.
The emotion has remained. Two years later my log
book was begun. It continues still.

CHAPTER FOURTEEN

MAN DETERMINES

WHEN THIS TREATISE WAS ISSUED
from the Macmillan Press in 1934 it bore the same
subtitle as it has today: *An Interpretation of the Southwest,* which indicates its purpose and its intended scope.
Although the design has never been abandoned nor
even substantially altered, *Sky Determines* has assumed
more manageable proportions as a book primarily on
New Mexico, the author's adopted homeland.

But what is an interpretation? And what does an
interpreter do? First, he concentrates his study on explanation rather than on narration. He asks himself,
"Why did this affair turn out in just this way rather
than in another?" He considers first its history, then
the contemporary scene, tries to read portents of the
future, calculates trends, examines old failures, ponders
significances, summarizes, reflects, deduces—and finally
guesses.

The present writer's worst guesses made thirty years ago related to two facts which no man could then foresee: That sleepy little Albuquerque, swept along on the new, rapid, swelling tide of federal spending would develop into the state's one city of metropolitan size, a population already of a quarter million or more. Second was the detonation of a giant bomb here on the desert. The date was July 16, 1945, a decisive day not merely in the annals of a state but of mankind. The bomb's impact on the world's peacetime activity is but dimly foreseen after twenty years. Some other guesses less than perfect are deeply embedded in the text where I have left them on purpose.

Inevitably the two titles of the book have become firmly welded together, and now a third title, closely related yet of contrasted emphasis is being merged with them. The third title is, of course, inevitably "Man Determines." But this socio-economic inquiry turns out to be, actually, much simpler than might have been anticipated. A pundit would organize his material to demonstrate step by step how this forbidding semi-wasteland was developed within a single century into a suitable—nay, even a desirable—habitation for civilized man, where possibly with a little luck he could make a living. Well, how came it?

The pundit could perceive clearly that in each generation, each decade, there had been a more or less orderly maturing in wealth-producing activities in one industry after another, in ranching, in agriculture, in lumbering, in manufacturing, in the extractive industries such as the production of oil, gas, of copper, of uranium, potash and coal. He would be tempted to say at once, with confidence, that the one great earth-shaking modification in the Southwest had been achieved through modern industry. Commerce determines, for money is the *sine qua non* of all civilized society.

Yet oddly enough we have coming up in next chapter the testimony of Lawyer Barreiro to the effect that in the Spanish-Mexican regime many people in this remote colony had never seen money.

If we moderns could forget a moment that we are not the only moderns who ever had an hour upon the stage of history; and that farseeing men now alive, statesmen, scientists, philosophers, are constantly occupied with the problem of water shortage which could perhaps be no more than a generation or two ahead, then we should be compelled to see for ourselves that civilization floats upon a sea of clear, pure water. To hammer a moment on the obvious, any student must see that the ranching industry here could not develop fully until water was obtainable all over the range; that large-scale agriculture was impractical until reserve water could be impounded for several crop seasons ahead. In explaining the Southwest, facts like these are needful too.

And to carry the explanation still further a series of articles in the *Wall Street Journal* were addressed to the country's leading industrialists (April 12, 1965). To show them how much water is consumed in industry it is pointed out that for each person in the U.S. the farmers use 500 gallons of irrigation water each day; that to process a ton of oranges into juice requires 700 gallons of water; that to brew one gallon of beer takes 13 gallons of water. The *Journal* tosses off a few other facts: for each gallon of crude oil refined, 5 barrels of water have been used; that the most insatiable users of all are agriculture and industry; that it is precisely in

the states of the arid Southwest, including California—
where growth is taking place fastest—that the water
shortage is becoming most critical. The region's demand is outrunning the supply. The situation is becoming worse because more of the nation is progressively
involved. It is not because some alarmists have begun
to cry "Wolf." For more than a dozen years the farseeing Department of the Interior has been concerned,
and now it is the President's turn. He is looking at
Guantanamo. Then there are the water-short islands
of the sea.

Lest anyone should wrongfully infer that shortage
is confined to deserts the *Journal* informs its readers
that owing to a 44-month drouth in the Northeast the
residents of New York City are not being permitted to
fill their backyard wading pools except during a six-
hour period each week.

A few months afterward, *Time,* in order to burnish
the drouth with a still brighter shine, ran a current
photograph of the Delaware River. Across a wide level
of boulders, black and forbidding, walked a bare-legged
boy without wetting his feet. The picture was dated at
Pond Eddy, N.Y., July 16, 1965.

In the same article it was stated that in restaurants
New Yorkers could not get a glass of water unless they
specifically asked for it. On pain of fine, residents were
forbidden to water lawns or gardens. Fountains were no
longer turned on, and all along the Eastern Seaboard
suburban lawns and trees were parching.

In an attempt to nail down an explanation *Time*
offered the following: "Cause of all the trouble is a
meteorological phenomenon that began four years ago
and so far has given no sign of abating: a predominantly
dry air mass that is stuck over the northeastern U.S. Un-

der normal conditions, the prevailing winds that sweep from west to east across the U.S. at altitudes ranging from one to five miles fluctuate between downhill (northwest-southeast) and uphill (southwest-northeast) courses, which produce alternating dry and wet weather. On the uphill course the air rises, eventually cools off enough to produce condensation, clouds and rain. Just the opposite happens on the down hill cycle: air flowing from northwest to southeast moves lower as it reaches the east coast, becomes warmer, drier, and loses its rain-making potential. Since 1961 the downhill flow has persistently hugged the northeastern U.S., producing the prolonged dry spell. Why? There are theories but no firm answer."

In an interesting sideline *Time* adds: "The Hudson pours hundreds of millions of gallons of water a day past New York City, but no one has ever adequately dealt with the problem of tapping the polluted stream for public use."

Said President Johnson recently: "There is no newer or more vital frontier for any of us than the one we must cross to a lasting abundance of fresh water for all mankind."

Did someone say loudly just now that in the Southwest "Commerce Determined?" Or that "Man Determined?"

Well, partly, friend. Partly!

In the old West there used to be a homely saying when a sick man had at least one foot in the grave, "There ain't nothin' wrong with me that whiskey cain't cure." But today the civil engineer treating his ailing patient hereabouts prescribes *aqua pura* in large quantities. It always works like magic, politically and otherwise.

Bringing water into the arid Southwest is not like stringing a mere telephone line into it—or a pipeline, or a highway, or a railroad. To bring water is to bring, as it were, a revolution!

When ruin at long last is laid side by side with reclamation we see black against white. Throughout the past, drouth has been an ever-present, consistent factor in retarding, opposing, thwarting human effort and the effort of the Machine. The record can be read everywhere from depleted fields where not enough native fertility persists to produce crops; where noxious weeds have substituted themselves for nutritious grasses; where denudation has left the overgrazed ground as bare and hard as a tin roof; where conflagrations have destroyed the virgin forest, leaving only bare poles in the desolation to be felled later by winter storms; where gullied mountain slopes are cut more deeply by each summer cloudburst; where March windstorms lift gritty red dust from New Mexico's Great Plains and drop it literally on Pennsylvania's towns.

Such are some of the horrid symptoms of man's impact on his elemental background. When a flooded river roars past in front of an observer he can see it sweeping a bridge away or engulfing an acre of land from its bank; but what he cannot see is the mud, sand, gravel swept past to silt up the nearest reservoir downstream to negate the work of a costly dam. The only reason for tiresome repetition of these hateful details is that they may be hated.

Man has always been the great despoiler of his domain. But has the land no defenders against those who use it so ill? None to undo all these wrongs? After an unconscionably long time, yes. There is now a corps of men, an arm of the federal government, committed to this task which is far too immense for any other agency. It is called the Department of the Interior and deserves recognition from every man interested in conservation.

It has its own seal, its own emblem which is a statement of its purpose: a massive buffalo bull behind which are the mountains and what I should understand to be a setting sun. The date is March 3, 1849, a time when the vast herds were dwindling after decades of savage, insane, pointless slaughter across the width of the Plains. Clearer than all words the seal says, "Be mindful of the Buffalo." Then beside it is printed like a belated act of penance this: "In its assigned function as the Nation's principal natural resource agency, the Department of the Interior bears a special obligation to assure that our expendable resources are conserved, that renewable resources are managed to produce optimum yields, and that all resources contribute their full measure to the progress, prosperity, and security of America, now and in the future."

Inspired by two beneficent, and epic examples of that Department's current work I have preferred to point the reader's attention first to one of them—the great San Juan–Chama Project. In the presence of that big engineering work by which irrigation water is brought from one side of the Great Divide across to the other, imagination is touched somehow in thinking of the humble Mexican farmers of the past in their green, little, well-leveled valley fields of corn, laboriously guiding the dimpled water with a shovel—the sons of San Ysidro, patron of all who cultivate that art.

Here is a work of a great magnitude. The Desalting Program for brackish and salt water, is destined to be still greater, for we can see now only its small beginning. The experts say that reclaimed drinking water is probably not too far in the future. But irrigation water for the fields is now not even on the horizon. (*Wall Street Journal,* April 29, 1965.)

When we speak of the herculean task of modifying a whole environment, we do not speak of the aggregate of shallow wells, of acequias and little diversion dams, but of the whole vast complex of structures—dams, reservoirs, canals, and powerhouses, which collect, impound, conserve, distribute the water resources of half a continent more or less. Only on such a scale can we really speak of modifying environment. But here man has truly determined, and on a lesser scale will continue to determine, because in each generation his dominion widens. This bright aridity of the Southwest yields ever more and more to water—to grateful, pure, holy water.

When I wrote the following more than three decades ago it seemed exaggerated praise to some. But there is more water now; so there is less caviling:

"Perhaps nowhere in the world is the natural setting nobler than in New Mexico—more beautiful with spacious desert, sky, mountains, more varied in rich, energizing climate, more dramatic in its human procession, more mellow with age-old charm. Endowed with sunshine that stimulates, and winter chill that toughens; with silence, vastness and majestic desert color that offer a spiritual companionship, it has enough. Here if anywhere is air, sky, earth fit to constitute a gracious homeland, not alone for those who occupy themselves in the world's work, but as well for those who study and create, for those who play, those who sit still to brood and dream."

CHAPTER FIFTEEN

A GRINGO CONQUISTADOR

CONQUISTADOR IS A PROUD word, an imperious, haughty word laden with romantic associations from a historic past; *gringo* is a proletarian sort of word without a history, or rather a history freighted with the sullen reproach of generations.

The American exploitation of the huge block of Spanish land between Texas and the Pacific Ocean is not one of our nation's most illustrious chapters. Our opponents—they could hardly then be called a nation— were a people alien to us in language and name, in religion and in every other aspect of culture. And while they were weak, we were strong. So we won.

It has taken them more than a century and two world wars to merge into the diverse stream of our national life and still the process is incomplete. Indeed among the older, more aristocratic families, I fancy it is still possible to detect a latent condescension for American ways—especially for the bare Protestantism of the newcomers in comparison with the pageantry of their ancestral Catholicism. And that pride reaches perhaps into their music—for they are a musical people, and they must retain a secret contempt for the limitless cacophony that rises to the skies above America. And as for ornamentation, they seem to ornament everything they touch. In our functionalism of glass and steel, do we? No wonder we need interpreters.

To Americans the earliest interpretation of the Spanish Southwest was the work of an American soldier, Lt. William H. Emory, who was attached to General Kearny's command in the Mexican War. Emory, of the Corps of Topographical Engineers, states that since it was expected Kearny's route would lie across unexplored regions he (Emory) and the officers assigned to duty with him "would be employed in collecting data which would give the government some idea of the regions traversed." Stated baldly, he was to find out whether the Great American Desert, so-called, was worth taking by force, and if so, whether it was worth keeping. Naturally he would make notes on the people too.

At that date, while Army intelligence doubtless had a fund of knowledge about Mexico proper, they knew next to nothing about its northern provinces. Apart from the rivers, the hinterlands of New Mexico and what was later to be named Arizona were virtually unmapped, and, except for the Catholic missionaries, almost unexplored. It is hardly too much to say that between the Rio Grande and the Pacific there was then no spot on the earth's surface whose position was precisely known until Emory's map provided the latitude and longitude. But by the time the Army of the West had reached the tiny Pueblo of Los Angeles, the whole endless route had passed under the eye of a skilled mathematical observer. And along the way he had measured streams, calculated gradients, studied contours, estimated drainage areas, everywhere noted the water resources of the thirsty land, and at night had taken readings on Arcturus, Alpha Lyrae, Procyon and others of the greater stars as data for other map makers in the future.

The following survey of the native New Mexicans as they appeared to Emory, the gruff soldier, somewhat more than a century ago is drawn by the writer from his book *Lieutenant Emory Reports* (The University of New Mexico Press, 1951). It must be remembered that in Emory's time there was no trace of today's hushed admiration for all things Spanish—architecture, crafts, music, dances, cookery, pageants—that has entirely reversed the condescending attitude the victorious Americans had in 1846. In fact, the Spanish graces and amenities have since happily captivated the Anglos in much the same way as the classical Greek culture enthralled the Roman conquerors in the Augustan Age.

At the end of the Mexican regime, the question before the practical Emory was simply, "What kind of people are living here?" His superiors in Washington would expect an unvarnished answer. He reported as correctly as possible what he saw, then as a realist deduced the impending change that would probably occur at the war's end.

In New Mexico, Emory and the brash, vigorous Americans like him saw a simple agrarian people who matched their conception of the downtrodden peasants of the Middle Ages. Their existence was incessantly shadowed by the Indian Terror, oppressed by the institution of peonage, denied for the most part the protection of police and the courts, without any adequate system of public education, without organized commerce by which the products of their labor could be exchanged for the goods of ordinary civilized life. And among the people was noted a picturesque but decadent aristocracy wasting its days, apparently, in gambling, fandangoes and political machinations.

To the thoughtful observer of today their proletarian life might have suggested the lament of the poor in the great German poem Faust: "Thou shalt do without, do without. That is the everlasting song." To the merciful priests who lived among them, spent their life in ministering to them it was something else. "They have their Church," said the Friars, "and though they seem conquered by fate, they have a something within themselves that the maulings of fate have not conquered—hope perhaps, or trust in the unseen, over-arching, compassionate world of saints and angels."

What the Anglos then believed was perhaps half truth, half untruth. But there was no doubt that the Mexicans—and the name at that time was perfectly proper—were still using some agricultural practices that belonged back in the Old Testament era. A plow was still a sharpened tree fork, perhaps strengthened with an iron point. And as late as October 1947, a Mexican farmer at Quarai—I saw this myself—was threshing his bean crop by treading it out of the dried hulls with his horses' hoofs; and the frijoles were being screened by means of a bull-hide hand barrow. For the transportation of burdens they had nothing more advanced than a pack horse, for certainly the primitive and ponderous *carreta* was not. Their placer mining, a modified form of starvation in which *colors* of gold were washed from arroyo sands, was equally primitive. Lieutenant Abert, one of Emory's men who visited the workings near Tuerto, described them thus: "We saw many miserable-looking wretches, clothed in rags, with an old piece of iron to dig the earth, and some gourds, or horns of the mountain goat (*sic*) to wash the sand."

Only in the livestock industry, and more especially in sheep raising, were the natives engaged in an enterprise of any magnitude. New Mexico was then the most favored province in the republic for sheep, but since they sold for only a dollar a head the profits were small and there was always the danger that Indians would drive off the flock and kill the herder. In short, agriculture was only subsistence farming.

There was no industry. And, except for that which came across the Plains, plus the trickle that came up along the Rio Grande trail, there was no commerce. The only income that kept money in circulation, as we learn from Don Pedro Bautista Pino, was the federal salary paid to the governor and his assistants, and to the one hundred twenty-one soldiers on garrison duty at Santa Fe. Pino said that in New Mexico, "until recently the majority of its inhabitants have never seen money." (*Three New Mexico Chronicles*, The Quivira Society, Albuquerque, 1942). And there existed in the province, as Emory pointed out, a system of peonage which had many of the evils of slavery without its advantages. By it a man could be held in lifelong bondage for a debt of less than a hundred dollars, and when he became too old or infirm to work, no master was responsible for his keep.

But a change was at hand. Harbingers of the change had arrived long before the American army. The prairie schooners of the Santa Fe Trail had already begun to revolutionize old ways of life and with them came Yankee workmen who made their contribution of technical skill to the backward commonwealth. Lawyer Barreiro (*Three Chronicles*) in 1832 had already begun to take notice of them. He says: "A few Anglo-American craftsmen are established in New Mexico. . . . It is to be expected that the natives of the country will learn something in the foreign shops, or at least that they may be stimulated by observing the excellent work of these foreigners. Among the foreign craftsmen there are tailors, carpenters, blacksmiths, hatters, tinsmiths, shoemakers, excellent gunsmiths, etc, etc."

Thus it is clear that at the back door of the United States there was then a country with many American ties, which at the middle of the progressive nineteenth century was still living, as it were, in the Dark Ages. All this Emory saw, and a thousand similar things. By them he was readily persuaded that the unspoken though already half-formulated policy of his government was wise, enlightened, necessary and in the larger sense not inhumane. He did not consciously or openly slant his findings toward annexation. Yet evidences are numerous that he was aware of his government's aim and that he supported it by discovering a multitude of facts that would argue for it. And in that direction his *Notes* exerted an immense persuasiveness.

The preceding digest of Emory's conclusions is taken from this author's introduction to the famous *Notes of a Military Reconnoissance* by Lieutenant W. H. Emory, a reprint published by the University of New Mexico Press (Albuquerque, 1951) under the title *Lieutenant Emory Reports*.

The grand and not totally unexpected conclusion of the whole adventure by the United States is summarized thus at the end of the same introduction:

"At the close of the Mexican War a Boundary Commissioner, John R. Bartlett, was sent to run a line round the prize. But Bartlett's survey proved unsatisfactory; and after the Gadsden Tract was purchased, Emory was sent to redraw the line.

"Safely inside when the last degree of latitude and longitude was reckoned, lay the goldfields of California, the undeveloped silver deposits of New Mexico, the copper of Arizona, unguessed riches in petroleum, gas and oil, the great pine forests and wide-flung grazing ranges that stretched between Texas and the West Coast, the surpassingly rich valleys in which agriculture was to reach its final climax—there on the Great American Desert."

CHAPTER SIXTEEN

THE NEWCOMERS
WHO MOVED IN

THE FIRST QUESTION TO WHICH
we addressed ourselves was: "What kind of people lived
here during the Spanish regime?" The second which
we now come to is: "What kind of newcomers from the
outside joined the native people, merged with them,
or more accurately, moved in on them?" To cover the
ground on this one we shall need to walk with seven-
league boots. Rightly it would call not for a few para-
graphs, not for a chapter, but a book, or a series.

But we have glimpsed a few of the needs already.
The first need would be for soldiers. The colonists were
an enclave of civilization pinched together along the
Rio by two bordering areas of savagery. And the second
need perhaps, oddly enough, would be for lawyers and
then for courts without which lawyers would be useless.
When there was "no law west of the Pecos" there was
also no safety for life nor property, no civilization in
fact. Society can hardly hold itself together without an

agent to collect the taxes required to pay for governing itself, a sheriff armed for public protection, and a scribe for the keeping of public records.

And the sheriff without a courthouse, even though he has a six-gun, would leave the gilded chariot of Justice to be pulled not by two chargers, but unanchored at one end, unbalanced—in short a one-horse outfit.

So long as there were no banks, the business of society was merely barter; so long as there were no books there could be no public schools; and while there was no teacher with his book, knowledge could not be disseminated or handed down. And where there was no engineer with a wheel—as a civilizer he was only a little less effective than a teacher with a book—roads would be only rough trails, bridges only rocky fords; and without a dam no water could be impounded for a season, two seasons or three. Without a merchant and without a store as distinguished from a petty shop, there could be no reserve supply of any commodity for the people; without the physician and his hospital there could be no protection for them in time of pestilence.

When the professional classes arrived from the States they brought services which the native people could not provide for themselves—expensive service, of course, which intensified the ancient distinctions already existing between the poor and the *ricos*.

Further immigration brought in numbers of skilled Americans—blacksmiths, miners, freighters, masons and carpenters, with ranchers, of course, leading the procession. And in the unequal competition with these skilled workmen whose services were naturally in great demand, the unskilled natives, almost without tools, found only the poorest employment. The consequence was inevitable. The well-to-do became richer, the poor only poorer. Thus came an unfortunate segregation into classes as old as human society, a separation for which nobody was entirely to blame and which to this day has not entirely disappeared.

For one who has long lived in New Mexico, and who shared in the bitter experiences of the Great Depression, the immense advance of the Spanish American people in these latter days has been a matter of profound gratification.

But it is only when attention is narrowed to individuals that the varied, interesting and cosmopolitan nature of New Mexico's population becomes apparent. Here follows a list from the writer's acquaintance which might be matched by many another who knows the state well. Most of them, past and present, stayed long enough to be *bona fide* residents, not merely persons on a voting list.

There was Old Doc S——, a saddlemaker by trade. He was a superb craftsman, or rather an artist who made his living by turning out hand-tooled saddles, bridles, "chaps" for the men who work cattle. His steel buckles might ultimately wear out, his leather never.

C. J., born in New England, is a mineral surveyor, whose services are in demand for marking out the bounds of mining claims. His results have to be of high accuracy on steep, difficult mountain slopes. He finds his happiness in random prospecting for metals, but is always attentive to volcanic intrusions, faulting, crystals, and has an eagle eye for brachiopods that have lain dead in the limestone a hundred million years.

B. K. is a "remittance man," a type no longer common. His father, an Eastern broker, puts up money for his son's Western wardrobe, his saddles, boots, horses and other properties which go with playing cowboy.

He is an alcoholic—a rather clean vice, I suppose.

Mrs. D. E. and her husband are a middle-aged couple who live on a remote mountain ranch where they are engaged in the production of mohair. The road to their home is long, and in winter choked with snow, but guests from many states find their way to the hospitable door.

Mrs. W. E. with her husband operates a dude ranch. It is the life she loves. She is entirely at home on a pack trip into the high country, equally so at a party among her guests. Daughter of an Easterner and graduate of an Eastern school, she is the perfect hostess.

K. D., who held a minor position in a greenhouse, is an amateur archaeologist. Within narrow limits he probably knows more about his specialty than many professionals. Recently he sold his collection of baskets, bowls, stone axes and other artifacts to a museum, where it will be preserved permanently.

And there was J. C. O. L., who worked as reporter on big Eastern dailies until TB overtook him. Living in Deming at the time of Pancho Villa's raid, he was the first to get it on the wire. His recovery progressed to the point where he became editor of the *Silver City Enterprise*. There he chronicled the happenings of his state not as finished literature, but as the kind of news from which literature is devised—ore discoveries, mine accidents, cowmen's quarrels, scientific expeditions, backwoods funerals, all the romance and tragedy of the Southwest. He succumbed to the disease at sixty.

A Jewish pack peddler there was who used to make the rounds of the silver camps on foot in the early days. I knew him only as an infirm oldster who had grown very rich. When he died the papers described him as one who "had prospered in spite of his honesty." Sam, one of his sons who became a scholar, divided his time between San Francisco and Deming, his native village. Once when a Presidential Special on the Southern Pacific passed through Deming, it stopped there to take Sam aboard.

This enumeration must end somewhere, but not without mentioning an inheritor of an old and distinguished family name in the East—La Farge. Oliver La Farge was a Harvard man who earned his niche by one brilliant novel. He married a Spanish American girl from a remote mountain village in northern New Mexico, and added to his fame by telling her story to *The New Yorker*.

Another, Ernest Thompson Seton, known to millions of boys for his wild animal stories—I never tired of them—settled during his later years in a village close to Santa Fe, named it for himself, and there spent the rest of his life meditating, dreaming, writing of the Southwestern scene. No man of his time or any other was more deeply versed in lore of campfire and trail.

Still one more: R. K. He had a modest income which permitted him to spend his life as an amateur ornithologist—the best. The collection of bird skins which he had spent his life in amassing later served as the basis for the authoritative *Birds of New Mexico*.

By stopping here I shall be accused of slighting our pioneers and the sons of the pioneers who made money in this poor land—lawyers who contended stoutly in Washington for justice to the Indian tribes; financiers who brought to this big, unwieldy territory resources for the development of its mines and ranches; traders who bought and sold turquoise, silver and rugs.

And still a class of men among the most gifted and most sensitive of all is unmentioned—the artists. It is claimed that now this state has more men and women deserving the professional title of artist than any other state. They and the writers and craftsmen of many kinds have had their share in the honorable company of those who in the past have helped to gentle this harsh land.

At this point it would seem admissible to mention without comment another group of highly skilled individuals who have arrived in recent years—the scientists and other professional scholars. Included within their ranks are indisputably the physicists and chemists and engineers engaged in defense work at Los Alamos, the White Sands Missile Base, and Albuquerque. Here belong also members of college and university faculties, physicians and surgeons, members of the legal fraternity and other learned professions.

The new City on the Hill, as Los Alamos calls itself, boasts of having among its inhabitants more holders of the Ph.D. degree, proportionally, than any other city in the world. Another notable fact is that a large per cent of them are alumni of venerable ivied institutions in the East or else of proud new ones in California; that their cells across New Mexico are made up of fairly recent arrivals. For instance, there is now in Albuquerque a flourishing club of former Ivy Leaguers, whereas at the 1935 commencement I could discover in the University faculty procession not a single crimson doctor's hood—the shyly arrogant badge of a Harvard education. At that time, to tell the truth, a Harvard man was an obscure and perhaps faintly objectionable individual; yet today he is much emboldened by the knowledge that his name is on the roster here with nearly three hundred others.

Here an illuminating comparison might be made between the population of Clovis and of Silver City. The former is on the eastern side of the state beside the Texas line, and the later is in the extreme southwestern corner, close to Arizona and the Mexican border. Using the term culture in its wider sense to include occupations, religion, recreation and intellectual climate, one may see instantly that the culture of the latter is purely Western, while that of the other is definitely Middlewestern into which Southern influences have been blended. Sixty years ago, when Clovis was only Riley's Switch, Silver City was already a substantial village of adobe and brick which housed two thousand persons and was governed by a mayor who was a Princeton graduate. But today, in spite of its greater age, it has only about a third of the population and possibly less than that fraction of the other city's wealth. Clovis has grown rapidly and now spreads out for miles across the plains.

In the second and third decades of the century, Silver City had four or five good-sized tuberculosis "sans," and had achieved the standing of a semi-fashionable health center. Its superb, stimulating climate had caused many of the health-seekers after arresting their disease to settle there permanently. Among them was current a significant saying: "A short life and a merry one," and the motto had a part in creating the tradition of sophisticated gaiety that has persisted there ever since. In this worthy enterprise they were assisted by the Army doctors and their ladies from neighboring Ft. Bayard, which had been converted meanwhile into a Veterans Hospital. The doctors were men who, having served the flag in many quarters of the world, carried with them their own cosmopolitan ideas of a good time. Furthermore there was always a sprinkling of mining engineers in the village, a hardy outdoor breed who liked their whiskey straight and plentiful. They were no more famous than the preceding groups for regularity of church attendance. Most of them in fact, seemed to consider church-going an undesirable show of piety, and since there was always a large, uncontrollable factor of luck in their profession, they were persistently schooled in spite of themselves to feel indulgent toward gambling.

Nor were the ranchmen willing to be outdone in the pursuit of pleasure. Living on remote homesteads, they had little opportunity for the conventional practice of religion, and their trips to town for the purpose of trade and dentistry (so-called) had a quite understandable tendency to blend the elements of pleasure with business. It is not hard to see that a devil-may-care tradition of gaiety mixed with rowdiness would inevitably develop and thrive in the place.

For many years the population of Silver City hung near the five-thousand mark. Approximately half were Spanish-Americans who lived much to themselves. That left a population of about equal size engaged in the Anglo pursuits of town life, but seasoned to an unusual degree with imported cosmopolitan spice.

If the intellectual climate of the town was varied and bracing—and the influence of Western New Mexico University has been large and rapidly increasing— the religious climate was less satisfactory. To be sure, there is as much openhanded friendliness as can be found anywhere; also there is a gratifying absence of censoriousness and hypocrisy. But the churches of the community have somehow failed through the years to leave a deep mark upon it. In this respect, as in almost every other, the town prides itself on being "Western," free from Bible-Belt interference.

At this point the contrast between Clovis and Silver

City emerges most clearly, for Clovis proudly and defiantly claims to be a part of the Bible Belt. Lying as it does on the border of Texas, the city has two Southern Baptist churches of what might be called metropolitan size and several others of lesser importance. So deeply is their crusading zeal felt throughout the length and breadth of the community that even the Methodists concede their superior weight. Their mores prevail. They set the standards—standards oftentimes illiberal, but clear and bracing always. The Roman Catholics claim only a small percentage of the population, and even so, a large part of their numerical strength lies in the Spanish-speaking colony. Thus the city is overwhelmingly Protestant with a roster of more than thirty denominations. And in addition to the major ones there are many less-known "fancy religions," as they are uncharitably called.

Among them there is a competition in good works which sometimes degenerates into unchristian polemics and name-calling. In addition, by their militant efforts to modify manners and reform morals, they not infrequently give their critics some justification for calling them public meddlers. For many years Clovis was one of only two or three good-sized towns in all of New Mexico which did not allow high school dances in the school building.

The somewhat abnormal number of churches may or may not account for the fact that in the town there is a great deal of true, sincere religion. There is indeed so much of the genuine article abroad that it encourages, as it does always and everywhere, the circulation of the corresponding counterfeit coin. Hypocrisy flourishes in Clovis because there it is good policy to appear religious. In Silver City hypocrisy hardly exists, because, unfortunately, there is so little need for it. Toleration itself may become a vice.

Next to religion it is in commerce that the greatest difference exists between the two towns. In Clovis everybody is engaged in getting ahead. The natural resources are there to develop, and the whole population is aggressively engaged in developing them, hence in the town there has never been a leisure class like the healthseekers formerly in Silver City. Nobody ever comes from the East to Clovis to settle down and play through his years of retirement. Yet in Silver City and in the villages tributary to it, there have always been people who possessed the leisure, the taste and the financial means to read, paint, study, collect Indian artifacts, hunt, loaf and picnic, and party to their heart's content. In Clovis everyone who has money now has made it himself and is busily engaged in adding to it. In the other town there are many who have had money a long time and think more of spending it in gracious living than amassing more of it.

So Clovis forges ahead and nowadays scarcely recognizes its one-time rival as a member of the same league.

Some of the immediately preceding material was drawn from my brief interpretation called "The People of New Mexico" which the Division of Research, Department of Government, UNM, authorized in 1947. Thomas C. Donnelly, now president of New Mexico Highlands University, stated at the time in his foreword, "Care is taken in each study to gather facts with fullness and accuracy and to draw conclusions with impartiality." Could the reader determine in which town the writer's facts "gathered with fullness and accuracy" caused him to be threatened with legal action? (It was Silver City.)

The examination of a town on the east side of the state should properly be balanced by one on the west side, and then both by one on the north side, the City of the Holy Faith, the Villa Real de Santa Fe.

Someone is bound to say here, "Why bother? It's just another state capital. Aren't they all alike—Santa Fe, Phoenix, Denver?" But after all, there *is* a subtle distinction between the first two. One is ten times the size of the other—an ultra modern city of half a million souls, looking for all the world like acreage transplanted bodily from California; the other still a Spanish village, a tight village though it has the state's official buildings, a grand opera, and artists and writers galore. And Denver—well, it is a great American city, great in any man's language. Yet when it began to have a fine-print rating on the map about 1860, Santa Fe was then a settlement already about two hundred fifty years old and, one may assume, already sophisticated. Santa Fe, perhaps the least American of all our cities, clings the most tenaciously to its Mediterranean heritage. In fact not many years have elapsed since its state legislature was bilingual, the business being conducted both in English and in *la lengua castellana* or what then passed for it.

Santa Fe is in love with its past. It has its own distinctive style of architecture, a style based upon adobe which has been employed for thousands of years in Arabia and the near East. And during its famous fiesta, oldest of American observances, both natives and visitors seize the opportunity to dress up, the señoritas in black silk with mantillas and high tortoise-shell combs. Santa Fe alone, unique, with no runner-up anywhere, desires no growth and would haughtily require if possible a written examination of the wealthy and gifted who aspire to live there, meditate and create among its juniper-dotted foothills, saunter along its quaint, crooked streets, brood and dream in its winter sunshine.

The brief excursion into the nature of New Mexico's population must come to an end without so much as a glance at the Indian people, because they did not come in after the annexation. Omitted also for the same reason is detailed consideration of today's Spanish Americans. The notes of the three towns already discussed fall naturally enough within the narrow classification we have chosen for ourselves, which was "the newcomers who have moved in." According to our best judgment it would be wiser to omit also the thirteen thousand inhabitants of non-typical Los Alamos.

Yet in the briefest account of New Mexico I am constrained to announce what seems to me a remarkable phenomenon in any population anywhere: the assembly at one spot and at one time of *so many intellectually superior families*. The mothers must surely be superior; the fathers by the mere fact of their employment at the great Los Alamos Scientific Laboratory have demonstrated their group superiority; and their children demonstrate annually in college entrance examinations a commensurate superiority of their own.

Finally, in regard to "the newcomers who have moved in" I am reminded of a remark which Mr. Frederick Simpich of *The National Geographic* once made to me. "In the course of my work I have gone everywhere, seen everything. But when I retire I wish it could be to some place between the Rio Grande and the Rio Colorado." The same attractions that he appreciated have drawn and held a host of others. The present writer is one of them.

CHAPTER SEVENTEEN

GILA: THE RUIN OF A RIVER

THE GILA DOESN'T BEGIN AS
the Gila River. It begins as Gilita Creek, which is a
melodious Spanish diminutive, almost suggesting en-
dearment, Little Gila. You must be sure not to mis-
pronounce the name and call it Jilla or something else.
It must be called Hee-la and Hee-lee-ta, unless by chance
you are a local rancher, in which case you probably say
Hee-lay. It is guessed, although nobody knows for sure,
that the original is an Indian word meaning "spider."

The upper Gila country is a cold mountain fastness, and in the main an unspoiled fastness it will always
be. The middle reach of the stream was in the seventies
and eighties a series of well-grassed valleys, unplundered,
unharvested, the fairest in all Arizona. The lower reach
as one nears the Rio Colorado is no longer a river at all
but a wide stripe of burning sand, the water having all
been appropriated.

High above the Gilita, not far below the mountain summits, are two springs close to the ten-thousand-foot level, although neither may be shown on your contour map. One is Bead Spring in whose chill waters many beads and jewellike arrowheads were once found long ago; the other is Hummingbird Spring. High in the Mogollons (pronounced almost "Muggy-owns") there are several species of hummers, but the species meant must be, I think the *rufous,* most gorgeous of all. You may see them probing for insects in the azure larkspur blossoms about the first week in August after they have already returned from nesting in Canada. This kind is really special: body like metallic copper brilliantly burnished; gorget, a rich scarlet so that when it catches the sun it kindles into an outsized flying ruby.

But clear above these two highest springs are giant icicles from whose stiletto points, about February, water begins slowly to drip. From such icicles (some of them ten feet long which I have photographed) and from such water drops the Gila takes its real beginnings.

At the summits of the highest peaks in the range mast-like spruce trees almost brush the eleven-thousand-foot level; below them by a vertical half mile or more where it becomes comfortable to camp in summer, the night chill takes the temperature down to the low forties; and the afternoon rains, which are likely to come almost daily, produce in one's tent a clamminess which extends downward to the level of the upper pines.

At the foot of the steep mountain slopes along the stream's edge the ponderosa pines leave off and the cottonwoods begin; but the two species blend hardly at all, and keep their identity like layers in a cake. At the point where the stream emerges from the steep mountain canyon the cottonwoods take over and with surprising directness air temperature rises, the stream spreads out, current slows and begins at once to lose its clarity and take on a reddish hue. These steps occur in order all over the Southwest but nowhere else does the transition from snows and spruces to sands and sahuaros occur so dramatically as along the Gila. Between these two extremes lie, or used to lie, the famous "desert grasslands" of Arizona as they are called.

Back in the thirties I was authorized by the then new Soil Conservation Service to write a history of the upper and middle Gila Watershed. So early one calm, chill January morning at Lordsburg, I encased myself in a fur-lined flying suit, fur-lined moccasins and helmet, and while the engine was warming up snapped on a chute which patted me loosely on the rear side, climbed clumsily aboard. It was an entirely open plane built for observation at low altitudes.

My first impression was the light color of the soil and the extreme bareness of the creosote desert. From on high the creosote bushes looked like isolated dots which did not coalesce, whereas from eye level on the ground they were projected one against another into a compact green band. Soon we were passing flat-topped tablelands—mesas—interbedded with layers of black lava. On some of the low bare mountains there was a dusting of snow, while on higher peaks in the far distance there were visible great irregular blotches of immaculate white in the sky. Here and there over the tawny surface of the earth drastic overgrazing had changed the color of the ground itself. Where patches of ripened grass caught the full sunlight it suggested the yellowed, coarse fur on a coyote's skin; yet across the nearly invisible strands of a barbed wire fence where all grass had been eaten away the bare soil approached the color of chocolate with a faint reddish tinge.

On the red hills near Clifton, Arizona, the tailings dump near the smelter stood out clearly in its chemical tints as a reminder of the immense industrial effort there in the past. Then northwestward we flew, looking down upon the astonishingly bare Ash Flat, which resembled nothing so much as an elephant's hide, flat, wrinkled, earth-colored. Then onward over the low, rounded, treeless Gila range, and a series of deep, imposing canyons eroded into a black rimrock; still farther ahead we saw the comforting gleam of water across the desert, the cerulean blue of the great San Carlos reservoir.

Soon the plane banks and begins to turn. The range of the giant cactus lies below us. We have passed from the spruces of New Mexico down to the sahuaros of Arizona; and without a pause we are wheeling back upstream from the sands to the snow which lies perhaps ten feet deep in the darkly shaded mountain folds.

The sharply-pointed stone peak of Mt. Turnbull, culmination of a treeless desert range, recedes to the rear, and before long we are above geometrical fields of alfalfa in a narrow valley. We have seen something of the land's anatomy, an underlying stony foundation covered with a few inches of gravelly waste. The desert is not pretty, but lying in its magnificent light and color it has an intoxicating, unearthly beauty all its own, of mornings and evenings.

Flying low enough to be noticed by some nibbling Herefords, we continue back to the Lordsburg plain and the landing field. The most barren, cut-up area which we saw was a dry tributary of the Gila called now the San Simon Wash, but in Mexican War days, when it rated the dignity of being a link in the international boundary line, it was Santo Domingo Creek. Nowadays it is a lifeless-looking greyness which resembles a magnified design carved out of roadside mud by a rain. The "creek," so called, is only a sanded, irregular gash in the earth that from the air suggests the infinitely crooked root system of a tree. It looks like a place accurst.

Yet it has not always been so, for in 1850, the boundary commissioner, J. R. Bartlett, spoke of following a dry ravine some eight or ten miles to a reedy place called by various local names, El Sauce, Willow Marsh, San Simon Ciénega. Bartlett says, "It seemed to be the basin where the waters collected from the adjoining mountains and slopes. Here was great abundance of water, which from the rushes that grew on its margin, I suppose to be permanent. Grass was also plenty here. Lieut. Whipple found the latitude to be 32°05′ 09″, longitude 109°02′ 06″. That is exactly correct for San Simon Creek. It is a common, well-documented fact that in the Southwest many other springs have dried up from human misuse of one kind or another."

That monstrous wound in the earth, floored with sand deep and bone-dry, with vertical, crumbling walls twenty feet high, one hundred to three hundred feet apart, sixty miles long, I could not forget. In the eighteen fifties Willow Marsh . . . forty years later a mild little arroyo which the freight wagons could easily cross . . . and look at the accursed thing now! Between those wide-separated walls a vacancy filled only with air and black, morning shadows . . . the cause, the wrecking force, being nothing more dynamic than water in motion. It seemed incredible. And the displaced earth—where was it now? Spewed out somewhere downstream by furious floods to bury fertile irrigated fields under a wash of gravel. The facts lay before the eye, and in addition were documented in writing, in old photographs, and living tradition. Later I was to see often the horrendous *barranca*—to use the Mexican word—but never without a certain dread. Fanciful though it was, those black shadows came at length to seem an evil monster there lying in wait. The real Gila Monster was there—Erosion, mancaused Erosion!

In that country there is a black, sinister, poisonous, seldom-seen creature which haunts the southern Arizona desert. All who go upon the hot wasteland have heard of it and all fear it. Its name? Gila monster! It has a fierce reptilian hiss. But otherwise it seems to have a rather peaceable disposition, unlike other denizens of the land. The monster, I might add, is about sixteen inches long, no thicker than a lady's wrist, too slow to run away, too big to hide itself readily. Actually the monster is only a lizard. But this other monster is more inimical than all lizards put together, for it is the one which was and still is creating concern to the Department of the Interior in far-off Washington, the one to which I gave my small service that summer. On this greater threat I would bestow the name Gila Monster, not any longer on a humble reptile.

The ruin of the Gila is a story too long and too varied for a routine, sober treatment. Then, besides, the ruin took place at haphazard rather than in any systematic fashion. There was no one set of good guys, in fact no one set of bad guys who were uniformly the villains in every piece.

Terrific man-caused erosion took place along the stream and its tributaries not as the acts of nefarious "interests," but as often perhaps by the mistakes of "nesters," poor men who were also ignorant. Not seldom they put the plow into land that should never have been broken. An example. Along Duck Creek on the New Mexico side of the line a colony of "dry farmers" from Oklahoma settled in the seventies, and with the encouragement of a series of wet seasons planted crops. Another wet season convinced them they were on the road to wealth. Then in its irregular rhythm drouth returned and ruined them all. And with their tragedy the land itself was ruined, for every furrow of the naked acres became a gully, deep, deeper until it could swallow a farm wagon. The spectacle is there to this day.

The ranchers suffered in their way from similar ignorance. They overstocked the unfenced country; the drouth returned, the cattle starved. And for them there was a double jeopardy, because at Washington in the halls of Congress, gentlemen passed land laws for homesteaders that almost starved them, too. Major J. H. Powell, who understood the arid Southwest, argued and pleaded for a homestead allowance of 2,500 acres per family; Congress set the figure at 160 acres; congressmen who thought they knew were often then as now ignorant, or under pressure or both, as well as being men often of goodwill.

And the miners. When the Indian menace ended with the imprisonment of all Apaches on reservations, prospectors swarmed out eagerly over the hills looking for metal. When they found silver they went suddenly from rags to riches—riches which evaporated suddenly after the great era of the seventies ended and the white metal's price dropped on the world market for reasons over which they had no control. Then the "camps" became ghost towns, hideous with tin cans, denuded of forest.

If it was copper they found, they were luckier, for

electricity was on the way to becoming civilization's most useful slave, and they had discovered in the red metal a conductor to lead and tame it. Where copper ore showed its presence by a green stain the miners beat a path to it. Then a mine and the smelter, and after that the tailings dump—along with the poisons. Without thought of harm the industry disposed of the waste material in ways closest at hand, as was natural. Ultimately the highly charged solutions found their way to the Gila and so were distributed through the soil where the farmer had planted his seeds. There was hell to pay. Litigation began. An action starting from an Arizona village reached at last the Supreme Court of the United States. There damages were awarded to the farmer, and the copper company had to pay in full for its pollution of the good earth, the grain giver. The case is well known.

Another despoiler along the Gila's course was the forest fire, sometimes caused by lightning but oftener by a fisherman or a hunter in the high country. Nowadays big fires, as the technique of fighting them improves, are becoming rather rare. When an alarm goes out by telephone the well-trained rangers go into fast action. If the threat appears extreme, Indian "smoke-jumpers" with their parachutes may be brought in as technical experts.

From my log book I draw some details of a big fire in the Gila National Forest in the summer of 1939:

Into the Forest Service field headquarters rolled a green truck with its quota of tired men who were being relieved after twelve hours of duty on the line. Clothes were sweat-stained, faces smeared with charcoal grime. The truck approached through cool, lovely morning shadows, but the background above it was a mountain on fire. After it had passed I kept watching a burning pine snag. The trunk, thirty or forty feet tall, was now only a column of shining charcoal from the ground up to a terminal jet of flame that burned oddly like a torch among the green pine boughs. In and out amidst the smoke circled a pair of bewildered ravens. Back in the murkiness somewhere they had a nest, probably now with their young.

Later I followed a steep, rocky trail far back into the forest to the edge of the conflagration proper. There a little wanton flame writhes like a bright serpent underneath some oak brush. A surprising heat comes traveling back from it, and a man with a shovel remarks to his companion, "That comes as near to burning them rocks as anything I ever saw." Farther along the trail I encounter a man with a forester's heavy rake standing guard over a blazing log. The ground near it is already burned safely bare, but his job is to prevent it from breaking loose upon the steep slope and rolling a thousand embers into the canyon below. After an all-night vigil he looks sleepy. He tells me that during the night he had seen three deer running aimlessly in and out of the fire. His story was punctuated by a dull, heavy noise. A charred trunk eaten through at the base had crashed full-length to the ground.

Later on from a point of rocks jutting out into the canyon I saw something below me that at length justified the cheaply misused word "inferno." Far down a puff of wind catches a cloud of smoke, bends the point of it backward into the shape of a great fishhook. And then, there at the end of the shank, a breeze whips the fire suddenly into the green pine tops. There is the hiss of a vast frying of pitch. With the sickening sound comes also a traveling red flash, and then the upshooting of a mushroom of smoke that is no longer greasy white, but sinister black. Almost like an explosion the cloud shoots skyward telling watchers all over the mountains that another new crown fire has broken out. The flame no longer grovels along the ground but leaps with a tigerish ferocity upon the tallest trees and overwhelms them in a red cloud.

In a forest fire the lumberman loses his logs, the stockman his green pasturage and often his stock. The woodcutter loses his fuel and the hunter his sport, for in a forest of charred poles there is no game. The nature lover, too, loses something real.

This big fire like so many others, was man-caused, it was widely believed. With lifted eyes and fervent emotion we sing of America,

> *I love thy rocks and rills,*
> *Thy woods and templed hills.*

Contemplating a mountainside of blackened pine trunks I surmise considerable overstatement among the singers.

In our examination of the Ruined River we reach now the place where we must consider Arizona and the Cow. And the Cow, it must be said at the outset, should be completely absolved from blame. She came not of her own free will; she was brought—mainly by American ranchers; but when she lifted up her eyes and beheld the prospect she realized she was in the bovine heaven and at once decided to settle down and do her best to deserve the good fortune she had come into.

The Saga of the Cow will not perhaps be interesting to all, but to all it should be definitely instructive. In the West, and especially in the Southwest, it has a social and economic significance that is truly immense. The gentlemen of the Department of the Interior may not all be cow-lovers, but for nearly a century they and their allies in the Department of Agriculture have been aware that the Cow's problems collectively are their problems. To put it another way, the magnitude of the effect can be explained only by the magnitude of the cause, the cause being the power-driven jaws (by hunger, that is) of heaven knows not how many hundred millions of animals that have grazed here within the last century or so.

Statistics there must be. But statistics are no good unless they all start from a uniform base, and this writer during his study many years ago for the Soil Conservation Service discovered that in Arizona the Territorial Governors' reports and the figures released from Washington seemed frankly in some years to be describing two altogether different industries—and that without considering the fiction collected by county tax assessors everywhere.

NUMBER OF CATTLE

Arizona (county by county)		Government Estimate
1890	636,016	604,170
1891	720,940	725,004
1892	644,209	761,254
1893	491,812	882,154
1894	423,292	649,502

Above are the figures for the five critical years ending in 1894. The left column purports to give the actual number county by county from Arizona; the right column gives the government estimate from the Department of Agriculture. Neither of the contestants rounds off three figures but pretends to be accurate to the final digit. And, oddly, neither total is consistently higher or lower than the other. Here accuracy is only an illusion, and the fact that I have included these census reports does not create any accuracy which the columns do not themselves possess. These statistics show merely that a lot of cows were in Arizona, and that a lot more got lost somehow between Washington and Phoenix.

Coronado in 1540 brought cattle into the Southwest. But whether any of them survived until the first Spanish settlement nobody knows. We are not on solid ground until near the year 1870. By that time the Apaches, prisoners of war, were herded into reservations. From childhood they were warriors, not farmers and of the arts of peace they knew not one. So the white man's government out of common humanity had to feed them lest they starve. At San Carlos, Arizona, sixty-four beeves a week were slaughtered for them; and the man who purveyed the meat was Sigmund Lindauer, earlier a Jewish peddler who, as we saw a few pages back, prospered "in spite of his honesty."

By 1872 cattle could be turned loose to graze with a degree of safety from the Indians. That was the year in which General Howard signed a treaty with the Chiricahua ("Cherry Cow") Apaches, the same year Col. H. C. Hooker in Sulphur Springs Valley founded Sierra Bonita Ranch, the first in the Territory.

The region then was in its virgin condition, for up to that time through fear of the Apaches no man had dared to leave his mark upon it, and Mexican ranching had touched only its fringe. As another matter of record a colony of Mormon farmers took out from the Gila a large irrigation ditch at the new village of Safford the following year. All at once civilization with all its virtues, and all its evils, had begun to invade Apacheria.

Cattle by the thousands began to arrive. In 1872 it is recorded that Hooker brought in 15,000. Of these, 4,000 were brought in a single drive from Texas. John Chisum, the famous cattle king of New Mexico, a little later brought in a herd of 4,000 more and settled them in the well-grassed Aravaipa Valley not far distant. About the same time shorthorns arrived from Oregon, purebred Durhams from California and of course the thin-bodied, rangy longhorns from Sonora. Ten years later came the Herefords and were discovered to be the best breed of them all.

And thus at a phenomenal rate expansion continued year after year. Windy promoters constantly added their excited dreams to the high-pitched reality until capitalists from the East, adventurers from everywhere, even noblemen from the British Isles were also fired by accounts that read like a prospectus from paradise.

And why not? It was new, unfenced, unspoiled country and every man, or so it seemed, had an equal chance, with the rewards going to the able and industrious; and no sneaky government was there to hobble the conduct of the strong and aggressive. And it was even claimed that the cost of producing beef on the open range was one tenth the cost of producing it anywhere else.

Above all the Cow was there hastening to spread her image and populate the land from valley grassland to mountain top. If a man's resources allowed him to own a hundred cows he could reasonably expect then, in those pristine years at least, that they would produce annually ninety calves—which would bring him a bounteous profit.

Arizona was then and would always be, so the

newcomers thought, a land of milk and honey. The cow critters could stand knee-deep in grass and do nothing but eat three hundred and sixty-five days out of the year. The promoters did nothing, of course, to soft pedal reports that the Great Plains in the eighties had a series of arctic winters. Cattle by the thousands froze to death in the great snowstorms, it was reported—gleefully—in Arizona's winter sunshine. The herds had no epidemic diseases—then; poisonous plants were rare, and the rich grama grasses would fatten a steer for the market without grain feed. Only an insufficient water supply in the streams lay between the newcomers and wealth; and artesian wells would soon remedy that, it was believed.

By word of mouth and by official reports the intoxicating message was passed. In 1885 Governor Tritle, although the estimate of the Department of Agriculture was 217,000, reported the number of assessed cattle at 435,000. Allowing for those the assessor failed to find, he set the total, with possibly pardonable exaggeration, at 652,000. And about that time he stated also that there is no quicker or surer road to fortune than cattle raising in Arizona." With this kind of opiate, both public and private, tyro ranchers so innocent of botany they could not tell a poisonous loco weed when they saw one, nor distinguish needle grass from good grama grass—they came, all kinds and from everywhere, eager to travel the "quickest and surest road to fortune." The herds were reckoned now in six figures—or seven.

And yet not all were fools, nor con men, nor gunslingers, nor failures. But then not many of them were empire builders, either.

In the early nineties came the Drouth, and not far behind, the Floods. The Cow had spread abroad her image by this time over the land in multiples of one million, two millions, or you name it; had scuffed narrow trails deep into the dusty pastures with her sharp hoofs; with her prehensile tongue had devoured the grass down to the naked dirt, and the young shoots of willow, grapevine, live oak, mountain mahogany, wild cherry, rose, *estafiata,* Apache plume, even rabbit brush and every other browse plant that raging hunger could dictate. The sunburned slopes began to approach the bareness of a tin roof, and when a heavy shower occurred the water collected into the dry arroyos like nozzles and wasted itself violently in muddy torrents.

When whole months would pass without rain, waterholes would dry up. The deep-bored wells, and windpumps with steel tanks at their feet were then many years in the future. All this was famine, but it was not yet starvation.

For relief let us turn our eyes aside a moment. . . . For ages in the forest solitudes the burnished-copper hummingbirds with the ruby throat—"sunbirds," as the Taos Indians call them—had haunted the spring which bears their name. Engelmann spruces in peace had there reached their normal girth of about twelve feet, but once long ago a fan-shaped flame swept that mountainside as a mower's scythe sweeps standing grain. Dead trunks, whitened like bones, still stand as stark reminders there, but many more lie prostrate on the earth in tangled confusion where winter storms now from the west, now from the north felled them on the high slopes.

Downstream along the Gila's course are poisoned spots of soil, as already noticed, and from sources of incipient side canyons are spread little fans of gravel and coarse pebbles spewed out by floods long past. Seen from a plane, havoc wrought by the herds stands out sharply across the tilted terrain where a wire fence separates two different degrees of overgrazing.

In all this visible demonstration of man's impact how fares the farmer's record? Surprisingly well, I should say. This must be in part because in Arizona the irrigator is likely to be a Mormon, and the Mormon is likely to be by nature a man of reverence, whose villages are invariably well-kept, and whose poor in times of depression are not abandoned to public charity. The Mormons care for their own. Along the Gila the irrigator has been in the main not the aggressor but the victim, the simple reason being that both by creed and tradition he is committed to making the desert blossom.

With a hint that the Mormon farmers deserve to be called the Gila's best friend among those who carelessly released conflagrations among its forests, some who allowed chemical wastes to pollute the stream or poison the soil, others who unchained the forces of erosion, and loosed the violence of baleful floods, it is well to warn the reader that this brief essay does not pretend to chronicle the whole history of the arid Southwest from the beginning up to the present and undertake projections for the future.

Up to the seventies, the Gila was a fairly clear stream in its middle reach. But in the eighties and nineties came the great flash floods and wholesale erosion, with the ruin of diversion dams, the silting of irrigation ditches, the leaching of alkali from the eroded subsoil. The silt, as farmers began to discover, had a colloidal property that was injurious to growing crops.

Our title, be it remembered, was The Ruin of a River, and the ruin was now well advanced. As to where it could be called complete there might be a difference of opinion, but when it reached the stage where Professor R. H. Forbes, a University of Arizona observer, could call it "The World's Muddiest River," this writer is willing to concede that the once lovely Gila had been ruined—period. The final ignominy of all was reached at the same time, give or take a half decade. That step lies only a little ahead.

In a country that is well grassed, generously watered and not sunburned, erosion seldom becomes a major peril. But in the far Southwest the ecologist finds all the routine processes of nature greatly magnified, just as the student of abnormal psychology finds ordinary process of the human mind greatly disordered and magnified in the paranoiac. Here the ground cover is permanently thin because of aridity; here the moods of nature both in sunshine and cloudburst are frequently violent; here the equilibrium of things sits, as it were, balanced on a knife blade. Hence it is that drouths and floods occur so surprisingly together. For generations the Gila has been naturally subject to flooding, as the historical records show; yet in reality the increasing denudation of the watershed hardly causes the floods. Rather it accentuates their frequency and their ferocity.

Over and over we have referred to the ruinous effect of overgrazing the native grasses; yet it must not be forgotten that timber cutting was another great factor in the ruin. Mines are naturally great users of lumber; in the early days their small locomotives were all woodburners; and also immense numbers of small trees were cut for fence posts and firewood. There being no substitutes for wood, wood was used. More denudation!

Consequently floods grew higher, wider, and the load of silt they carried grew thicker until the river's current was no longer water; it was a hideous, evil-smelling emulsion which engineers could measure in percentages. In 1906 at Clifton, Arizona, a copper-mining town lying on a tributary a few miles upstream from the parent stream, five mine locomotives were trapped in silt and water in their own roundhouse. Even wider was the inundation at Safford at 8:00 A.M. on October 14, 1916. An old photograph taken at that time shows the Gila as a young Mississippi, albeit somewhat more turbulent.

Possibly the highest flood of all may have occurred in September 1941, five years after Soil Conservation Service had spent fabulous sums on riprap, cribbing, bank protection, jetties and water spreaders. That was a famous wet year from Los Angeles to Texas. That year photographs showed the river as a standing lake of indefinite width.

Such record-breakers are introduced here for one single reason—to show the prodigious load of silt carried by the world's muddiest river. The source of the silt? Most of it was clawed out from the expensive, irrigated bottomlands owned by the Mormon farmers. And it was deposited where? Washed up along the channel in high banks, and also precisely where it would do the most harm—behind the Coolidge Dam, filling up the San Carlos Reservoir which had been calculated by its engineers to have a useful life of fifty years.

Unlike tax assessors, engineers are men trained to mathematical precision and the use of refined instruments. In 1916 an engineering study of the Gila for the Department of the Interior was made by Mr. Frank H. Olmstead. Among other astonishing facts he discovered a ten-fold increase in the width of the channel.

According to the U. S. survey made in 1875 the river channel in the township just above Safford averaged 138 feet in width and occupied an area of 103 acres. Olmstead's measurements showed that instead of 103 acres, the same channel length then occupied 1,500 acres. What extraordinary force had moved those 1,397 fertile acres? The floods had simply swept them downstream as mud. Even more of a heartbreak, doubtless, to those Mormon farmers in the Safford valley was the utter disappearance of 1,100 acres of their irrigated land in the year 1916. This ruin was revealed by an actual plane table survey. Olmstead's report was sent to Washington with the simple statement there existed in engineering practice no known precedent for such flood control. The World's Muddiest River indeed!

Now a final, backward look at the Report of the Chairman of the Arizona Livestock Commission. It showed 1,500,000 animals. . . . And a year or so later it was reported, "All ranchmen concede that it [the death loss] was not less than 50 per cent. . . ." The Chairman, though probably not an engineer nor a statistician, would doubtless have managed to get within a half million of the correct figure on the death loss. That would leave how many. . . . how many dead animals, the victims of starvation, lying there in the river bed with tongue stretched out desperately toward the last pool of water. And the stench . . . and the stench rising and drifting across the burning landscape. . . . The final ignominy!

All this tragedy had required just about twenty years of folly, from 1872 until 1893.

CHAPTER EIGHTEEN

THE REGION'S
INSATIABLE THIRST

THROUGH WOLF CREEK PASS
in Colorado the highway rises from the vast drainage
area of the Rio Grande, proceeds westward over the
high ridge of the San Juan Mountains and descends
by way of the San Juan River into the equally vast drainage of the Rio Colorado. Historically these are the two
great rivers of the West, and the pass itself is not by
any to be taken unadvisedly or lightly. Shall we pause
and look around here on the roof of America? Wolf
Creek, a swift, cold, small stream, always calls to mind
one of the great predators of the mountains. Another
name for him is lobo, or loafer wolf; never coyote,
which is a minor, commoner species altogether.

Your car climbs up the grade in the huge saddle
without laboring, but presently you begin to feel a
distinct drop in the temperature as you near the twelve-
thousand-foot level, and discover that, whereas you had

been coming upstream, you are now going downstream. If you are a good observer you will find opening up vistas of the titans that tower far above you along the Continental Divide. In winter the comb of this roof is an inhospitable region of snowfields, talus slopes, incipient glaciers, landslides, and snowslides where life ventures only at its own peril. Here is a realm given over to totally impersonal processes like freezing, thawing, grindings, erosion, which is a world-shaping operation that is forever transporting the heights downward to sea level. It is a boreal domain ruled by forces primeval, inhuman, inanimate, and uniformly hostile.

Yet withal it is not a world beyond human concern, because for the western two thirds of America it is the main supplier of an indispensable commodity—water. Down from its high snowy folds and corrugations go streams for the needs of teeming cities along the Pacific Ocean, for populations on the great central plains, and far southward toward the Gulf of Mexico. Furthermore, their water in transit is not merely water; it is weight in motion and therefore momentum. Momentum harnessed at damsite is power, and power—well, it makes the world go. And all this water traces its ultimate source straight to the drip of sharp icicles atop the Great Divide.

Exactly on the Divide in Wolf Creek Pass careful measurements of the snowpack in this winter of 1964-65 show that the precipitation is now the highest in years. So the men on snowshoes confidently predict that the runoff in the San Juan will be unusually generous next April and May. But there is on the way now to always dry Albuquerque a double bonus, something new and dramatic: the new San Juan–Chama

Project, a vast federal undertaking. Though it has been in the incubating stage several years, construction began only in January 1965. Now the Department of the Interior is at work bringing water from the San Juan *through a tunnel in the Continental Divide* down the open channel of the Chama to Albuquerque.

A ponderous machine known as the Mole drills the big hole into the mountain; the tunnel is lined with concrete at the same time, and the Mole goes forward on his laborious way. And he has a long way to go—in fact, twenty-seven miles. At its upper end the tunnel will be eight feet in diameter with a capacity of 520 cubic feet of water per second; in its middle five-mile reach, a capacity of 550 cubic feet; at its lower end in the Azotea (roof) tunnel, diameter will be 11 feet and capacity 950 cubic feet per second. That will be for the dry Southwest no inconsiderable bonus of water!

Beyond this point, the writer suspects, no amount of clarification will lure his readers to give time and attention enough to understand the San Juan–Chama complex. So we are about to leave behind us and pass now from what Sky Determined to the consideration of what at his best Man Determines for peace and human welfare.

The San Juan–Chama project began more than a dozen years ago from the perception that 1) Albuquerque is fast growing into one of the important cities of the Southwest, and that its growth is certain to be hampered unless its municipal water supply is greatly increased; 2) that in spite of the Elephant Butte Reservoir, irrigation in the Rio Grande Valley will be limited because water is limited there, as well as in the depressed areas of northern New Mexico; 3) that the distressing poverty among the Navajo people, owing to their rapid increase in population with a corresponding shrinkage in water and other natural resources requires adjustment—in spite of their recent big income from oil and gas.

While water might not be the total answer to all these needs, it would do more than anything else. But in this dry land where would the water come from? Where could one find water here that doesn't already belong to someone else? True, there was water that a growing, aggressive city might possibly get, but it was clear over on the other side of the Great Divide. And already leagued against Albuquerque was Arizona, Utah, Texas and California in sisterly jealousy. And if ever the authorization could be obtained from Congress, plus another indispensable matter, the appropriation, various bureaus and agencies would have to be satisfied and pacified also, such as the Bureau of Indian Affairs, the developers of Fish and Wildlife, the public health people (they were worried about the mosquitoes) the road builders and others who might be expected to be the most closely concerned—the Bureau of Reclamation. The exploratory work was itself an earthmoving job that required several years. . . . And it wasn't the kind that is done by bulldozers!

Along with the vast task of logrolling—also not done by bulldozers—and persuasion and fact-gathering, a small army of men examined every tributary of the San Juan (which is itself the largest but one in the whole system of the mighty Colorado) . They were testing the suitability for trout, estimating the beaver population, counting the number of archaeological sites, and so on and on. Obviously, if the project were to be approved it would be a federal job of first magnitude. And that is was.

The plans finally accepted were hardly less imposing than the reality itself will be—an immense complexity with something for everybody except the hydroelectric interests; something for the evergrowing municipal water needs of Albuquerque, something for the irrigation farmers down along the Rio Grande and elsewhere, something for flood control, a big reservoir for water storage, something for the fishermen, a great deal more for the pampered trout, the boat owners, the bathers, the water skiers. A prominent economist of the University of New Mexico is busy nowadays persuading people that water is too valuable here to use for crop irrigation. It should be used, he says, for recreation.

Opposition to the San Juan—Chama project has so far been comparatively silent, but not absent. In the engineers' project book some long letters were published even before stakes were set, so that no state's partisans were deprived of their say. It was said among other things that the cost of improving the land was in many places greater than the land was worth. I do not pretend to say how much merit some of these rebuttals contained, nor from what quarter they came. But I know that among lawyers it is axiomatic that where there is irrigation there is litigation. Probably it will not be different here.

In the book for all to read are the carefully calculated "benefits" expected from the federal money spent, and on them will be disagreements. What engineer can calculate them on his slide rule? Just how can anyone calculate the "benefit" of a vacation? or of an education? or of a fast ride on water skis? or of a symphony? From which end of the slide rule will you select the logarithm? Possibly it might help here if I quote two well chosen words of Latin; *Cui bono?*, meaning, "To whom is it a benefit?" For many the benefit of a symphony would be about two bits. But then, again. . . .

Once years ago in Deming, I met a well driller, a driller of water wells. I inspected his equipment, and then we fell into conversation. His was an interesting trade, he felt, with a large element of pure luck, for no man could tell exactly what is buried in the earth nor where. He thought himself, and quite rightly, a very useful member of society, for he was a producer of one of life's most necessary and valuable commodities—pure water. And what little wealth he had amassed, he had produced for himself instead of taking it away from some other man as profit. Very respectfully I told him as an admirer that he was a true member, like an Indian Rain Priest, of the Sky Powers cult.

Indeed in an arid country like New Mexico, many of us who live here a long time come finally to feel a kind of mystic gratitude to the sky, the lightning, and the life-giving rain clouds. In fact, for more than thirty years I have kept a written record of every sizeable rain that has fallen on my roof. What more than that could even a Hopi shaman do? Had I lived in the Holy Land, a dry, bright country like ours, I probably would have aspired to leave for posterity a well, a deep, pure well like the Patriarch Jacob's three thousand years ago with its rope and bucket.

When I asked Senator Clinton P. Anderson's permission to quote from him on the treatment of saline water in our state, he graciously promised—because he, too, is one of the Rain Brotherhood—to write me some material himself for this third edition of *Sky Determines*. I quote him here:

"My mind has been constantly attracted to the suggestion of Ross Calvin that in our Southwest 'Sky Determines.' Sky decides what areas can be habitable, what agricultural lands can be grazed, which acres are subject to reduction of row crops and which can best be turned to the production of cotton.

"But is there a new force ahead of us? Will there be a day when sky no longer so completely determines and rain clouds will not be so totally important to us? Will the desalinization of the brackish water in our State and the conversion of saline water in coastal areas change the water supply picture?

"I think so, and I think that as we read Ross Calvin's book carefully, we should bear in mind that increasingly larger, more efficient desalination plants are coming on the line all the time. One of these is at Roswell, New Mexico.

"Two giant vapor domes, rising 92 feet above the barren New Mexico landscape, dominated the scene on a hot July day in 1963, when more than a thousand persons gathered four miles east of Roswell for the dedication ceremonies of the first one-million gallon per day brackish water conversion plant in the United States. Secretary of the Interior, Stewart L. Udall, Representative (now Senator) Joseph M. Montoya and I joined with several other members of the Congress, State and local officials to participate in the program. In his remarks, Secretary Udall said, 'Today for the first time in New Mexico, we will begin to utilize hitherto unusable salt laden water by processing it in this unique new "water factory." This plant is a pioneering venture. This will be a "fact factory." The information it supplies will help us draw on the vast brackish water resources of this and many other areas of the West to provide a new source of fresh water.'

"The plant was one of five built by the Department of the Interior's Office of Saline Water following the approval by the Congress in 1958 of a Joint Resolution which it was my good fortune to introduce in the Congress. The act authorized the appropriation of ten million dollars for five plants to 'establish on a day-to-day operating basis the optimum attainable reliability, engineering, operating, and economic potential of . . . the process selected by the Secretary of the Interior.' The law specified the general location for the plants including one for the treatment of brackish waters 'in the arid areas of the Southwest.'

"More than fifty cities in the Southwest asked to be considered as the site for the brackish water demonstration plant, providing a clear indication of the level of interest in the potential utilization of desalted water.

"One of the reasons Roswell was selected as the location for the desalination plant was because of the very high salinity of the brackish water available there, thus providing a challenging test for the desalting plant. Public Health Service states that good drinking water should not contain more than five hundred dissolved parts of salt per million parts of water (ppm). The raw feed water delivered to the Roswell plant contains approximately 16,000 ppm which is about half the salinity of sea water.

"The process utilized at Roswell is a distillation cycle known as forced-circulation vapor-compression. A number of mechanical and operating difficulties have been encountered. One by one these are being solved, but all of the problems have not yet been surmounted. Careful records of the technical difficulties are being kept and an accurate evaluation of the process is being made. While these problems are being eliminated, engineers are continually seeking ways to improve the process to make it less expensive. The plant has operated at design capacity on a number of occasions, and gradual improvements are anticipated. Much valuable operating data has already been obtained from the construction and operation of this plant, as has been the case with the other operating plants.

"The Roswell plant is just one 'test tube' in the Government's program to develop low-cost sea or brackish water conversion processes. As the frontiers of knowledge are extended through fundamental research studies, through engineering developments, and through the construction and operation of experimental plants, the cost of winning fresh water from salty sources is being reduced.

"President Johnson succinctly summed up the importance of the saline water conversion program when he stated 'There is no newer or more vital frontier for any of us than the one we must cross to a lasting abundance of fresh water for all mankind.' "

One of the most striking facts noted in the preceding is the announcement that more than fifty cities in the Southwest asked to be considered as the site for the brackish water demonstration plant. It was erected at Roswell, New Mexico, and for a good reason. There the water table (distance down to underground water) has long been declining, and with that the agricultural prospects also. The city has no oil wells, no gas wells, no potash mines in its vicinity; and in February 1965, seven of its water wells have had to be shut down because their salt content has been climbing toward the danger point (500 parts per million parts of water).

It just might be that if Roswell discovered the golden secret of desalinization her water wells might be even more valuable than wells of oil and gas.

The Department of the Interior has now in operation besides the experimental plant at Roswell four others located strategically over the nation—one on the Atlantic coast, one on the Pacific, one on the Gulf, and two in the interior. And how appropriate it turns out to be that New Mexico, one of the most arid states, has had an able and farseeing man in Washington who has sponsored and worked for the necessary legislation since its beginning.

BIBLIOGRAPHY

ALEXANDER, H. B. *The Great Spirit.* N. Mex. Quarterly, pp. 3-16, Feb., 1931.

AUSTIN, MARY. *The Land of Little Rain.* Boston, 1903.

BAILEY, FLORENCE M. *Birds of New Mexico.* Pub. by the N. Mex. Dept. of Game and Fish, 1928.

BAILEY, VERNON. *Life and Crop Zones of New Mexico,* in N. Amer. Fauna, No. 35, U. S. Dept. of Ag.

BAILEY, VERNON. *Mammals of New Mexico,* in N. Amer. Fauna No. 53, U. S. Dept. of Ag., 1931.

BARKER, RUTH L. *Caballeros.* Appleton, 1931.

BOURKE, JOHN G. *On the Border with Crook.* Scribners, 1891.

BRADFIELD, W. *Cameron Creek Village.* El Palacio Press, Santa Fe, N. M., 1931.

BUTTREE, JULIA M. *The Rhythm of the Redman.* A. S. Barnes, 1930.

California, National Forests of. Misc. Circular No. 94, U. S. Dept. of Ag.

CARTER, DIANA B. *Potsherds and their Significance.* El Palacio, Feb. 24, 1932.

CATHER, WILLA. *Death Comes for the Archbishop.* Knopf, 1927.

CHAPLINE AND TALBOT. *The Use of Salt in Range Management.* U. S. Dept. of Ag. Circular No. 379.

CLARK AND PRIEST. *Public Water Supplies of New Mexico.* Univ. of N. Mex. Bul. (Chemistry Series) No. 215.

COAN, CHARLES F. *Shorter History of New Mexico.* 2 Vols. Amer. Hist. Soc., Inc., 1925.

COOK, JAMES H. *Fifty Years on the Old Frontier.* Yale Univ. Press, 1923.

COOLIDGE, MARY ROBERTS. *The Rain Makers*. Houghton Mifflin, 1929.

Coronado, Journey of, ed. by G. W. Winship. New York, 1904.

COSGROVE, H. S., AND C. B. *The Swarts Ruin*. Papers of the Peabody Museum, Harv. Univ., 1932.

DARTON, N. H., AND OTHERS. *Guidebook of the Western U. S.—* The Santa Fe Route. U. S. Geol. Sur. Bul. No. 613.

DAY, P. C. *Summary of the Climatological Data for the U. S.—* Southwestern N. Mex. and Southern Ariz. U. S. Weather Bur.

DAYTON, W. A. *Important Western Browse Plants,* U. S. Dept. of Ag. Misc. Pub. No. 101, 1931.

DOBIE, J. FRANK. *Coronado's Children*. Southwest Press, 1930.

DUFFUS, R. L. *The Santa Fe Trail*. Longmans, 1930.

FERGUSSON, ERNA. *Dancing Gods*. Knopf, 1931.

FERGUSSON, HARVEY. *Rio Grande*. Knopf, 1933.

FEWKES, J. W. *Designs on Prehistoric Pottery from the Mimbres Valley, N. Mex.* Smithsonian Inst. Pub. No. 2713.

FEWKES, J. W. *Additional Designs on Prehistoric Mimbres Pottery*. Smithsonian Inst. Pub. No. 2748.

FOREST SERVICE. *National Forests of N. Mex. and Ariz.*

FORREST, EARL. *Missions and Pueblos of the Old Southwest*. Cleveland, 1929.

FORSLING, C. L. *A Study of the Influence of Herbaceous Plant Cover,* etc. U. S. Dept. of Ag. Techn. Bul. No. 220, 1931.

FRENCH, THE HON. WM. *Some Recollections of a Western Ranchman*. Stokes Co.

GARRETT, PAT. *The Authentic Life of Billy the Kid,* ed. by M. G. Fulton. New York, 1927.

Gila, National Forest. Forestry Serv., U. S. Dept. of Ag., 1929.

GRIFFITHS AND THOMPSON. *Cacti*. U. S. Dept. of Ag. Circular No. 66, 1929.

HAFEN, L. R. *The Overland Mail*. Cleveland, 1926.

HALLENBECK, CLEVE. *Climate and Health*. "New Mexico," Dec. *Pecos Valley*. Monthly Weather Rev., May, 1917.

HALLENBECK, CLEVE. *Climate and Health*. "New Mexico," Dec., 1931, pp. 9 *et ff.*

HEWETT, EDGAR L. *Ancient Life in the American Southwest*. Bobbs-Merrill, 1930.

HOUGH, WALTER. *Decorative Designs on Elden Pueblo Pottery, Flagstaff, Ariz.* Smithsonian Inst. No. 2930, 1932.

HUNTINGTON, ELLSWORTH. *The Climatic Factor as Illustrated in Arid America*. Carnegie Inst., 1914.

JAMES, GEO. WHARTON. *The Land of the Delight Makers*. Page, 1920.

JENKS, A. E. *Geometric Designs on Mimbres Bowls*. Art and Archaeol. May-June, 1932, pp. 137 *et ff.*

KIDDER, A. V. *Introduction to the Study of Southwestern Archaeology*. Yale Univ. Press, 1924.

LAUT, AGNES C. *Pilgrims of the Santa Fe.* Stokes, 1931.

LAWSON, W. P. *The Log of a Timber Cruiser.* Duffield, 1915.

LIGON, J. S. *Wild Life of New Mexico.* State Game Commission, Santa Fe, 1927.

LINDGREN AND OTHERS. *Ore Bodies of N. Mex.* U. S. Geol. Survey Prof. paper 68.

LINNEY AND GARCIA. *Climate in Relation to Crop Adaptation in N. Mex.* N. Mex. Coll. of Ag. and Mech. Arts, Bul. No. 113.

LINNEY AND OTHERS. *Climate as It Affects Crops and Ranges in N. Mex.* N. Mex. Coll. of Ag. and Mech. Arts, Bul. No. 182, 1930.

LUMMIS, CHARLES. *The Land of Poco Tiempo.* Scribners, 1925.

Minneapolis Inst. of Arts. *The Mimbres Valley Expedition.* Vol. XVII, 1928.

National Monuments, Glimpses of Our. Pub. of Natl. Park Service, Washington, 1929.

NESBITT, PAUL H. *The Ancient Mimbreños.* Logan Mus., Beloit Coll. Bul. No. 4, 1931.

New Mexico, National Forests of. Pub. of Forest Service, U. S. Dept. of Ag., 1922.

PAIGE, SIDNEY. *The Silver City Folio.* Geol. Atlas of the U. S. No. 199, 1916.

PRINCE, L. B. *Concise History of New Mexico.* Torch Press, 1914.

SAUER, CARL, AND BRAND, DONALD. *Pueblo Sites in Southeastern Arizona.* Univ. of Calif. Press, Berkeley, 1930.

SIMPICH, FREDERICK. *Arizona Comes of Age.* Natl. Geog. Mag., pp. 1-47, Jan., 1929.

SIMPICH, FREDERICK. *The Santa Fe Trail, Path to Empire.* Natl. Geog. Mag., pp. 213-252, Aug., 1929.

Smithsonian Miscellaneous Collections. *Prehistoric Remains in N. Mex.* Vol. 65, No. 6, pp. 62-78.

SWEET, A. T. *Soil Survey of the Deming Area.* U. S. Dept. of Ag., Series 1928.

THOMAS, A. B. *Forgotten Frontiers.* Univ. of Okla. Press, 1932

TINSLEY, J. D. *Forty Years of Climate in Southern N. Mex.* N. Mex. Coll. of Ag. and Mech. Arts, Bul. No. 59.

TWITCHELL, R. E. *The Leading Facts of New Mexico History.* 5 Vols. The Torch Press, 1912.

VAN DYKE, JOHN C. *The Desert.* Scribners, 1902.

VAUGHN, JOHN H. *History and Government of New Mexico.* State Coll., N. Mex., 1929.

WATSON, E. L. *Laughing Artists of the Mimbres Valley.* Art and Archaeol. July, 1932.

WEBB, WALTER P. *The Great Plains.* Ginn and Co., 1931.

WOOTON, E. O. *Cacti in New Mexico.* N. M. Coll. of Ag. and Mech. Arts, Bul. No. 78.

WOOTON AND STANDLEY. *Flora of New Mexico.* U. S. Natl. Herbarium, Vol. 19, 1915.

INDEX

Civil War, the, 203, 234, 242, 301,
passim
Clark, J. D., 69
Clifton, Ariz., 273, 350, 364
Cloudcroft, 70
Clovis, N.M., 309, 340 ff.
Clum, John P., 244, 250
Coahuila, 238
Coan, 206
Cochise, 232
Cochiti, 178
Cold Springs Fire, 112
Colfax County, 305
Collyer, Vincent, 225
Colorado, 71, 75, 309
Colorado River of Texas, 154
Colorado River, the, 21, 38, *et
passim*
Colorado spruces, 68
Columbus, Christopher, 176
Comanches, the, 58, 165, 210
Conchos River, 158
Conestoga wagons, 291, 297
Confederates, the, 244
Congress, the U.S., 243
Conkling, R. P., 297 ff.
Conquistadores, 6, 7, 142 ff., 328
Coolidge Dam, 364
Cooney, James, 243
Cook's Peak, 32, 126, 231, 296
Cook's Spring, 241 ff.
Cordero, Captain, 240 ff.
Corn Maidens, 74
Coronado, 6, 97, 148 ff.
Corvera, Captain, 186
Cosgrove, B. C., 132
Counter Reformation, the, 187
Cow Springs, 296
Crimmins, Colonel, 248
Croix, Teodoro de, 239
Crooked Canyon Fire, 111
Crook, General, 224, 246 ff.
Cross Mountain, 218
Crown of Thorns, 51
Cub Creek, 101
Culiacán, 145, 146 ff.
Custodio de San Pablo, 167

Dakota sandstone, 309

Damascus grapes, 15
Datil National Forest, 91
Day, P. O., 20, 21
De Anza, Governor, 214, 239
Delaware River, 323
Delawares, the, 251
Deming, 13, 57, 126, 248, *et passim*
De Neva, Felipe, 240
Denver, 345
Denver and Rio Grande R. R., 309
De Rubi, 238 ff.
Desalting Program, 326, 372 ff.
Desert, Mesa and Mountain, 5, 116,
125
De Sosa, 286
De Soto, 155
De Vargas, General, 178, *et passim*
Detroit, 163
Diablo Mountains, 92
Diamond A Ranch, 278
Digger Indians, 224
Divide, the Continental, 5, 16, 22,
60, *et passim*
Domitian, 168
Doña Beatriz, 149
Donnelly, Thomas C., 344
Douglas, Ariz., 278
Douglas fir (spruce), 19, 94, 95, 105
Douglass, Dr. A. E., 124, 174
Dry Creek, 101
Duck Creek, 353
Dudley, Colonel, 271
Durango, 164, 309

Earth Mother, 254, 319
Eastern Seaboard, 323
Eddy, Mr., 309
Egypt, 279
El Dorado, 8
Elephant Butte Lake, 75, 91, 287,
312, 368
Elephant Corral, 267
Elguea, Don Francisco, 236
Elijah, 168
Elizabethan romances, 145
El Paso del Norte, 29, 36, 159, *et
passim*
El Paso *Times*, 248, 297
El Sauce, 351

Sacaton Creek, 101
Sacramento Mountains, 35
Safford, Ariz., 358, 364, 365
Sahara, the, 33, 34
St. Joseph, 168, 199
St. Joseph, Mo., 298
St. Louis, Mo., 163, 189, 290
Salt Lake City, 298
Salton Sea, 85
Sam, 338, 339
San Carlos, Ariz., 358
San Carlos Reservation, 244, 247 ff.
San Carlos reservoir, 350, 364
San Carlos River, 91
Sandia Mountains, 198
San Francisco (St. Francis), 148, 176, 185
San Francisco, Cal., 236, 296
San Francisco Mountains, 92
San Francisco Street, 298
San Gabriel (colony), 160, 162
San Gerónimo (Taos), 184
Sangre de Cristo Range, 20, 68, 118, 121, 288
San Ildefonso pueblo, 184, 190 ff.
San Juan—Chama Project, 326, 367, 368, 370
San Juan Mountains, 366
San Juan Pueblo, 159
San Juan River, 57, 75, 116, 366, 367, 369
San Lorenzo, 216, 218
San Marcial, N.M., 85, 304
San Miguel Church, 184
San Miguel County, 305
San Simon Ciénega, 351
San Simon Creek, 241, 351
San Simon Wash, 350
Santa Barbara, 216
Santa Barbara, Mex., 158
Santa Cruz (settlement), 179
Santa Fe, 7, 69, *et passim*
Santa Fe Railroad, 301 ff.
Santa Fe Trail, 290 ff., 332
Santa Maria, Fr. de, 156
Santa Rita, 216
Santa Rita Mountains, 273
Santa Rita, N.M., 30, 79, 112, 305, ff.
Santiago, 150

Santo Domingo Creek, 351
Santo Domingo Pueblo, 10, 184, 194 ff.
San Vicente, 218
San Vicente Arroyo, 16, 86, 88, 89
San Ysidro, 27, 28, 326
Sapillo Creek, 93
Sauer and Brand, 280
Saxons, 170
Scientific Monthly, The, 85
Scott, Sir Walter, 272
Senecu (pueblo), 178
Serra, Fr. Junípero, 179
Seton, Ernest Thompson, 339
Seville, 150
Sherman, Gen. W. T., 225
Sherwood Forest, 273
Sierra Blanca, 238, 244
Sierra Bonita Ranch, 358
Sierra de las Uvas, 287
Sierra del Gila, 129, 238, 249
Sierra Madre, 249
Signal Peak, 103, 106
Silver City *Enterprise*, 250, 338
Silver City, N.M., 16, 25, 69, 70, *et passim;* 340 ff.
Simpich, Frederick, 346
Sinaloa, 155
Sioux, the, 251, 300
Skeleton Canyon, 251
Sky Father, 254
Sky Powers, the, *passim*
Smithsonian Institution, 127, 135
Socorro County, 296
Socorro, N.M., 159, 266, 288, 296
Sonora, 66, 92, 155, 156
Sonoran Zones, 12, 13, 15, *et passim*
South America, 187
Southern Baptist Church, 343
Southern Pacific R.R., 266, 299, 304, 339
Southwestern Museum, 103
Spain, 6, 284
Spanish American War, 179
Spanish Catholicism, 216
Spanish livestock, 287, 289
Spanish-Mexican regime, 322
Spanish regime, 335
Spanish Southwest, 329

Springfield rifle, 234
Steeple Rock, 75
Stetson hats, 308
Stevenson, Mrs. Matilda, 191
Stevenson, R. L., 302
Stone Age, 223
Sulphur Springs Valley, 358
S U Ranch, 250
Sun Father, 158, 191, 192
Sun People, 173
Sunshine State, 11

Tabira, 278
Taggart, Frank, 266
Tanos, the, 185
Taos, 70, 179, 209 ff.
Taos Pueblo, 184, 192 ff.
Tartary, 176
Te Deum, 185
Teguas, the, 185
Tennessee Cabin, 107
Tesuque Pueblo, 118, 183, 188
Tewas, the, 6, 158, 191
Texas, 11, 34, 35, 155, 204, *et passim*
Texas *Almanac*, 295
Thomas, A. B., 238
Thor, 170
Thunder Bird, 134, 190, 198
Thunder Mountain, 150
Tigua Province, 160
Tiguex, 151, 156 ff.
Time, 323, 324
Titan King's Palace, 83
Toledo swords, 54, 149, 286
Tonti, Lieut., 201
Topeka, Kans., 301
Tovar, Captain de, 149 ff.
Transition Zone, 12, 17, 18
Tres Castillos, 248, 249
Tres Hermanas Mountains, 31, 48, 60
Tritle, Governor, 360
Tropics, 20, 34
Tucson, Ariz., 236
Tuerto, 332
Tunstall-McSween Faction, 270 ff.
Turkeyfeather Pass, 107
Turkey Flat, 105
Turner, Sheriff, 271

Twitchell, R. E., 147, 161, 185, 225, 247
Tyrone, N.M., 305
Tyuonyi (ruins), 119

Udall, Stewart L., 372
Ulysses, 148
Union Pacific R. R., 301
U.S. Army, 246 ff.
U.S. Bureau of Indian Affairs, 369
U.S. Corps of Topographical Engineers, 329
U.S. Dept. of Agriculture, 279, 357, 360
U.S. Dept. of the Interior, 323, 326, 364, 367, 374
U.S. Geological Survey, 307, 312
U.S. Land Office, 207
U.S. Post Office Dept., 294, 296
U.S. Public Health Service, 373
U.S. Reclamation Bureau, 312, 369
U.S. Soil Conservation Service, 349, 357, 364
University of New Mexico, 344
Ursa Major, 76
Utah, 369
Utes, the, 210

Vacapa, 146
Valkyrs, the, 250
Velasco, Fr., 183
Vera Cruz, 164, 288, 293
Victoria, 183
Victorio, Chief, 31, 232 ff.
Vildosola, Captain, 239
Villagrá, Captain, 160
Villa Real de Santa Fe, 345
Virgin, the Blessed, *passim*

Walker, Rev. Samuel, 187
Wallace, Gen. Lew, 269, 274
Wall Street Journal, 322, 327
Ware, Dick, 267
Warm Springs Apaches, 232 ff.
Wars, Indian, *passim*
Washington, 91, 313
Washington, George (Negro), 266 ff.
Wells-Fargo Express Co., 266

Western New Mexico University, 342
West Fork (Gila River), 72, 101
Whipple, Lt., 351
White Creek, 101
Whitehill, Sheriff, 266
White Sands, the, 39, 40, 42
White Sands Missile Base, 340
Whitewater Baldy, 18, 72, 107
Whitewater Creek, 101
Whitewater Mesa, 93
Wild Horse Mesa, 31
Willow Creek, 72, 103
Willow March, 351
Willow Mountain, 94
Wilson Dam, 312
Wolf Creek, 113

Wolf Creek Pass, 366, 367
Woodhouse jay, 16
Wooton, E. O., 282
Wyoming, 106

Xenophon, 156

Yankees, the, 209
Yankee workmen, 333
Yaquis, the, 246
Young, "Parson," 267
Yuma, Ariz., 38, 40, 75, 296

Zaldívar, Captain, 160
Zia Pueblo, 178
Zuñi-Albuquerque Trail, 143
Zuñis, the, 70, 71, 184, 223

PUBLISHER'S REQUEST

The Publisher thinks it is time I should introduce myself. Well, at noon on January 10, 1927, with wife and small son I landed in the village of Silver City, New Mexico, a healthseeker, down and out and broke. Not too far from forty, I found life beginning, as they say. The new world of desert, mesa and mountain, plus the return of health, and seven years of pondering produced Sky Determines.

Life as an Episcopal clergyman was resumed before long in the tiny parish there, which allowed leisure for travel over the country and study, plus a great many field trips among the foothills. Detailed notes furthered by such tools as binocular, camera and magnifier, were made on each trip, the collection being called my Log Book, a record which I had begun in my home state, Illinois, at the mature age of twelve. Later on I began to mine the mass of data and discovered that it had some literary possibilities as an interpretation of the country. That's the way all this started.

The Log Book continues. It will be turned over, I may say in passing, at a determined date to the University of New Mexico Library and there preserved in the archives. Doubtless it will have no readers for the first century or two; but anything, anything if preserved long enough will interest the archaeologists who rediscover it and then write an introduction and notes for it. (I should know!)

Of course there had been some schooling before arrival in the Southwest—high school which had begun at twelve, then college, then the graduate school, where two Harvard degrees were collected (one of them a Ph.D. in philology) then a hitch in Seminary followed by ordination. Along the way there had been also some teaching in Syracuse University and Carnegie Tech at Pittsburgh.

And in the historic Old Trinity Parish, New York, I had been three years a curate—a minor job which, however, carries a bit of prestige. Then after a time came the forced rustication in the Southwest, followed by two long rectorships, one at "Silver," the other at Clovis, where the people at length pooled their efforts to build that small, jewel-like Franciscan adobe church, a noble structure, and famous, too.

So after a long, obscure ministry there came inevitably in due time retirement—though I could still smack a soft-ball and run the bases. (In youth I had been a track athlete as well as a Latinist.)

And now a life not altogether lonely, with grandchildren, with a small walled-in garden, with leisure for study (in which my life has been mainly spent) and for the cultivation of a literary style which aspires afar off toward the ease and grace of classic English prose.

Though often I have written articles on the Southwest for tourist readers, I'm seldom satisfied to bring these to an end until they turn interpretative, i.e., answering the question, "How did the country happen to turn out thus?" This book follows the same trend from narration to explanation, and so likewise does Lieutenant Emory Reports *and also* River of the Sun. *This the books have in common, all being a three-part study of the same grand theme.*

But the garden—shall I tell you about it before you go? A garden is a great revealer of a man's philosophy you know. A rendezvous mine is for honeybees in larkspur, hollyhock, apple tree; a park for great yellow butterflies, and an evening haunt for repining katydids which warn that frost lurks in the chilly nights ahead. A sanctuary, too, it is also with something for its many birds—bright cherries for the robins, blue-skinned, green-fleshed damson plums for the linnets; crimson-twigged woodbine berries for tanagers and flickers; unspecified diet for sparrows and warblers. Even for the hatched larva in April there is a tender young apple—with a drop of poison.

Fair in form and function is the bronze sundial, which recalls for the hours of solitude former seedtimes, recurring snows and winter nights, hopes, regrets, partings, time's injustices.

If ever in my garden I should need a walking cane, I have ready a blackthorn shillalah which was dried and seasoned in an Irish chimney long ago. So run the years accumulating into slow decades, the fifth, sixth and so on as the century nears the last third of its annual circuits . . . October's here already!

Ross Calvin